D1566246

BLUFFING TEXAS STYLE

BLUFFING TEXAS STYLE

THE ARSONS, FORGERIES, AND HIGH-STAKES POKER CAPERS OF RARE BOOK DEALER JOHNNY JENKINS

Michael Vinson

University of Oklahoma Press : Norman

Library of Congress Cataloging-in-Publication Data
Names: Vinson, Michael, author.
Title: Bluffing Texas style : the arsons, forgeries, and high-stakes
    poker capers of rare book dealer Johnny Jenkins / Michael Vinson.
Description: Norman : University of Oklahoma Press, [2020] |
    Includes bibliographical references and index. | Summary: "An
    examination of the life, career, and mysterious demise of rare book
    dealer, gambler, and forger John Jenkins"—Provided by publisher.
Identifiers: LCCN 2019030989 | ISBN 978-0-8061-6495-3 (hardcover) |
    ISBN 978-0-8061-6542-4 (paperback)
Subjects: LCSH: Jenkins, John Holmes. | Antiquarian booksellers—
    Texas—Biography.
Classification: LCC Z473.J4 V56 2020 | DDC 381/.45002092 [B]—dc23
LC record available at https://lccn.loc.gov/2019030989

The paper in this book meets
the guidelines for permanence and durability of the
Committee on Production Guidelines for Book Longevity
of the Council on Library Resources, Inc. ∞

Copyright © 2020 by the University of Oklahoma Press,
Norman, Publishing Division of the University.
Manufactured in the U.S.A.

All rights reserved. No part of this publication may be reproduced,
stored in a retrieval system, or transmitted, in any form or by
any means, electronic, mechanical, photocopying, recording, or
otherwise—except as permitted under Section 107 or 108 of the
United States Copyright Act—without the prior written permission
of the University of Oklahoma Press. To request permission to
reproduce selections from this book, write to Permissions, University
of Oklahoma Press, 2800 Venture Drive, Norman OK 73069, or
email rights.oupress@ou.edu.

For my mom and dad,
Veora and Robert Anderson,
and my brother and sister,
James Vinson and Eileen Dyer

"A mask tells us more than a face."
—Oscar Wilde *Pen, Pencil and Poison*

Contents

Acknowledgments

I would like to thank Megan von Ackermann, a wonderful reader, travel companion, contributor of ideas, and my accomplice in this endeavor. She never tired of hearing yet another detail about the "Johnster," as I took to calling him. J. P. Bryan Jr. provided wonderful stories and insights about his friend John H. Jenkins. He was also kind enough to let me use his ranch in Big Bend, Texas, to write part of this book. Alfred Bush, retired curator of Western Americana at Princeton, and occasionally Ted Lusher sat patiently listening to early versions of this book during summer evenings on Alfred's patio in Santa Fe. His glasses of wine and bottles of beer helped too, I think.

Nearly thirty years ago, Kevin MacDonnell began amassing research about Jenkins, which included FOIA requests from the Bureau of Alcohol, Tobacco, and Firearms, along with many other research files. He generously made all of his files available for my use, and it is not too much to say that this book could not have been written without his research assistance. Russell Martin, the director of the DeGolyer Library at Southern Methodist University, and his staff were especially helpful during my visits to the John Holland Jenkins Papers in May and October 2017, and I thank them as well for travel grants for research.

Gregory Gibson (author and novelist) gave a close reading to an early draft of this book, and I thank him for his suggestions. Holly Webber did invaluable developmental editing on this book, and it was a pleasure to work with her. I will be relying on her keen insights again in my next book. Michael Hicks, Travis

McDade, and Ron Tyler read early drafts and offered valuable suggestions.

I would like to thank the Book Club of California for the opportunity to speak on Jenkins at the Kenneth Karmiole Lectures in 2018, and Gregory Thompson of the Rare Book Society of the University of Utah for the same privilege in 2019. These opportunities to speak helped to hone this book, and I am grateful.

There were many others who provided research leads, anecdotes, and suggestions—Kenneth Rendell, William Reese, Michael Ginsberg, Ron Tyler, Terry Bellanger, Phillip Wajda, and Michael Heaston stand out. Any errors that remain are mine.

Prologue

On Sunday afternoon, April 16, 1989, Kaye Freeman found a body in the Colorado River thirty miles from Austin, Texas. Freeman was putting bait on her line, casting it out, and trolling it back, hoping that a large catfish would bite. A man named Robert Donnell was driving from Austin back to his job switching freight cars in Beaumont. He'd watched his son play in a Little League baseball game and took the lazy farm-to-market road to Bastrop instead of the busier highway. He pulled up his 1973 blue-and-white long-bed Ford at the same boat ramp where Freeman was fishing and noticed a late-model Mercedes with its driver's door left open and a flat rear tire. He walked around the car and spotted a wallet on the ground.[1]

Donnell picked it up and rifled through it but found no cash or credit cards; then he hollered down to Freeman and her family, "Hey, where's the fellow that was in this car?" Kaye Freeman thought it was strange that the scruffy-looking man didn't walk over to them first and say, "Hey, how's the fishing?" like any normal Texan would have done. Before she could respond, Donnell jumped in his pickup and slammed the door. He then drove to Bastrop and turned the wallet in to the sheriff's office around 5:30 P.M., telling them that someone had abandoned the car. Taking the wallet to the sheriff's office wasn't too surprising for Donnell; he came from a Texas family with deep roots in law enforcement, and in fact his uncle had been sheriff of Bastrop County.

An hour later, around 6:30, Bastrop County dispatch sent a sheriff's deputy, Jim Burnett, to the river to check out the abandoned car.[2] Just before the deputy arrived, Freeman cast her bait in the shallower waters close to the riverbank. Her hook snagged, and when she pulled it a body bobbed to the surface among the tangled branches of a willow on the bank.

By the time Burnett arrived at the bridge, he had a much bigger problem than an abandoned Mercedes. John H. Jenkins III had been shot once with a large-caliber gun pressed to the back of his head. The bullet exited through the left temple, taking with it part of the brain and skull.[3]

The next day numerous rare book dealers from the West Coast to the East Coast called each other with the news of Jenkins's death. Rare book sellers describe their close-knit community this way: when a dealer in New York sneezes, one in Los Angeles says gesundheit. To the tight circle of brokers, the sudden death of an especially influential bookseller like John Jenkins was momentous news. One of Jenkins's oldest friends, the director of the Texas State Historical Association, echoed the sentiments of many when he said, "I'm just thunderstruck."[4] Years later, most rare book dealers of a certain age could recall where they had been when they heard the news of the violent finish to Jenkins's flamboyant life.

In 1975, Jenkins engineered the largest rare book coup of the twentieth century—the purchase of the legendary Eberstadt inventory of rare Americana. The selling price was for over $2.5 million, and it garnered him coverage in the *New York Times* and the *Wall Street Journal*. But his career as a top-tier dealer and scholar began long before that. He had a history book published by the University of Texas Press on the day he graduated high school in 1958, with a resounding endorsement from famed Texas folklorist J. Frank Dobie. He edited and published the ten-volume *Papers of the Texas Revolution* and authored a massive bibliographic guide to the history of Texas called *Basic Texas Books*. One scholar called it the best research tool ever created for Texas.[5]

Hollywood appealed to Jenkins. He dabbled in movies and helped to finance the highly profitable 1974 horror film *The Texas Chainsaw Massacre*. He invested in oil wells, and at his peak bought the campus of Westminster University near Mexia, Texas. Jenkins even once went undercover with FBI agents to help them recover a cache of hand-colored Audubon copperplate engravings stolen from Union College, which later gratefully gave him an honorary Doctor of Letters degree. The dark side of Jenkins's rare book dealings showed itself in the many forgeries of Texas historical documents that passed through his hands and, late in his career, in two office warehouse fires of suspicious origin.

Dick Bosse, the proprietor of the oldest antiquarian bookstore in Dallas, knew Jenkins from many rare book trades.[6] Bosse exemplified the streak of independence that made most book dealers such poor employees in other occupations. He once typed up a rare book catalogue on the cattle trade and outlaws, and in between sips of Lone Star beer he mailed it to customers with the cover title "Shitty-Shitty, Bang-Bang."[7]

Bosse self-deprecatingly said he was just one of many antiquarian nickel-and-dime hustlers, but he thought Johnny Jenkins the most important rare book dealer in Texana.[8] One longtime customer described Jenkins as the P. T. Barnum of rare books, clever and manipulative but also a hell of a researcher: "He built an empire on Texana."[9]

To describe Jenkins only as a dealer in Texana is too limiting; Bosse also thought Jenkins was probably the most creative rare book dealer of his century. Jenkins handled and placed great works and archives of literature related to such well-known writers as Jane Austen, Herman Melville, and Mark Twain. He appraised over seven thousand IRS donations of rare books and manuscripts. He imagined and pioneered categories unknown to other rare book cataloguers in the 1970s, including catalogue listings on JFK, NASA and space exploration, anti-Vietnam protests, and even the civil rights movement, long before social history was a fashionable academic trend.[10]

———•———

Jenkins's short stature made him feel inadequate, and he compensated by wearing a white felt Stetson cowboy hat with a high crown. Sometimes Jenkins would remark wistfully to his rare book manager, Michael Parrish (who is 6 foot 2 inches), "I wish I had your height." Jenkins had read that the average male height was 5 foot 7 inches; thereafter he could say of his slightly shorter

5 foot 5 inch frame with a straight face: "For a short person, I'm actually pretty tall."[11]

Jenkins's friends and customers genuinely enjoyed his company. He cultivated his persona of being extremely pleasant by carefully sowing self-deprecating remarks about himself. His pale baby face irritated him when he wished to be thought more mature, and he tried a mustache at different times. Later Jenkins's young face became more rotund, but he still had little color because he avoided the sun. For any admiring audience, his smile was all teeth matched with eyes that sheened like freshly waxed used cars.

Unlike many other rare book dealers who avoided forays in the public eye, Jenkins loved publicity. He mastered the unforgettable entrance, once showing up at the normally reserved autumn Boston Rare Book Fair with his Stetson hat in a pinstripe suit, shiny alligator cowboy boots, and full-length dark mink coat, puffing away on a Cuban cigar.[12] One acquaintance thought that what Alice Roosevelt Longworth said of her father, Theodore, applied equally to Jenkins: "He always wanted to be the baby at every christening and the bride at every wedding."[13]

———— • ————

Jenkins's luxurious lifestyle sparked outlandish speculation about motives for his death. The high life requires constant sources of cash and credit, and there were certainly financial crises in Jenkins's life. One included an IRS audit of his business taxes and a lawsuit over a defaulted $1.3 million loan on an oil well in West Texas. The week before Jenkins's death, an Austin bank had foreclosed on his publishing business and business premises for his failure to pay on a $600,000 loan. There had also been a suspicious fire at his business, with nearly a million dollars in insurance claims under an ongoing arson investigation.[14]

Jenkins was once a successful blackjack player who counted cards and raked in the chips, until the casinos banned him. Later he played high-stakes poker in Las Vegas under the sobriquet "Austin Squatty," and he had lines of credit at twenty-three different casinos. Two months before his death, he won one of the early rounds at Amarillo Slim's Super Bowl of Poker in Las Vegas with a $99,000 prize; yet after his death rumors circulated about massive gambling debts.[15] Had mobsters from Las Vegas gone after Jenkins for uncollected debts? There were the two Audubon thieves with known mafia connections who received long prison sentences after Jenkins turned them over to the FBI. Was Jenkins's death a revenge killing from the mob?

———•———

The rumors that Jenkins's death was connected to the sale of the many forged Texas documents he sold were just as disturbing to rare book collectors and dealers. There were two other Texas dealers who also handled the forgeries, but no one sold more than Jenkins. The Texas forgeries were of the type that rare book dealers call "black tulips." The name comes from the Dutch tulip bloom speculation bubble of the 1600s and is a metaphor for something so rarely seen that a collector might have one chance in a lifetime to buy it.

Two black tulips haunted the dreams of Texana collectors. First was a copy of the printed plea for help from the siege of the Alamo authored by Col. William B. Travis, known colloquially as the Travis "Victory or Death" letter. Before Jenkins sold them to delighted Texans, there was only one known copy of the Travis letter. Suddenly twelve more of these rare documents appeared on the market, sold largely through Jenkins.[16]

The other black tulip of Texana was a copy of the Texas Declaration of Independence, published when Texans thumbed their noses at General Santa Anna in 1836. At the time there were only five known genuine copies of the document, and only one had appeared at public auction in the previous hundred years. That had been in the famous Thomas W. Streeter sale of Americana at Parke-Bernet in New York in 1966. Now, twelve more copies appeared and were sold, again, through Jenkins.[17]

Rare book dealers enjoy boasting among fellow dealers about how many copies of an especially rare item they have handled. Western gunfighters notched their pistols, but rare book dealers tally these transactions in their catalogues, and their printed record is a kind of provenance and genealogy for these rare books. Jenkins, however, who was always so eager to gloat about almost anything, nearly never recorded any of the Texana black tulips in his catalogues, and, even more oddly for a publicity hound, never issued a single press release about any of his Texana discoveries.

———•———

A tongue-in-cheek keepsake printed when Jenkins came to address the Western history enthusiasts at Yale in the late 1970s said he was the "enfant terrible" of the rare book world. The author of this in-house satire continued: "In 1840 Captain Richard King stated, three kinds of people come to Texas nowadays—preachers, fugitives from justice and sons-of-bitches." Showing the mixture of wariness and affection that Jenkins elicited in the profession, the author concluded: "Which of these descriptions applies to Jenkins is a closely held secret."[18]

Secrets need masks to protect the deeply buried things and to project images of success and wealth. I met Jenkins once and got a small taste of his effortless persona. I worked at a rare book library in Dallas and occasionally ordered relatively cheap Texas and Western imprints from the Jenkins Company catalogues. A month before he died, I saw John Jenkins in the book exhibitor hall of the annual Texas State Historical Association meeting. After I worked up the courage to approach him and introduce myself, he turned to a collector standing next to him and said, "This is Michael Vinson—he's our best customer." Though Jenkins charmed and flattered me, even I knew then that if I were their best customer they were in a heap of trouble. Little did I know how much.[19]

Oscar Wilde, who said, "A mask tells us more than a face," believed disguises magnify personality traits.[20] If true, the personas Jenkins projected—successful businessman, expert rare book dealer, high-stakes gambler—show what Jenkins wanted people to believe about him. The examination of his masks may not uncover the true Jenkins, but it will make visible the chasms in his own ego, the places where, for whatever reason, Jenkins felt least secure. Jenkins's ultimate mask and secret was also his final one. Was he murdered? Or was his death a suicide, staged as a murder?

1

Born a Trader

Jenkins liked to tell people he was born a trader. The only words of caution that his doting parents ever received about Jenkins's propensity for grand schemes came from his pediatrician when he was four or five years old: "You have a hyperactive boy here." At his birth an uncle gave him a $100 U.S. savings bond and ten years later Jenkins cashed it and began collecting coins.[1]

His father, J. Holmes Jenkins Jr. (1907–84), encouraged his son's treasure-hunting instincts. Holmes had a successful graphic design business in Beaumont, Texas, a thriving community of around 100,000 people. He had begun by illustrating the company magazine for Magnolia Petroleum Company and later worked for Hooper Engraving, before opening his graphic arts business in 1951.[2] He and his wife, Sue Chalmers (1909–85), were active in the city's social circles. They served in the early 1960s as king and queen of the Neches River Festival, and Holmes was president of the Beaumont Country Club and also served on the Beaumont city council. Though not wealthy, they were comfortably upper middle class. Johnny was their only child, and they gave him every advantage.[3]

The young coin trader soon learned that he could quickly multiply his collection by buying rolls of pennies, nickels, dimes, and quarters at the local bank on a Friday. Then at home on the weekends, Jenkins sorted them at the kitchen table and kept the more valuable or collectible coins. All he paid was the face value of the coins plus his sorting time. But he felt hamstrung by having only enough money to take out five or ten dollars of coins at a time, so his father signed for a temporary loan at the bank for fifty dollars in his son's name for weekend credit, due back every Monday morning. Then Jenkins could take home fifty dollars' worth of coins to sort through over the weekend. Later Jenkins claimed he had a $5,000 line of credit when he was only twelve years old, but even fifty dollars in the early 1950s was a week's worth of minimum wages.[4]

Jenkins joined the American Numismatic Association and by age fifteen was the corresponding secretary of the Beaumont Coin Club. He took his duties seriously and reported on the club's activities to the national collecting journal, *Numismatist*.[5]

Jenkins's proudest moment came at age fourteen when he invented a new method of cleaning and restoring coins. He published his method in a letter to *Numismatist*, which Jenkins later claimed caused a "sensation" in the numismatic world.[6] Although this sounds impressive, experienced collectors would likely have recoiled in horror from the teenager's advice. Collectors are almost universally cautioned not to clean their coins because amateurs who try to improve their coins' appearance often end up damaging their resale value.[7] Such a public mistake of judgment shows the disadvantages of being a juvenile self-taught collector, especially one in haste to cast himself as an expert.

The letters and papers from Jenkins's boyhood have the same odd banality and resonance as Jay Gatsby's plan for self-improvement in F. Scott Fitzgerald's novel *The Great Gatsby:* at the funeral, his father brings his childhood copy of *Hopalong Cassidy* with Gatsby's handwritten note on the endpaper: "Read one improving book or magazine a week." In eighth grade Jenkins kept a reading list of books, with his reviews of them. He found Raphael Semmes's *Rebel Raider* interesting, for example, but like most history books it had a bad ending, particularly if you loved the Confederacy. Jenkins read some fiction; he wondered why Earl Stanley Gardner's Perry Mason book could not be considered good literature (except for the foul language), but he thought the Hardy Boys in

The Criss-Cross Shadows far-fetched. Of *Gone with the Wind*'s story of the romantic lost South, he had one word: "excellent."[8]

Jenkins's family encouraged his love of the Confederacy with gifts of more books on Texas and the Civil War. His first antiquarian book, an 1866 first edition of R. L. Dabney's *The Life and Campaigns of Lieut.-General Thomas J. Jackson*, was given to him by his Bastrop cousins, the Kesselus family, and dates from this time. There were other Civil War books Jenkins devoured, including Douglas Freeman's *Lee's Lieutenants*, Henry Steele Commager's *The Blue and the Gray*, and James Ferber's *Texas, C.S.A.*[9]

Just how rich his Confederate dreams were can be seen in his boyhood crafting of a new persona. When he was eleven at summer camp near Uvalde in West Texas, he asked his parents to address their letters to Lt. Col. Johnny Jenkins, which would be read out loud at mail call, and his father happily indulged him. Later he wrote to his parents that after mail call "everybody calls me Colonel to kid me." Ever impatient, Jenkins asked his parents for a promotion to general in his next letter.[10]

The next year Jenkins created a handmade certificate of enrollment in the Confederacy. At the top was a small picture of a Confederate flag between two hand-drawn wreaths that read:

This is to certify that JOHNNY H. JENKINS has officially seceded from the United States of America and has become a loyal officer in the Army of the Confederate States of America on this first day of July in the year of 1952 A.D.

R. E. Lee [signed in black ink]
Commander in Chief of the Army of the Confederacy

Jeff Davis [signed in black ink]
President of the Confederate States of America

Johnny Jenkins [signed in black ink]
Confederate.[11]

Even his classmates at Dick Dowling Jr. High School in Beaumont knew about Jenkins's romantic love of lost causes. In the year after the Supreme Court's *Brown* v. *Board of Education* landmark decision, the student newspaper wrote a prophecy about

what class members would be doing in twenty years. They fore-
cast that Jenkins would be the president of the "New Confederate
States of America."[12] Jenkins eventually outgrew his wholehearted
admiration of the Confederacy and became a lifelong liberal. But
his boyish fantasies of being larger than life never left him.

A neighbor boy younger than Jenkins remembered his singing in
the shower every morning. Their houses were close together and
on the many warm and humid days in Beaumont he could hear
the other boy's voice drifting out the open bathroom window. The
current country or pop hits didn't appeal to Jenkins; his favorite
song was "You Are My Sunshine," a smash hit in Louisiana in
1939 when it was recorded by the Pine Ridge Boys.[13] The song
was so popular that the writer Jimmie Davis became governor of
Louisiana in 1944. Jenkins also improvised upbeat ballads in the
morning showers, usually about himself, like "I'm going to be the
best—." Once in the front yard the neighbor boys teased Jenkins
about his morning shower performances, but Jenkins just laughed
them off.[14]

Jenkins took that happy and confident attitude to the poker
games he played with his friends. Originally known as "bluff," the
game of poker took hold in the South during the Civil War, where
many young soldiers brought it home when the war ended. One
of Jenkins's cousins described their games as a pastime that Texas
boys have played for 150 years: "Poker is one of our sports."[15] Jenkins's father, Holmes, played a weekly game at his home, which
Jenkins's mother, Sue, discreetly referred to as his "literary club."

As a seaport, Beaumont often played host to visiting sailors, and
in the 1950s the city officials looked the other way when it came
to gambling and other illicit pursuits. There were betting parlors
on Main Street for horse racing as well as houses of prostitution
for entertaining sailors and locals. The most famous of these were
Rita Ainsworth's Dixie Hotel, on Crockett Street in downtown
Beaumont, as well as the Marine and Boston hotels.

The flagship Dixie refused to admit boys of Jenkins's age (because
their dads and uncles might be there), but they were welcome at

the Marine and Boston. The afternoon matinee rate of five dollars at these two boarding houses allowed even teenage boys to gain initiation to the sexual mysteries of life.[16] One boy thought that parents didn't really mind, because a professional was better than getting a teenage girl into trouble. Jenkins's next-door neighbor believed growing up that gambling and prostitution were legal in Beaumont, because they were everywhere in his town. Even the Beaumont Country Club hosted late-night poker games.[17]

That risk-friendly atmosphere and the love of gambling stuck with Jenkins throughout his life. At their weekly "poker game bull sessions," he and three high school buddies played bourrè (in Texas spelled "booray"), a five-card game imported from the Acadian region of Louisiana. Players each put in one chip at the beginning of a hand, trying to win the most tricks to win the pot. A player who won no tricks was "bourrè" (drunken) and, as a penalty, had to match the money in the pot for the next round.

After one game at Jenkins's home in spring 1957 (when they were juniors), Johnny and his pals came up with the idea for a trip across the United States and Canada. Each boy vowed to get a job at the beginning of summer to earn enough money to pay for gas and food. To save money on motels, the states where family relatives lived dictated the itinerary. Secrecy was half the fun, and Jenkins didn't tell his parents until a month before the trip. They ended up traveling 7,000 miles across twenty-three states and Canada during August 1957.[18]

———— • ————

Jenkins started his first scholarly project while still in high school, editing the memoirs of his great-great-grandfather. John Holland Jenkins's (1822–90) adventurous life included fighting as a boy in the Texas Revolution, later with the Texas Rangers, and finally under Col. Rip Ford in the last battle of the Civil War in Texas. The *Bastrop Advertiser* originally published the old soldier's "Recollections of Early Texas" in 1884. Young Jenkins began actively researching and writing the book in 1955 during the fall of his sophomore year. By February he reminded his mother she had given him permission to skip school so he could work on the project; he optimistically planned to finish between fifteen and twenty pages that day. He also bragged to her that the Alabama state archives intended to purchase a copy after publication.[19]

Jenkins spent the summer of 1956, between his sophomore and junior years, in Bastrop with his mother's parents (Owen and Lutie Chalmers) so he could continue his research, but it wasn't all dreary work in the archives. He told his mother he was having a swell time, but that she wouldn't think he was getting much done on his book, since with the help of "scheming aunts" he had had two dates in the previous twenty-four hours. Jenkins sometimes showed a sentimental sense of history. To his mother he signed off one of his letters, "My pen is bad, my ink is pale; My love for you shall never fail. From a Confederate soldier's letter written in 1863. Love, Johnny."[20]

In that same summer, Jenkins finagled an invitation to J. Frank Dobie's home to talk about his project. Dobie (1888–1964) was one of the most famous Texas historians and folklorists of the 1950s. He had published best-selling books about the lore of Texas history, and it took courage for a teenage boy to ask for an interview. Jenkins recalled that he was "scared as one can be of one of his heroes," and he thought he would make a fool of himself. The teen's historical interests intrigued Dobie, and he sank back in his chair with a grin to draw the young man out. The two carried on a lengthy conversation about Texas history until Dobie's wife finally interrupted with the news that it was time for Dobie's nap. Jenkins left a copy of the memoirs with Dobie, who promised to read them and get back with him.[21]

Not long after that, Jenkins's aunt Kate wrote telling him of an encounter she had with the historian at a doctor's office in Austin. She happened to be carrying one of Dobie's bestsellers when she heard a man's voice boom behind her in the elevator, "I see you have a copy of my book!" She turned around and there was Dobie, "pleased as punch." When she asked Dobie to inscribe the book to Johnny Jenkins, he mentioned that he was looking forward to Jenkins's book project. Dobie told her he had read the reminiscences and found them interesting.[22]

Like most aunts, she had some words of caution for Jenkins as she advised him to write a thank-you note to Dobie and not to say, "Why did you have to scribble in my book?" Apparently Aunt Kate had once written an inscription in a book she had given him and had later heard a complaint from him about the writing in it.[23] Jenkins the collector would treasure any book autographed by its author, but Jenkins the teenager probably just thought his aunt's writing marred his copy.

Eventually Jenkins needed a completed manuscript, but he had hundreds of pages and notes scattered around his room at home and no idea of how to organize them. In the summer of 1957 (between his junior and senior years), he was lucky enough to have the brother-in-law of his next-door neighbor drop over for a visit. David Carlson was a history major at Southern Methodist University and had worked as a research and teaching assistant. After Jenkins bragged about his project and then showed Carlson his home office's mess of notes, Carlson offered to help him get it organized. He spent a week with Jenkins in his room, sitting on the floor and sorting the piles of notes according to where they would appear in the book.[24] This timely help enabled Jenkins to finish the manuscript. Unfortunately, he never acknowledged Carlson's contribution in his book.

Dobie told Jenkins to take the edited manuscript to the University of Texas Press with his recommendation that they publish it. Although there was some tussle with the editorial board, the press eventually agreed to publish the memoirs. The agreement included the proviso that the book, *Recollections of Early Texas*, have a foreword by Dobie to guarantee sales.

Jenkins proudly noted that he received his first copy when he graduated high school in May 1958.[25] Dobie saw a hopeful future for the young historian. He wrote in his foreword that he did not support this publication because Jenkins was such a young editor but because he was such an able one. "Many a Ph.D. thesis shows less scholarship and less intelligence than Johnny's editorial work and is not nearly so interesting."[26]

Publishing a book with a university press while still in high school would be exemplary, but Jenkins could not resist embellishing his story. He told people he actually wrote the book secretly in high school without his parents' knowledge. In October 1958 (when he was a college freshman) he was on a panel of

University of Texas authors, and the program coordinator asked if it was true he had worked secretly on the book: "How did you manage such a momentous, long-time project without your parents catching on?"[27]

Jenkins said the secrecy of his book project was a comedy of errors and white lies. It had almost but not quite caused him to lose his girlfriend, get him expelled from school, and nearly gave his grandmother, his teacher, and his great-aunt a collective nervous breakdown.[28] Jenkins had a captive audience and could not resist adding that, if the Press would print a paperback edition with his girlfriend on the front cover in a scanty bathing suit and use the title "Passion on the Prairie," he "would soon be a millionaire." That brought the house down.[29] Jenkins could not have failed to note his audience's enjoyment of his audacity and storytelling skills, even if they suspected that his tales were exaggerated.

Even as a young author, Jenkins quickly mastered the nuances of self-promotion. Just before he graduated high school he promoted a meet-the-author signing day at a bookstore in Beaumont that netted him nearly $300. That was not an insubstantial sum in 1958, considering that tuition at the University of Texas was $100 per semester.

Later, during Jenkins's junior year in college, he excitedly wrote his parents that there was a new weekly ABC radio program called *Meet the Colleges* that would tell the story of his writing the book. Each week the program profiled a different college with a docudrama-style radio broadcast, and for the University of Texas they would do his secret book story. The one-hour episode would have music and actors playing the parts of Jenkins, his parents, Dobie, and others. The radio drama would be broadcast over the summer, and they promised Jenkins script approval.[30] There are no surviving scripts for this radio episode. Was it ever really seriously considered? I doubt that Jenkins worried about the possibility of exposure of his exaggeration to his parents. If they called his bluff, he always had another story to tell.

Jenkins's proclivity for self-invention stayed with him throughout his life. He happily created personas for any occasion, a motif that recurs often in his life, whether he wore his Stetson cowboy hat to an auction at Sotheby's or a jacket emblazoned with "Austin

Squatty" to the World Series of Poker. Jenkins knew his own reputation for enhancing tales, and later in life when recounting a
caper he would ask listeners, "Do you want the story or do you
want the truth?"

———•———

Jenkins became a student at the University of Texas in September
1958 and pledged with the Delta Tau Delta fraternity. He told a
friend that pledging was hell. He did 298 pushups during a three-
hour work rally and could hardly raise himself from bed the next
morning. But his fraternity friends loved card games too. He won
a trophy in the Goodall-Wooten dorm gin rummy tournament. It
was a two-foot-tall statue of Venus.[31]

Jenkins's most formative influence at the University of Texas
came as a result of his experience working in the Texas state
archives. About a month before Jenkins started school he got a
phone call from the state archivist. Dorman Winfrey had probably heard about the history wunderkind through his participation
in the Junior Historians of Texas, and he called to see if Jenkins
needed a job while he was at school. Jenkins was "flabbergasted"
but thought it was typical of Winfrey to give a chance to a young
man interested in books and history.[32]

Winfrey started Jenkins at $1.25 per hour (25 cents an hour above
the federal minimum wage of $1.00 per hour) with the added ben-
efit that he could work up to forty hours a week if he wanted.
Winfrey gave Jenkins another perk as well: because he was editing
Texas history materials for the archives, he would pay him for any
Texas history books Jenkins read in his spare time at the same
rate. Jenkins told his parents that the book they gave him, Lon
Tinkle's *Thirteen Days to Glory*, and all the reading he did would
count too: "It's a damn good deal."[33]

Why did Winfrey offer Jenkins such an enticing deal? Jenkins
told his parents that all the other state archives workers were
political appointees "who couldn't care less about Texas history,"
so Winfrey needed someone to supervise their work.[34] Though
it seems unlikely that a part-time freshman college student was
supervising the work of full-time appointees, one thing was clear:

Winfrey was taken with the young man and excited to groom another future enthusiast of Texas history.

The archives job fit Jenkins well. He said it was the first job that he looked forward to every day.[35] Since the archives did not yet have its own building, Jenkins worked in a Quonset hut at Camp Hubbard (just opposite Camp Mabry off the MoPac highway) in Austin. He took full creative advantage of the fringe benefits of his position. Upperclassmen were given first choice in class registration, meaning that freshmen and sophomores might miss classes or times they preferred. But Jenkins asked Winfrey to write notes for him certifying that he needed to register early because of his job in the archives. Winfrey complied each time, asking for the earliest registration time for Jenkins because of his work schedule in the archives.[36]

The state archives offered occasional serendipitous encounters that Jenkins enjoyed. One Friday afternoon he went to the archives to see if he could "scratch up" anything for a book he hoped to write on Edward Burleson (1798–1851), the colonel who accepted Santa Anna's sword of surrender at the Battle of San Jacinto and who later served as vice-president of the Republic of Texas under Sam Houston. Jenkins had a personal connection to Burleson. His great-great-grandfather Jenkins (subject of his first book) had lived in Burleson's household for a time while a young man.[37]

One afternoon Winfrey and Jenkins were drinking coffee and talking about Burleson when a lady visiting the archives from Tennessee overheard and interrupted them. She told them they should read the *Recollections of Early Texas* that "little boy wrote" because it had some wonderful accounts of Burleson. Then she turned to Jenkins, telling him that maybe the book would inspire him to do something like that. Jenkins wrote to his parents about the meeting, noting that the woman had bought and read his book in Tennessee. He concluded with a proud sentiment that any author would recognize: "Little things like that are worth a lot more to me than the money angle."[38]

The archives gave Jenkins valuable experience. It didn't hurt to have Winfrey as his mentor, nor that Winfrey continually tried to improve his job. When Dorman Winfrey became the University of Texas archivist in 1960, Jenkins followed him (at the beginning of his junior year) and got his pay increased to $1.45 per hour, because his work in the university archives was so "desperately needed."[39] There were other perks, including the good news he told his parents early in 1961 that Winfrey had got Jenkins his own office upstairs in the Barker Texas History Center.[40] Jenkins had another reason to strut to his classes.

Jenkins's experience in the archives coincided with the frenetic tenure of Harry Ransom. As chancellor, Ransom dramatically increased the rare books and archives collections at the University of Texas. Jenkins excitedly told his parents in the fall of 1961 that Winfrey had selected him to do a reorganization of the archives in preparation for moving into a new building. This meant that he could come and go as he pleased with two assistants to do his "dirty work."[41]

This promotion came about because the governor offered Dorman Winfrey the position of state librarian at $12,000 per year. Ransom, though, did not want to lose another important staff member to state government. He offered to match the state salary if Winfrey would stay and take the position as head of the Barker Texas History Center with some additional inducements. Ransom would give Winfrey free time to finish his Ph.D. and write for historical publications, an unlimited travel budget, and virtually unlimited resources for historical acquisitions.

According to Jenkins, Winfrey accepted the position with the additional proviso that Ransom let Winfrey keep Jenkins as his assistant, and the new arrangement would begin in October. Jenkins carefully enumerated the benefits: higher pay for fewer hours; a campus staff parking permit; travel with Winfrey (with absences excused, as Jenkins carefully pointed out to his parents, who worried about his grades). More important to Jenkins, he would get to associate with Ransom and the "top, very top men at the university." Jenkins and Winfrey celebrated by opening a bottle of champagne.[42]

Winfrey took Jenkins along to give him firsthand experience in deal making when the archives were considering the purchase of historical papers. They went to Corpus Christi to try to buy some rare documents. Jenkins told his worried parents that President Ransom got him excused from classes and the board of regents had authorized Winfrey to spend $10,000 on the acquisition. But Jenkins, who had been bartering coins and collectibles for nearly ten years on his own, told his parents that they had gotten the unidentified owner down to $8,000, and they expected that "she will go down even more." Jenkins thought that their acquisition of these documents would be a big feather in both his and Winfrey's caps.[43]

After starting work in the archives, Jenkins met a law school student working there, Jaime S. Platon, whose parents were from Puerto Rico and Brazoria, Texas.[44] Jenkins and Platon were crows of a feather for risks and adventures. The two young men took a trip as college students to Fidel Castro's Cuba in the year after the revolution, which later became part of Jenkins's mythology. Castro's fight against the established regime captured the imagination of Jenkins. He wrote in his diary early in 1959 after hearing the news of the revolutionary's victory that his hero had finally won out over the Cuban dictator, Batista. Jenkins's naïve enthusiasm disregarded rumors that Castro had made a deal with the communists and would seek to become a dictator.[45]

In the summer of 1960, Jenkins and Platon wrote to the student organization at the University of Havana asking to observe Castro's revolution firsthand. Jenkins, ever the hopeful collector, also hoped to meet Castro and get his autograph. The student organization gave them a warm reply, offering to put them up in dormitories and to let them eat at the student mess and to charge them only student rates. Platon and Jenkins flew to Key West and then to Havana, where Jenkins wrote his parents trying to ease their minds. He assured them he was safe from indoctrination, and that his hotel, the Havana Hilton, was one of the best, "on a par" with the Hotel Beaumont.[46]

Even though soldiers were walking the streets with rifles, knives, and machine guns, the Havana students invited them to drink beer and share their dinner. Ever the entrepreneurs, Jenkins and Platon also bought large quantities of Cuban cigars to bring back to Texas. Although they did not get to meet Castro, they got a fairly close view of him in the great Havana public square where at least 300,000 Cubans cheered as Castro tore a U.S. treaty to pieces.[47]

Platon knew Spanish and immediately understood the travel implications of Castro's tearing up the treaty; soon there would be no airline flights out of Cuba. Platon grabbed Jenkins by the arm and told his friend, who spoke no Spanish, "We have to run." They raced to the hotel, dumped all of their clothes on the floor, filled their luggage with boxes of Cuban cigars (and revolutionary pamphlets and broadsides), and caught the last Pan-Am flight from Havana to Miami.[48] That haul alone kept Jenkins in Cuban cigars for years.

Archive work and deal making came more naturally to Jenkins than classwork. At college he had all the trappings of a scholar, with a bedroom to himself at the fraternity, three bookshelves, three filing cabinets, and a desk, but his grades never matched the expectations suggested by his bookish clutter. That did not stop Jenkins from adding one more academic accoutrement. He loved new technology and told his parents that he had purchased a Smith-Corona electric portable typewriter wholesale at $145, lest they wonder about their spendthrift son, and "it was really a dandy."[49]

Jenkins told his parents in the fall of his freshman year that he could make A's if he spent every minute on schoolwork, but that he felt that would be wasting his time in college since grades really just didn't mean that much. Besides, his fraternity had a poker game; he mentioned playing for the first time in three weeks, winning a dollar.[50]

Jenkins's attention to his grades also ranked behind his romantic life. He told a friend during his freshman year that he had broken up with his high school sweetheart, a process that took six long-distance phone calls and two trips home, but that he had now met a wonderful Chi Omega girl, who was one of several girls Jenkins dated. The only downside Jenkins saw was that she was causing him to get lower grades, though he admitted that they were already "pretty rotten."[51] Two years later Jenkins tried to reassure his parents that his dating life did not have to hinder his grades. He and his current girl were giving up dating for two weeks to get ahead on their grades and were even giving up a fraternity hayride with beer so they could go to the library and study. "How about that?"[52]

Sometimes Jenkins's archives job helped his grades. Winfrey, who probably knew Jenkins badly needed a boost to his GPA, told him that while he was working in the summer he could take the seminar in historical writing for state archivists. It would be two hours per day in Austin, and Jenkins would get three hours' credit with an A in a history course.[53] The other good news about working in the archives during the school year was that he was making nearly $100 per month, "and that ain't hay." Besides, Jenkins bragged to his parents, he had not cut a class in two weeks.[54]

Another indicator of Jenkins's poor grades was his Selective Service (draft) registration. In his junior year of college, the draft card ranked him in the lower quarter of full-time male students in his class. That same year (1961) Jenkins failed both his German and biology courses and was placed on scholastic probation.[55] The two failed classes must have weighed on Jenkins's mind, particularly since his plan was to attend law school at UT after graduation. He told his parents he was having so much trouble in school that he was thinking of quitting his job in the state archives. But he did not know how to tell Winfrey.

A letter from his parents complaining about his grades, like the draft Jenkins was enclosing for them, would work nicely. Jenkins asked his parents not to date it, since he didn't know for sure when he would show it to Winfrey. Jenkins's suggested draft ran: "Dear Johnny, Since you have been having so much trouble this semester with your schoolwork, and your mid-semester grades are so low, we think it would best if you would not work anymore for the rest of the semester. It is more important that you get your biology and German behind you, etc., etc."[56] It appears that Jenkins never used his parents' pre-written excuse.

———◆———

Jenkins's parents gave him a cabin in Bastrop for his high school graduation gift. It became his idyllic getaway from the pressures

of college classes and grades. His father had built the cabin of
heavy Oregon pine on the exterior with white pine paneling on
the interior walls, on nearly one-third of an acre facing the Colorado River. The cabin sat just west of rural downtown Bastrop
near Fisherman's Park, next to a bend in the river, and from the
porch Jenkins could watch the occasional fisherman drifting
downstream in his boat casting for bass. They sited it twenty-six
feet above the flood stage, which seemed a safe location. Reflect-
ing on it in his journal, Jenkins wrote that it was a "college boy's
dream" cabin and he couldn't wait to use it. "Mother and Dad
have been really kind to me."[57]

Jenkins kept his fraternity poker trophy of Venus at the cabin,
his growing collection of history books, and a record player for
parties. In a bit of college boy humor, he and his new girlfriend
Maureen Mooney nabbed a metal sign from a military site west
of Austin on one of their first dates: "Warning—Missile Silo."[58]
He generously let his friends use the cabin, though later he had to
post some house rules on the refrigerator:

> To Whom It May Concern. The upkeep on this place is high and
> I therefore suggest to all who stay here for the purpose of poker
> playing, love making, drinking, "studying" and other unmention-
> able pleasures that you help me out by replenishing the liquor sup-
> ply, buying food, providing transportation, and feeding the can on
> top of the icebox with something besides the IOUs that keep crop-
> ping up there.

With a typical dramatic if anti-Semitic flourish, he signed his
notice "John Jenkinstein."[59]

Bastrop was a small town and Jenkins's mother had many relatives there, so it is not too surprising that his parents eventually
heard about the student parties at the cabin. They had misgiv-
ings, and Sue wrote him about a year after he started college that
she and his father were not at all happy with how Jenkins used
the cabin. Although they had honored Jenkins's request by putting the title in his name before he was twenty-one years old,
his parents felt entitled to make a few rules since they were paying for the taxes, utilities, insurance, and repairs at the cabin.
His mother warned him that his parties were not proper and the

gossip was hurting her family in Bastrop. The new rules were straightforward: no girls, that was "O.U.T. absolutely!"[60]

Family might gossip about Jenkins's cabin revelries, but they stepped up to help him when the Colorado River flooded on October 29, 1960, damaging the cabin and its contents. It was the worst flood in Bastrop since 1935. Jenkins's uncle and cousin worked with him in a rowboat using flashlights until eleven at night trying to save his estimated thousand books, but nearly all were waterlogged and ruined under six feet of water.[61]

Fortunately for Jenkins, there was some insurance on his book collection; his father wrote him about a month after the flood that he had not yet received the money from the claim.[62] More important, this was Jenkins's first experience with collecting insurance on his book collection—something that would play a much larger role in his rare book business in the 1980s.

———•———

Despite his poor grades, Jenkins planned to attend law school in the fall of 1962, in part for a career but also to avoid the draft, a concern shared by his parents. This concern was not too unusual. Many upper-middle-class families were fairly successful at helping their sons avoid the Vietnam war draft, and Jenkins's parents were near the pinnacle of Beaumont society. Jenkins's mother wrote with draft avoidance advice in the fall of his senior year at UT (1961), asking if it would not be more helpful for Jenkins to go directly into law school, in case after graduation his named "popped up fast on the draft list?" She also wondered if it would be better to try to defer the draft by not graduating at all? But Jenkins's father quickly wrote to say that the plan of avoiding graduation would be a sure way to get called up. His mother, like all mothers who believe in the most dire of consequences, added one note of caution to the letter with this admonition: "Please destroy the letters that I write to you that you wouldn't want read," especially by a suspicious draft board.[63]

In the fall of 1961, Jenkins had been dating Maureen Mooney from Dallas, and he fell hard for her. Jenkins wrote his parents, "Did I tell you? She was one of the ten most beautiful of the

University of Texas last year."[64] By the middle of the following
March they were engaged, and there was no longer any need
to worry about draft deferments (the deferment for marriage
remained until 1965). The couple set a June 5 date for their wedding at Perkins Chapel on the Southern Methodist University
campus in Dallas.

Everyone who knew them says Maureen became the love of his
life. Every letter to her was signed "Love, Johnny." During their
engagement Jenkins showed promise of becoming a responsible
businessman. He kept Maureen informed on the monetary prog-
ress of their affairs: paying off a loan of $900 so they would be
"completely out of debt, selling coins and bonds for $410, getting
the Clara Driscoll Scholarship ($200), selling $360 in coins to a
collector in LaMarque, and sending $250 in antiquarian books to
a man in New Jersey on approval."[65]

The two were separated for a time while Maureen left school
to recover from mononucleosis at home in Dallas. Jenkins told
her that if she got lonely she was to call him collect at the cabin
in Bastrop. He added that he did not want to risk a call when
her family might all be sitting around and keeping them from
"talking mushy." Another detail of his letter may be familiar to
couples who dated in the early 1960s. Jenkins hoped that his calling Maureen's father didn't cross them up on their stories. "He
didn't seem to like your being home so late."[66]

Despite his efforts to recast himself as a solid soon-to-be-married
man, Jenkins's flamboyant nature showed itself in excesses, such as
his dangerous driving. After a visit in Dallas for New Year's with
Maureen, Jenkins got a speeding ticket from the Texas Department of Public Safety. His father paid the ticket, with a note at the
bottom to his son that he wanted to know about this ticket. Holmes
had already paid several of his son's tickets and had warned him
about speeding. Jenkins's fiancée soon joined in the family efforts
to have him drive more safely. Maureen wrote him before one of
his visits up to Dallas, "Do NOT DRIVE FAST—Don't get a ticket—
Don't kill yourself on the road. If you do, I'll kill you!"[67]

Jenkins played the admiring and cooperative, if sometimes
absent-minded, fiancé. He had minimal interest in the wedding itself, telling Maureen only that the plans sounded "really

neat" and asking her to keep reminding him of anything he was supposed to do to help: "I'm pretty much a nit-wit about things like that."[68] The honeymoon, however, was his department, and it became another channel for his extravagance. Jenkins planned an around-the-world trip by jet for two, which ended up costing nearly $4,000 for both of them. He sold several of his coin collections to pay for the trip and later bragged that it had cost $35,000. There was little need to inflate the original figure. In 1962, $4,000 was a substantial sum of money—by comparison more than enough for a new car. He was still unsure about how he would finance the honeymoon in early April, telling Maureen, "We'll make it somehow, though, I think."[69]

Jenkins's worries about paying for the honeymoon drove him to pester the dealer in Fort Worth for news about the sale of his coins. It didn't take much to become the center of Jenkins's attention. Just owe him some money and watch the telephone ring. The dealer wrote back, chiding him for his impatience: "You sure got ants in your pants!" But the same letter told him that the collection had sold for $4,500, and the dealer enclosed $3,000 in payment. To keep Jenkins from phoning him every day, the dealer told him to be patient; like many collectors, he had purchased more than he could afford to pay for at that moment, but he was still good for it.[70]

After getting the payment in hand, Jenkins confirmed to Maureen the travel details for the nearly eighty-day trip. The honeymoon would start with a flight to Hawaii and then include stops in Hong Kong and Japan. The next leg of the trip would be to South Vietnam, Thailand, and Burma. From there the couple would travel to India, East Africa, and Egypt, then Israel, Turkey, and Greece. They would go on to Italy, making stops in Naples and Rome and then through France and Switzerland, Germany and the Netherlands, with final stops in Ireland, Scotland, and London before flying to New York and back home.

Before leaving, Jenkins left a close friend a long list of instructions for handling his business and collecting affairs. If the draft board asks about him, for example, he tells his friend to say he is on vacation but not where, only that Jenkins will return to attend law school starting on September 12 (1962); if Jim Cope sends him any money, go ahead and deposit it, but don't tell

Cope where Jenkins is; if R. O'Hare sends money, go ahead and deposit it and he can know where Jenkins is; W. C. Young owes Jenkins money but will make the check out to Rick Barnes—sign it Richard Barnes and go ahead and deposit it for Jenkins; if any books or packages come, accept the delivery but don't pay for them; and, "if Mrs. Rosa Todd Hamner from Houston writes, don't answer at all." A detailed set of instructions from a young and complicated man.[71]

Jenkins was impulsive as a collector and as a honeymoon tourist. He stopped shaving during the trip and grew a beard, to the surprise of Maureen, especially since she knew Jenkins's mother would never approve. Among Jenkins's tourist purchases were a movie projector and camera from Hong Kong, Buddha statues from India, a camel saddle from Egypt, some rare maps and documents from dealers on the Left Bank in Paris, gold clocks, and an antique beer stein from Germany. On the final morning of the trip, just before they left London for home and seeing their parents again, Jenkins came out the bathroom with a smoothly shaven face. Maureen looked at him and said, "You coward!"[72]

After Jenkins's return to the University of Texas, he continued his coin trading and antiquarian documents businesses. He wrote his parents that he had been doing "extra good" on coin trading the past two weeks, because of an explosive spiral in the price of the 1950-D Jefferson nickel. Many people thought the nickel might be "real rare" and wanted to get in on it.[73] Jenkins had been hoarding these nickels for some time, and he was not the only dealer doing so. A pair of coin dealers in Wisconsin put away over 100,000 of the 1950-D nickels, and the release of the Denver Mint numbers showing it to be an unusually low coinage only fueled more speculation. One of Jenkins's acquaintances had purchased a roll of the 1950-D nickels for the face value of $2 (forty nickels) and traded it during the peak of the '50-D nickel boom for a beach house near Rockport, Texas.[74]

Jenkins was sanguine about the possibility of future profit, noting that even if the nickels turned out to be relatively common it would still be a year or two before anyone knew for sure—unlike today, when the era of the internet and instant knowledge means that such a boom is unlikely to last long. Besides, right then they were a "hot item," and Jenkins was more than willing to trade them. Jenkins hired his fraternity brothers at $1.25 per hour to search through rolls of nickels, just as he had done on weekends for himself years earlier in Bastrop. Only a few years later the collecting bubble for 1950-D Jefferson nickels burst, but not before Jenkins had cashed in and taken his profits.[75]

Around this time Jenkins handled his first major archive. He had acquired the Civil War letters of W. T. Martin from a scout in Fort Worth, who had bought them at an auction of the Martin family plantation in Natchez, Mississippi. Martin had a distinguished career as a Confederate major general and later as a state senator in Mississippi. Jenkins bought the archive of some forty letters and 250 documents largely on his instincts. He told his parents in the fall of 1961 that he had shown the papers to Winfrey and some other history professors, who had taken them on approval for examination. He was relieved to have that off his back for a few weeks.[76]

Soon the historians and archivists came back with another question about the collection: were there any more documents? Collectors with some experience in these matters need to know if there will be future acquisitions required (and more money), so Jenkins inquired of his scout in Fort Worth. The scout responded that the papers had been in storage for several years, so Jenkins had everything the first time the scout had showed him the archive.[77] The university decided to acquire the collection from Jenkins that December for $1,650.[78]

Jenkins, true to form, celebrated his potential sale of the archive—before being paid, much less knowing it was sold—by buying one of the most desirable cars a young college man could afford: a 1958 Thunderbird coupe with a white body and turquoise top. He proudly gave his mother a ride around town in the Thunderbird, and she told him it was the "prettiest one" she had ever ridden in.[79]

In his last year of college the university police department prohibited Jenkins from taking his Thunderbird on campus because of three prior traffic violations.[80] Later, after his marriage when Jenkins went to trade in that first Thunderbird, the driver's side door had quit working. He told Maureen to drive the car and to stay inside it while he traded it in for a more practical station wagon. Then Maureen climbed out the passenger side and left with Jenkins in their new car, leaving the salesman to figure out how they had taken him.[81]

Such small deceits were not the only ones Jenkins practiced. During the summer of 1961, between his junior and senior year of college, Jenkins changed his business name to the Southwestern Investment Association.[82] The new name evoked a large firm's presence, and the firm advertised a larger inventory of coins for sale—nearly $5,000 in retail inventory, although the mailing address and phone number remained the same.

Any given coin advertisement from the Southwestern Investment Company resulted in nearly half of the orders being returned for refunds. Complaints typically read, "Each and every coin was over graded"; "This coin is terrible to be advertised as A.U. [About Uncirculated condition]"; "I am returning the roll of nickels because there is not one of them that will grade very fine or extra fine." Another collector threatened Jenkins's reputation and wished him no success in his new business: "I will relate this experience at our next coin club meeting as false advertising by a dealer and believe me it will not remain confined to our local vicinity."[83]

Even though the Southwestern Investments Company gained a poor reputation for coin grading, that did not deter Jenkins from upbraiding other dealers about their own descriptions. In August 1961 he returned two 1939 nickels in AU condition with this note: "Sorry—I can't grade these AU. Please send refund. John H. Jenkins. PLEASE! Look at Dunn & Brown as you grade coins!"[84] John W. Dunn and M. R. Brown published *A Guide to the Grading of United States Coins* (1958), which became the standard reference work for grading coins, but this criticism was a little rich coming from a dealer who habitually received requests for refunds for overgraded coins.

One collector was so incensed that he reported Jenkins's firm to the Better Business Bureau in Austin. Jenkins never bothered to answer their letter of inquiry and left blank their form for response. Not too surprisingly, by the following year (1962) the firm's poor reputation caused Jenkins to stop advertising or dealing under the Southwestern Investment Company name.[85] His experience illustrates the hazards of venturing in business without a mentor, much less a sound moral compass. The opportunities for profit seemed too immense for Jenkins to pass up. Buy coins cheaply at a lower grade, then sell them for more at a higher listed grade. If only half the customers return their orders, the dealer still comes out way ahead of the game, in money if not in reputation. In the collecting game, however, reputation is of paramount importance.

Jenkins was apparently admitted on a probationary basis to law school, but he continued his dealing and collecting. He told his parents that while visiting Maureen's parents in Dallas they had gone to some estate sales where the pickings were good. He bought some rare Texas and Confederate books that he sold to Morrison in Waco on the way home to Austin. W. M. Morrison was an antiquarian bookseller in Waco who participated in many trades with Jenkins. Morrison also explained to the young entrepreneur how he handled income taxes for his book sales, which Jenkins thought was an immense help.[86] Even then Jenkins seems to have been thinking at least as much about rare book sales as he was about becoming an attorney.

In fact, Jenkins later made no secret of his dislike for law school and desire to do something else. Law school final exams are intense, and the temptations to cheat are considerable. J. P. Bryan Jr. did not yet know Jenkins, but they sat next to each other in Professor Leon Green's tort class. Green was nationally recognized for his scholarship on the attractive nuisance doctrine in tort law and did not suffer fools in his class. Bryan had noticed that his seatmate had rarely bothered to attend any of the lectures; now, during the final exam, that student was cribbing his test answers.[87]

Bryan took the University of Texas honor code seriously. He waited in the hall after turning in his test and a few minutes later, when Jenkins emerged, challenged him directly about his copying. Jenkins confessed, his manner disarming, and introduced himself. When Jenkins found out his classmate was J. P. Bryan

Jr., he said, "Your dad buys Texana books from me."[88] The two law students realized they shared a deep passion for Texas history, and that became a bond. Bryan laughingly warned Jenkins that, if he had copied Bryan's exam answers, he failed. Jenkins failed that exam, but Bryan graduated from law school and later built a tremendous collection of Texas books and artifacts, acknowledging Jenkins's lasting influence as a dealer and friend. This collection has become the Bryan Museum in Galveston, Texas, which opened in 2015.[89]

The investigator of any life tainted by crimes such as arson and forgery is always curious about the point at which a dealer becomes a crook. The biographer would like to believe that overwhelming financial pressures cause a straight dealer to veer toward criminal impulses, but Jenkins enjoyed the thrills of risk taking. If poker was in his blood, an overgraded coin was just a bluff of a different type. The coin was the grade Jenkins said, until it was returned. Dealers selling overgraded coins are guilty of poor judgment, usually tinged with greed, but when is a dealer not motivated by greed? The question about Jenkins is, how early did he step over the line from poor judgment to larceny? There is one letter in his papers that suggests he crossed that line while still in college.

The letter is from his fellow Cuban adventurer and archives coworker Jaime Platon, and it discusses financial arrangements for stolen letters and documents from the state archives. He wrote Jenkins after graduating from the University of Texas law school and taking an internship with a law firm in Puerto Rico. Platon started with the good news, that he found himself in the happy circumstance of living right across the street from a "whorehouse." Platon then informed his friend that there had been no time for digging around in the local archives in Puerto Rico, but that he would soon put on his Sherlock hat, get out his "burglary tools and go to work." He reported that the autographs they were trying to sell "didn't do so hot." Platon had sold some autographs for fifty dollars, which he figured to keep, since Jenkins had made some small sales with "the bills" which he had kept.[90]

The bills Platon mentioned were Republic of Texas currency (still a desirable item for Texas collectors). Currency is a relatively easy item to steal from archives, since the notes rarely receive item-level description in the finding aids. Instead, currency and Republic of Texas bills that came in with someone's papers would most likely be identified in the finding aid or catalogue as "one folder of Republic of Texas currency," or in some such fashion, with no individual identification and only rarely an enumeration.

Platon thought he might sell some of their Republic of Texas bills to collectors in New York. At the same time, Jenkins ran this now incriminating advertisement in a national coin collecting magazine: "Have Good Stock All Texas Notes—Buy, Sell, Trade."[91] Jenkins also sold or traded these stolen bank notes to William Morrison in Waco, where they appeared in the addenda to his List 175. Morrison almost certainly had no idea they were stolen.[92]

Platon proposed that anything they sold from their proceeds should be spilt 50:50 if it was over $100, and sales less than that they should each keep without splitting. They had also stolen some duplicate books from the archives. Again, this was not a crime requiring great ingenuity, since printed items often come in with collections of papers and manuscripts but are usually catalogued separately long after the acquisition, meaning they could be easily taken before they were inventoried. Platon thought he might be able to get into a bank vault soon, presumably in Puerto Rico because he had met a friendly Englishman who was in charge of all the cashiers. He asked Jenkins to make him a list of the most valuable coin issues from 1900 on, and then he would "try to sniff some out for us—on the usual basis of course—theft."[93]

Platon went on to Jenkins that he had better not hear of any old books being sold "without a word towards Puerto Rico." He wasn't thinking evil thoughts about Jenkins's greed, "just cautious ones among thieves." Besides, the neighboring whorehouse was one of the better ones, with "real perfume," so Platon pleaded with Jenkins to make some sales and send him money for this new entertainment.

Jenkins's own letters from this era do not contain any confessions of theft, and his letter answering Platon does not survive in the archives. But his friend's detailed arrangements for disposing of stolen documents in concert with him are a powerful argument for Jenkins having engaged in criminal activity from the very outset of his career.[94] I will admit that the day I found this letter in Jenkins's papers was a glum one. Why did he keep this letter? Perhaps it was to have something on Platon later on, or it may have been ego, just like the Wall Street insider traders who are hoisted on the petard of their own emails.

I must ask one additional question about Jenkins. Why did he have an insatiable need to exaggerate and embroider nearly every story? For obvious reasons a child deprived of love might seek attention, but there is every sign that Jenkins's parents loved and adored their boy. As one friend told me, their sun rose and set on Johnny. They gave him a cabin for a high school graduation gift, they continually paid his bills while he was in college, and they took him on a trip to Europe in the summer after his sophomore year—after Jenkins's low grades kept him out of the UT Study Abroad program. They were immensely proud of their ambitious son and kept nearly every scrap of paper he wrote and every newspaper clipping about him. I think they thought he would be president someday. Jenkins had no want of parental love, support, or affection.

Jenkins exaggerated stories about his achievements for the same reasons that he drove flashy cars: because he wanted to be admired. The American Psychiatric Association defines such individuals as suffering from histrionic personality disorder. The symptoms include excessive attention seeking and deep need of approval from others. These colorful persons have lively and enthusiastic personalities that are often accompanied by volatile emotions and extreme behaviors. They have a constant craving for stimulation and often fail to see their own personal situation realistically. They become bored easily, and when presented with difficulties they prefer to withdraw rather than face them.

Anyone so afflicted will never have a car expensive enough or a story large enough to compensate. Every new purchase or tale of derring-do is only a temporary salve for that person's profound lack of self-worth. An insecure sense of self-worth is something common to everyone at one time or another. But to take advantage of a mentor and friend to commit larceny? Jenkins later spoke glowingly of his former boss: "I worked for Dorman Winfrey for several years, and he influenced my love of history, of books, of people and of life."[95] Yet Jenkins didn't mind raiding the state archives under his mentor's eye.

This divide in Jenkins's personality puzzled many who considered him their friend. Jenkins may be best understood as one man standing in a carnival funhouse of mirrors. His images might be too tall or too short, too wide or too thin, or bent into ridiculous curves. Some saw a young scholar, but others saw a thief or a fraud. At the center stood Jenkins the barker, bidding one and all to come and see the dazzling young Texan.

2

Trading Up to a Silver Cloud

Jenkins complained constantly about how much he hated law school. One afternoon shortly after failing his tort class exam, he was in Frank Dobie's backyard. The historian Walter P. Webb and university chancellor Harry Ransom sipped bourbon with Dobie and listened to Jenkins with amusement. Webb suggested that he become a historian, but Dobie wisely interjected that that would mean more graduate school, just of a different type. Then Ransom, "out of the clear blue, asked why I didn't become a publisher?" Jenkins related that, the more he drank, the better the idea became, despite his having no money.[1]

The idea of his own rare book and publishing business continued to percolate inside Jenkins's head. He found the money with a chattel mortgage on his coins and books for $3,000 in June 1963 and set up a publishing and rare book shop on 912 Congress Avenue in Austin, just a couple of blocks from the state capitol building.[2]

Jenkins wanted to buy a house as well, even though he was broke from his honeymoon and new business venture. He always was a betting man, and when he heard that a new fighter, Cassius Clay, was going to fight the champion, Sonny Liston, for the heavyweight boxing title in Houston, Jenkins put $1,000 on the underdog. When Clay won the match in an upset, Jenkins won $6,000, which he used as a down payment on his house in the toniest part of old Austin, 1 Pemberton Parkway (which also gave

its name to his publishing business, Pemberton Press). John and
Maureen had only one small scare in their new home. Late one
night a burglar broke in. When Jenkins heard someone down-
stairs in the middle of the night, he jumped out of bed, grabbed
his .38 Special revolver, and chased the unknown intruder out.[3] Of
course, this story is more important in retrospect, since it estab-
lishes that Jenkins owned a revolver.

By fall Jenkins told his parents that the new "store looks wonderful
now that everything is fixed up." It was no showy rare book emporium, but it was his house of treasures. Now all Jenkins needed
was more treasure to sell, so he fashioned some himself from a
local rare book store. One of Austin's more venerable antiquarian
bookstores was the Brick Row, originally founded in New Haven,
Connecticut, in 1915. It moved to New York in the 1930s, and after
the owner's death in 1953 Franklin Gilliam, who had worked in
the store, bought it and moved it to Austin in 1954.[4] Jenkins wandered in one day and saw that Franklin had a printed leaf from
the *Catholicon*, originally written in the thirteenth century as a
Latin dictionary for the Bible, and one of the first books to have
been printed on Gutenberg's press, around 1460. The pages from
the book are folio size (approximately 15 inches tall), and Jenkins
bought one of the leaves for his new store. After the store opened,
Franklin paid a courtesy visit and was quite surprised to see that
Jenkins had a sign on his wall, "Own a piece of history." Under it
were twenty tiny pieces of the original *Catholicon* leaf, each about
one inch square, individually matted, framed, and priced. Gilliam
had seen instances of historical carelessness before, but nothing
on the order of Jenkins's mutilation.[5]

The *Austin Statesman* ran a story on the new businessman,
"Young Tycoon of Texana." The story noted that the new store
had 7,000 square feet on two floors, and Jenkins told the reporter
that it would be set up like a museum, except that everything
would be for sale. Among the treasures the reporter saw in the
store were a letter from the Alamo from William B. Travis, two
rifles used in the Battle of San Jacinto, and a Bowie knife found

near the Alamo. The photograph with the story showed a bespectacled proprietor with a large Bowie knife in one hand and a book in the other.[6]

Michael Ginsberg was a rare book dealer from Massachusetts who was visiting Waco in 1963 to purchase some inventory from a local Texana dealer. He heard from the dealer that there was a "comer" in Austin he should visit, a young upstart named Johnny Jenkins. Ginsberg stopped by the new shop and remembered that the young owner looked like a college kid. Jenkins had a couple of bookshelves in his upstairs office and an enormous Kentucky rifle on the wall. The two booksellers were not far apart in age and they hit it off, especially since both were fans of another son of Massachusetts, President John F. Kennedy. Ginsberg remembered that Jenkins impressed him as quiet and respectful in "that Southern manner of not wanting to step on someone's toes." Ginsberg returned to Massachusetts with books from Waco, and a few from his new friend in Austin.[7]

The week before Thanksgiving 1963, Jenkins and Maureen took a break from setting up the new shop to visit a customer, Jenkins Garrett in Fort Worth. When Garrett offered them two tickets to the presidential banquet for John F. Kennedy during his visit to Texas, they eagerly accepted. Jenkins had no sooner finished his business with Garrett than he heard that the president had been shot. He went and stood outside Parkland Hospital in Dallas in time to see two priests rush inside while the crowd watched, with "some crying." Only a few moments seemed to pass when a pale hearse with a bronze-colored coffin made its way through the crowd.[8]

Jenkins remembered this as the most devastating personal tragedy in his life up to that point. As he recalled, "I was a wholesale, all-out, committed civil rights liberal, and to me at the age of 23, Jack Kennedy was a golden god." That evening in his office, Jenkins sat with the tickets to the speech in front of him and unburdened his soul to his typewriter, later publishing his thoughts as a keepsake in pamphlet form.[9]

The *Dallas Morning News* headline that Friday morning had read, "Yarborough Snubs LBJ," so Jenkins blamed Sen. Ralph W. Yarborough for the Democratic Party infighting in his Kennedy pamphlet. Jenkins's pamphlet said that Yarborough's complaint that Governor Connally had not invited him to a reception for Kennedy in Austin also showed Democratic Party divisiveness in Texas.[10]

After Jenkins published his accusations, Yarborough asked his old friend, J. Frank Dobie, how he should respond. Dobie told the senator that Jenkins's pamphlet was a hatchet job, and it was only quoting some "two-bit Texas journalists." Dobie told Yarborough he should be guided by Sam Houston's reply to a challenge: "I never fight downhill."[11]

The senator was more politic than Dobie, and he probably knew that the new publisher Jenkins would be on the Texas scene for years to come. Sometime in December 1963, Senator Yarborough made his way to Jenkins's new shop, introduced himself, and asked to discuss the pamphlet. Yarborough was also an avid book collector, so he may have had a little personal motivation for the visit as well. Jenkins did not yet have chairs in the office, but he took Yarborough to the back of the store, where they sat on Coca-Cola cases and talked for five hours.[12]

The senator's experience in politics had taught him to handle disagreements the way a wary cowhand approaches an unruly horse. He circled his opponents with talk for hours until they were ready to lie down and give up. But Jenkins was young and brash, and once drawn into a fight he would not back down. He offered counterarguments to every one of Yarborough's calm explanations. After much debate, Jenkins agreed to insert into each copy of the Kennedy pamphlet a sheet with Yarborough's objections, and another with Jenkins's refutations. But as in the earlier incident when Bryan caught him cheating on the law school exam, Jenkins showed his ability to transform what might have been an ugly encounter into a lasting friendship. Yarborough became one of Jenkins's best customers, often celebrating a successful campaign fund-raiser by indulging in a book-buying binge for his collection.[13] Yarborough later selected Jenkins as the public relations chief for the Texas delegation at the 1976 Democratic National Convention.[14]

The following year Jenkins showed his Kennedy enthusiasm by issuing his first catalogue devoted solely to the assassinated president. The introduction had the usual Jenkins aplomb: "This catalogue represents the largest collection of material related to John F. Kennedy ever offered for sale." The Jenkins Company catalogue featured eleven letters and manuscripts written and "signed by Kennedy," along with nearly five hundred other items.[15] Jenkins admitted including some "tasteless and worthless" items for the completest collector who must have everything. The autographed Kennedy letters were a particular coup.

The catalogue was illustrated with photocopied reproductions of the signed Kennedy letters. A careful buyer would have noticed that there were at least five different Kennedy signatures shown on the various letters, particularly in the ones written after 1954 (items 177–186). The problem for collectors is that in 1954 Senator Kennedy started having his secretaries sign his correspondence. There is nothing in Jenkins's catalogue indicating that the letters were signed by anyone other than Kennedy. Unfortunately for Jenkins, one of the close readers of his Catalogue 3 was the dealer from whom he had purchased the secretarially signed Kennedy letters, and that dealer's knowledge would cause problems for Jenkins later.

In 1966 a reporter described Jenkins as a youthful energetic prodigy. He was partial to wash-and-wear suits but drove a Rolls-Royce, collected antiques, and had already authored five books. Jenkins no doubt loved the description of himself as an eccentric intellectual, and he was even more pleased to tell the reporter that his new book-publishing concern and magazine could "become one of the milestones in modern publishing history."[16] That was some hyperbole, even by Texas standards.

His gift for charming others to join forces with him is illustrated by several other partnerships in the 1960s. Jenkins partnered with Raymond Brown to purchase the Country Store Art Gallery in Austin in 1963, and together they launched a new magazine, *Southwestern Art*, in 1966. The additional benefit of the magazine partnership for Jenkins is that he used his status as a publisher of *Southwestern Art* to get NASA press launch credentials for the Apollo 11 mission to the moon in 1969.[17] With Wolford "Lucky" Attal he owned an antique store on Burnet Road in Austin, which would later join with the Country Store Gallery to sell both art and antiques.[18] Another slightly more informal partnership was with Hollywood screenwriter and fine press designer William Witliff. When Jenkins met him in 1966, Witliff was the young sales manager for the University of Texas Press, and in 1969, after Jenkins purchased the equipment of the Adolphus Bindery in New Orleans, Witliff designed a new logo for the bindery.[19]

Jenkins's restless penchant for dreaming up new projects never seem to be interrupted by the fear that he might be overextended. When he was only twenty-six he started the first public library in his family's home town of Bastrop by renting space in an empty store and filling it with cheaper duplicate books from his store. He named it after either himself or his great-grandfather, who had been a sheriff in Bastrop County, the "John H. Jenkins Public Library." It does not seem to have been a great success, to judge by a letter to the editor of the local newspaper (admittedly written by Jenkins's younger cousin): "How many of you have been to the John H. Jenkins Library downtown? I have, but have always found it empty except for the librarian."[20]

Jenkins bragged that by 1965 he had written five books. This was true only if you counted pamphlets such as the Kennedy keepsake. But in 1965 he finished another substantive contribution to Texas history and bibliography. *Cracker Barrel Chronicles: A Bibliography of Texas Town and County Histories* dwarfed the only previous such compilation, H. Bailey Carroll's *Texas County Histories: A Bibliography* (1943), by several hundred pages.

No one who has not tried to compile a subject list for a historical bibliography should presume that such a book is a simple undertaking. Llerena Friend was a bibliographer who had authored

A Check List of Texas Imprints, 1861–1876. Reviewing Jenkins's bibliography for the *Southwestern Historical Quarterly,* she marveled at the young author's multiplicity of interests as an editor, author, publisher, merchandiser, and student and his undertaking a massive project that called for physical endurance and mechanical drudgery. Friend concluded that librarians, researchers, and collectors of Texana would be grateful for his efforts.[21] Another recognition of Jenkins's scholarly efforts came in 1966 with the Award of Merit for his bibliography from the Association of State and Local History. Jenkins carefully cultivated a self-deprecating air to go with his achievements, which endeared him to many people. To a friend Jenkins inscribed his copy of *Cracker Barrel Chronicles,* "My great bibliographical work, which has one county that doesn't exist and which leaves one out entirely."[22]

Sometime during his early years in business, Jenkins was visiting the Houston rare book shop of C. Dorman David when the esteemed Los Angeles rare book dealer Jacob Zeitlin (1902–87) dropped in for a visit.[23] Zeitlin was from Texas, but in the 1920s he had moved to Los Angeles, where he opened his antiquarian book business and established himself as an authority on books on the history of science. A little background on David and Zeitlin helps illuminate the rare book world as it appeared to Jenkins.

In the 1930s, one of Zeitlin's customers, Dr. Herbert Evans (1882–1971), asked the Los Angeles dealer to help him build the greatest collection of the history of science. Dr. Evans loved his rare books more than money and perpetually overspent.[24] His passion for collecting flourished for decades, and in 1965 when Zeitlin flew to London for the Sotheby's sale of the science library of E. N. de C. Andrade, he carried Evans's bids with him. Zeitlin knew that every bookseller dreams of being able to sit in Sotheby's London auction rooms and buy every rarity against all competition. He thought that with Evans's bids in hand this sale would be his chance. But on the first day of the sale he had to sit there while every great classic was taken by other booksellers, sometimes at bids twice as high as his limit. That night he called Warren Howell (of John Howell–Books in San Francisco, who was working with him) and told him the bad news.[25] Howell talked to Evans and called Zeitlin early the next day with good news: "Our friend said to triple all of your bids and don't let the next day's best books get away from you."

Zeitlin said it was a thrill to sit at the next day's sale with his pencil raised and to have "all of the plums fall into our basket." The English book dealers perked up as they saw Zeitlin winning bid after bid, and each of them tried to "draw our blood" by bidding higher. Each soon found it too costly to go up against Zeitlin's new unlimited bids. Finally the high spot of the sale came up— Thomas Salusbury's *Mathematical Collections* (vol. 2, 1665). This was the book Evans most desired. Salusbury's book contained the first English translation of Galileo's most important works. At the time only seven copies had been located, and this was the only one in private hands. There was a scholar-collector sitting next to Zeitlin, Professor Stillman Drake, the foremost authority on Galileo, who also wanted the Salusbury. Drake leaned over and told Zeitlin that he had placed a bid of £1,500 (around $4,000 in 1965) with the English dealer Bert Marley of Dawson's (the London firm).

Zeitlin glanced across the room, and Marley gave him a smug wave. Zeitlin told Drake that he would not bid on the Salusbury until the bidding had passed Drake's limit. The auctioneer opened the bidding and in less than a minute Zeitlin jumped in and started bidding. Marley did not stop at £1,500 and kept at it until he had the top bid at £2,800. Then Zeitlin raised the bid to £3,000 (about $8,000). The auctioneer looked at Marley, but he had to shake his head and the book was knocked down to Zeitlin, who looked up in time to see Marley stick his tongue out at him from across the room. Drake was deeply disappointed until Zeitlin leaned over and told him that Evans had authorized him to leave the rare book in Drake's care until he had finished his research on it.

More than anything, Jenkins knew he wanted to be that rare book insider, the Zeitlin who could drop in from the London auctions to Houston to trade. Dorman David was rumored to have been given a trust fund of over a half a million dollars by his father, Henry, who made a fortune in barite, a mineral used in oil exploration and known as "drilling mud." He epitomized the rare book dealer's favorite axiom: the surest way to make a million dollars in rare books was to start with two million.

David, like many young persons, gyrated between bouts of existential anxiety and a vaulting conviction of his own native genius. To his diary in 1960 he confided, "I feel myself being separated from other people by a wall of knowledge—their light conversation has a negative effect on me."[26] David did a brief internship with John Howell–Books in San Francisco; legend had it that David kept a cab waiting at the curb while he asked for a job. Larry McMurtry, who later worked for the Davids in Houston, speculated that Dorman's internship was short-lived because he was buying all the Texana high spots that came in the door, and Howell feared offending his long-standing customers.[27] Just as likely, David's brash confidence and trust fund meant that he could have his own business instead of working for someone else.

On his return to Houston, David chose one of the swankiest streets in the city, San Felipe, to build his rare book emporium. The surrounding neighborhood, River Oaks, is still among the top ten in the United States for home values. The store had two imposing wooden doors with brightly polished brass knobs, and the showroom had a mahogany banquet table and polished wood bookshelves that went up three stories.[28] David proceeded to fill them with purchases from the nation's leading rare book dealers. It was a fast way to build an inventory but a poor way to build a business. Even with customary dealer discounts of 10 or 20 percent off the retail price, he quickly had a stock of overpriced and thus difficult-to-sell rare books.

There was a grand opening of David's store, with a Japanese houseboy to serve wine or sake for added pizazz. Larry McMurtry did not attend the grand opening, but he wandered into the store a few days later, looking to augment his own collection of reference works for book trading. He found copy of A. S. W. Rosenbach's *Early American Children's Books*, which he bought for a "pittance," only to have David chase him down the street and plead for the book back for his own reference collection. As far as McMurtry could see, David did not have a reference collection, but he acceded when David proposed a trade of some Tarzan first editions—which were worth far more than the Rosenbach bibliography.[29]

David cultivated a bad-boy image for his new shop. The Catalogue 7 cover title offered Texas books "from a Recent Robbery"; in Catalogue 9 he used a wanted poster with his own name substituted for the outlaw. However clever David's marketing, it did not extend to his trading skills. McMurtry noted that David "always seemed to come out on the losing end of those trades."[30] David's ineptness accounted in part for why rare book dealers like Zeitlin were suddenly willing to make pilgrimages to Houston.

Jenkins hung around on the edge of David and Zeitlin's conversation, listening to their stories of rare books bought and sold. "Up to that time," he said, "I had only traded books to increase my personal reference library." Jenkins listened in awe for several hours, then sheepishly explained that he had brought David only one moderately rare Texas book and an old buckskin jacket to sell. David was interested in the book but refused to offer any money for the jacket. He finally offered to buy the book from Jenkins, as long as he could also buy the bottom button on the jacket. Jenkins happily agreed, and Zeitlin wielded the scissors to free the button.[31]

David's trades with Jenkins and other Texas collectors made for spectacular stories, even if Jenkins often got the better deal. Once David bought a 1957 Thunderbird convertible, then spent several thousand dollars installing a Shelby Cobra engine, a racing motor capable of nearly 500 horsepower. He repainted the car, and the night after it came out of the shop he drove up to Waco (about 225 miles) for a trading session with Bob Davis. Around 3 A.M., David fell asleep at the wheel and rear-ended a parked pickup truck. When the farmer came out to see what had happened, David drug himself out of the smashed Thunderbird, gave him a $1,000 for the pickup, and let him have the Thunderbird too. David then hitched a ride to Waco, but he had so many cuts and bruises that the driver took him to the hospital instead. "He had stitches all over his face and arms and his tongue was cut badly."[32]

Even though he was hospitalized, David still wanted to trade. He called Bob Davis and asked him to come over, and they had a trading session right there in the hospital room. At one point in the trade Bob could not resist teasing David and said, right out of a clichéd western, "Dorman, you speak with forked tongue."[33] Besides all of his bandages, David took away two Colt six-shooter revolvers. Then he booked an airplane ticket to Austin so he could trade with Jenkins.

On his way to the airport the next morning to pick David up, three or four police cars passed Jenkins with their sirens wailing. His first thought was, what has Dorman done now? Jenkins's hunch was confirmed when he saw police surrounding the plane. Finally, Dorman got off the plane with several police officers. He learned that David had boarded the plane with his sewn-up face and bandages and with two old navy Colt revolvers stuck in his pants, sat down, and said loudly, "Let's go to Cuba." While David blustered and complained to the police about his civil rights, Jenkins argued more effectively by telling the officers about Dorman's serious car accident. They eventually released him. What part of this accident may have been due to David's drug use is unknown, but eventually heroin addiction came to dominate his life.[34]

David was an important early customer of the Country Store Gallery. He indulged his tastes in art with purchases that were paid on time, probably to accommodate income from his trust fund. Sometime in 1964, David purchased a Julian Onderdonk oil painting for $3,500 (an early Texas impressionist who specialized in fields of bluebonnets), along with a signed John F. Kennedy book for $1,700 as well as frames and art supplies for just over $1,300, presumably for David's own artistic efforts ($6,525 to be paid with no interest in one year).[35] Later in October, David purchased three more paintings and a Charles Russell pencil sketch from the Country Store Gallery for nearly $3,000 and borrowed $2,000 in cash, to be paid back to the Country Store Gallery within eight months.[36]

How closely did Jenkins and David work together in the 1960s? In 1964, Jenkins sold a half-interest in his business to David for $7,000, which was only the first of many deals they would make together.[37] The partnership with the flamboyant David probably piqued Jenkins's interest for a variety of reasons, including the hope of profit and the chance to make professional connections, but at heart they were both seat-of-the-pants traders who were ready to take a bet on a moment's notice.

A short time after forming this partnership, Jenkins and David issued their first joint catalogue. The introduction stated that this was the largest selection of Texas autograph material in private hands, and that the two proprietors—Jenkins and David—hoped to issue many other joint catalogues in the future.[38]

The trading session with David that Jenkins remembered as his best was a famous three-way deal in Houston in 1966 that took eleven hours to complete. David had an antique racing car from 1923 and wanted a VW bus. A Rolls-Royce dealer in Houston had a VW bus and a late 1950s black Rolls-Royce Silver Cloud. He wanted some of Dorman's art objects and his antique racing car. Jenkins was in love with the idea of owning a Silver Cloud, judging it the "most handsome car Rolls-Royce had ever made," and he had some things that David wanted. Jenkins opened the trade by offering an ivory-handled Bowie knife from the 1840s, along with some very rare books, including a complete set of Gammel's *Laws of Texas*, beautiful copies of five other rare Texas books (Maillard, Kendall, Fiske, Parker, and Holley), and an eight-pound cannon. David had a Benjamin Franklin letter, a group of letters from George Washington Carver, several letters from Winston Churchill (Jenkins had been a fan since boyhood), a seventeenth-century manuscript on dueling, a sack of Mexican silver eight-peso coins, several boxes of fine Cuban cigars, a large quantity of rare wines, and an 1811 bottle of brandy with Napoleon's seal.[39]

By nightfall, the Rolls-Royce dealer got his antique racing car and objects d'art and David got his VW bus, Texas Bowie knife, a pile of rare Texas books, and the eight-pound cannon thrown in for good measure. Jenkins got his shiny black Rolls-Royce Silver Cloud loaded with 1,100 Cuban cigars, a large number of rare wines, the 1811 brandy belong to Napoleon, and the rare manuscript letters from Franklin, Carver, and Churchill.[40] When the giddy intensity of a trading session with Jenkins had passed, David often found himself with the short end of the of the bargain, and this trade was no different.[41] Jenkins was more than happy to take advantage of the Houston playboy, especially since he got his desired Silver Cloud.

Driving the Rolls-Royce around Austin thrilled Jenkins, and he admitted that he enjoyed "being haughty" with it. In April 1966,

Jenkins's draft number came up for the army, and he reported to Fort Bliss in Texas for basic training. One weekend, Maureen rode in the Silver Cloud (with a Jenkins Company driver) to El Paso to visit Jenkins, only to learn that his training sergeant had prohibited visits for the entire unit. Undaunted, the comely Mrs. Jenkins drove the Rolls-Royce up to the commandant's office, then got out wearing a "going to church" blue dress with alligator high heels. The commandant superseded the sergeant's prohibition, and Maureen got her weekend with John.[42]

Even though Jenkins enjoyed the admiring stares from strangers, the Rolls proved expensive to repair and had to be sent to Fort Worth or Houston for maintenance. He finally traded the Silver Cloud for a sporty Thunderbird for himself and a more practical station wagon for the publishing business.

After Fort Bliss, Jenkins was assigned to the U.S. Army Counter-Intelligence School at Fort Holabird, Maryland. He later bragged of learning how to pick locks. Though it is not known who Jenkins might have offended during his enlisted tenure, he spent the first part of his training taking care of a general's rose beds, and then later stocking shelves for the PX—both standard punishments for unsatisfactory enlisted men attached to intelligence units.[43]

The rare book business was never far from Jenkins's mind. One of the biggest rare book auctions of the century was about to take place that fall of 1966 at Parke-Bernet in New York. Thomas W. Streeter (1883–1965) was one of the most important and passionate collectors of Americana and Texana of the twentieth century.[44] The funds for his collecting came from his tenure as president of the Prudence Bond Company in the 1930s and from a shrewd investment in a gold dredge in Alaska, which during some years of the Depression era yielded an annual profit of $200,000 (equivalent to around $4 million in 2018); much of that went to his favorite rare book seller, Edward Eberstadt and Sons of New York.[45]

The Texas section of the auction was scheduled for October 26 and included 115 rare lots on Texas printed between 1806 and 1859. The sales took place over three years and ultimately realized more than $3 million for his estate (nearly $25 million in 2018 dollars).[46]

Everyone in the rare book world wanted to be at the auction. The *New York Times* reported that more than six hundred collectors, dealers, and curators packed the Parke-Bernet showroom for the sale.[47] Jenkins couldn't get leave from Fort Holabird, so he sent Maureen, who was living in Baltimore, in his place. She drove their station wagon through the Holland Tunnel but was so turned around when she exited in Manhattan that she pulled up by a policeman directing traffic to ask directions. He sent Maureen to "How-ston street," which she couldn't find, until she drove back and asked him to spell it. "H-o-u-s-t-o-n," he replied, and only then did she realize that New Yorkers did not pronounce the name the same way as Texans. Eventually Maureen made her way to the Waldorf Hotel, and the next day she wore her pearls and a tight-fitting yellow wool dress to the Parke-Bernet auction room on Madison Avenue.[48]

Maureen entered the sale room with Jenkins's marked copy of the auction catalogue. She could see the rare book dealers lined up around the back of the room, including the Massachusetts dealer Michael Ginsberg, who didn't recognize her. When the high spot of the Texas section—the 1836 Declaration of Independence—came up for bidding, she waved her hand as the bids went higher, prompting many of the dealers to wonder who the beautiful blond was bidding in the room for the high spot of the sale. Rare book dealers like to think that they know all of the major players at an important sale, so the arrival of a new bidder, and a young woman at that, caused rampant speculation. Maureen didn't get the Texas Declaration, but it made a new record price, $7,000, and she enjoyed jumping in and out of the bidding during the sale of the rest of the Texas items.[49]

After Jenkins finished his intelligence training at Fort Holabird, he and Maureen returned to Austin. He took up buying, selling, and trading constantly with David, and even though David usually had the more desirable items Jenkins was the better trader and got the better part of the deals.[50] After one trading session with Jenkins, David wrote him an IOU to be paid within ten days: "1 print case and 1 complete lot of paper," plus two bottles of Chateaux Haut-Brion (from a French vineyard dating back to the 1423), along with five other bottles of wine, "all my intercoms," and some cash due to David from a forthcoming sale. The expensive wines were part of the haul that David made in a trade with a Houston country club.[51] Jenkins wanted the intercoms because he was enamored of technological gadgets and loved the idea of being able to bark orders throughout his store from the sanctity of his desk.

The mention of the complete lot of antique-style paper is notable because it was replica paper. David, in one of his bouts of extravagance, had ordered 500 pounds of it from a factory in England made to the specifications of paper used in Texas during the revolutionary period.[52] This would mainly be of interest if someone were planning to produce reproductions of Texas historical documents. Perhaps David was contemplating his future facsimile project for Texas broadsides when he ordered the antique paper.

David was impulsive in trading. Once, after Jenkins and his wife had left his rare book emporium, David opened the second-story window and asked Maureen if she wanted that sapphire ring she had seen earlier. "Sure," she said. She started to go back inside the gallery when David hollered "Catch!" and tossed the ring out the window. Maureen looked up too late and the sapphire ring shattered on the sidewalk.[53]

Eventually, despite David's access to his trust fund, his poor impulse control, and free spending landed him in financial trouble. By 1965, Jenkins decided that although he had profited from trading with Dorman David it probably wasn't such a good idea to be a business partner with someone who was a wild card. When David was again short on cash, Jenkins took the opportunity to repurchase his half-interest in Jenkins's firm.[54] Jenkins was once again the sole proprietor of his business, and David was temporarily reprieved from his financial difficulties.

Though Jenkins was the cannier trader, it would be a mistake to simply regard David as a rich boy whose friend was taking advantage of his foolish good nature. It is now known that at this time documents were being stolen from archives all over Texas. Jenkins obviously contributed to some of this trafficking as an undergraduate when he worked at the state archives, but it would later come to light that Dorman David had been behind a series of much more brazen thefts.

I didn't find any evidence that David ever confided any of his illicit activities to Jenkins, but they must have been aware of each other's thefts. In September 1967, Jenkins bought seven original letters from David with Texas revolutionary signatures such as Henry Smith, provisional governor of Texas in 1835, and Thomas J. Rusk, one of the heroes of the Texas Revolution.[55] But after taking them back to his Austin shop, Jenkins found that two of the letters were from the Texas comptroller's papers and were listed in Binkley's *Texas Revolution Correspondence*.[56] Jenkins realized that he could no longer list such letters in his catalogues without extreme risk to his business reputation.

Jenkins returned the letters to David explaining, in rather carefully chosen words, that he understood that for many years up through the 1940s the state archives had released papers that were considered unimportant. Jenkins told David that some of the documents were traded for items needed by the archives, and many others were left for years unattended in the basement of the capitol. Jenkins concluded that it seemed the state did not intend to try to recover the papers lost during those times. However, he preferred not to deal in those papers whenever possible. By choosing his words carefully, Jenkins obliquely acknowledged that the letters were stolen, yet he refrained from making any direct accusation. Jenkins's comment about the unattended papers in the capitol basement sounds like something from his own firsthand experience. This conscious tact on Jenkins's part implied his conviction of David's guilt.[57]

As long as there was no danger of anyone realizing where documents came from, Jenkins was still ready to wheel and deal. He told David in January 1968 that he was ready to come to Houston for another poker game, reminding David that he still owed Jenkins twenty-five dollars from a previous poker game and mentioning a deal for seventy-five Texas autograph documents from David. Jenkins was just more careful not to implicate himself now with any documents that might be listed in published library collections.[58]

The most important partnership Jenkins formed in the 1960s was also his most secret, which he kept from even his closest friends.

Dallas oilman Robert A. Venable (1939–96) was a classmate and Delta Tau Delta fraternity brother of Jenkins. Venable was impressed with the Jenkins Company sales of $535,000 in 1968 (over $3.5 million in 2018 dollars), and in 1969 he became a half-owner in the Jenkins Company.[59] Suddenly Jenkins had a line of credit of $100,000 from Venable (around $700,000 in 2017 dollars) that he used to buy the equipment of the Adolphus Bindery in New Orleans as well as scout for other acquisitions. Why did Jenkins keep this partnership a secret? I can only surmise that he preferred people think he gained his additional capital from his own efforts and not from selling out to a partner.

Disaster struck the Jenkins Company's new partnership on June 22, 1969, when a fire swept through the printing plant at 1414 Lavaca Street. A passerby noticed smoke coming out of the southwest part of the building around 7 A.M. The fire was on the second floor; Jenkins Publishing Company leased the first floor and basement in the building. The fire started in a couch in a room used for music practice on the second floor, where a cigarette from a very late visit the night before apparently smoldered and then ignited. Jenkins lost his "layouts and plates" for many books, as well as the printing equipment.[60]

Roger Conger, one-time mayor of Waco and an enthusiastic supporter and collector of Texas history, wrote condolences and sent his best wishes to Jenkins after hearing about the disastrous fire. The only consolation he could offer Jenkins was that, since the fire affected the publishing side of the business, "perhaps no original documents were destroyed." Although the rare book and document inventory was not harmed, the fire's impact on the young businessman was immense. Jenkins later told a friend that the fire "left me reeling and almost put me out of business." The curious investigator must wonder how much, if any, this experience contributed to Jenkins's later fires at his rare book warehouses in the 1980s.

The fire seems to have been the impetus for Jenkins and Venable to look for a warehouse where both the publishing and rare book companies could be housed under one roof. Now with Venable's financial backing, such a warehouse became a reality when they purchased eight acres south of Austin next to the freeway and erected a 20,000-square-foot metal building. Jenkins instantly took to calling it "the plant," as if it were his factory.

The new financial backing also meant that Jenkins could make a serious play for the inventory of one of the oldest antiquarian bookstores in the country. Lowdermilk's of Washington, D.C., was founded in 1872, and William H. Lowdermilk adopted the practice of purchasing fifty to one hundred copies of new government documents and storing them in the basement. He probably bought these quantities against the day when they would be declared out-of-print and would then bring higher prices. When Lowdermilk sold his establishment in 1897, the new owners continued the practice of stockpiling government reports and documents.

One antiquarian bookseller recalled being able to roam the Lowdermilk basement in the 1950s and finding such original reports as Powell's survey of the Colorado River or Fremont's explorations of the West. During the store's heyday, Ulysses S. Grant used to browse there, and Theodore Roosevelt purchased many books for his library from Lowdermilk's. Lowdermilk's was rightly touted as one of the nation's great second-hand bookstores, a "Gutenberg's midden of all manner of civilizations."[61]

In 1944, Randolph Adams, director of the Clements Library, attended a bibliographic conference in Washington where the scholars wondered if the books from Jefferson's original library could be gathered again. They wanted not just the same titles but Jefferson's original copies. In theory, this was possible because each of Jefferson's own volumes from his library carried his hand-penned marks at the bottoms of certain pages. After book pages are printed, they are folded into signatures before they are cut, and in the eighteenth and early nineteenth centuries the signatures were identified by letters of the alphabet printed at the bottom of the first page in every fold. If eight pages are printed at a time (making the book an octavo), then the first page would have a letter "a" printed in the blank margin below the text. Then the binder could fold and sew the pages together correctly. Jefferson added a hand-penned capital "T" just in front of signature "i," and a "J" just after the signature "t." Jefferson used the letter "i" to mark his copies because signatures were marked according to the Latin alphabet, which had no "j." Adams wandered into Lowdermilk's with time to kill after the conference and casually asked if the store had ever had any copies of Jefferson's own books. He left Lowdermilk's that day with three books from Jefferson's original library, each marked in Jefferson's hand with an inked "T" on the "i" signature.[62]

Literary treasures could also turn up at Lowdermilk's. One February day in 1950 the American poet Charles Olson, a friend of Ezra Pound and William Carlos Williams, wandered into Lowdermilk's. He wanted a cheap reading copy of D. H. Lawrence's *Fantasia of the Unconscious*. The Lowdermilk clerk barely restrained his excitement: "But look—we've got a Lawrence collection!" "My God," Olson said. He could hardly stand while the clerk brought the collection out. Olson found himself with not only Lawrence's original editions but some of his paintings as well. Olson saw one painting by Lawrence that he had to own, "of a man pissing against a brick wall into a bed of daffodils." Though the Lawrence collection was too expensive for the poet, Olson arranged for its purchase by the Library of Congress and received the watercolor as a finder's fee.[63]

Jenkins heard through the bookseller grapevine that the entire Lowdermilk inventory would be offered at auction because the building had to be demolished for Washington's new subway.[64] Even though the premises were closed to customers, he got permission from the owners to scout Lowdermilk's cobweb-covered shelves "pretty thoroughly" in the summer of 1969. When the auctioneers began chanting descriptions such as "60 shelves, miscellaneous subjects, 13 sections, 23 shelves, 12 rows and 3 piles on the floor and about 2,000 objects," Jenkins piled all in with his bids. Among his purchases were hundreds of books published in the 1870s, 1880s, and 1890s, which were still in the original wrapping paper and cartons in new condition. When his staff opened the boxes, they found books with the autographs of William Howard Taft, Woodrow Wilson, Confederate general Samuel Cooper, Julia Ward Howe, and scores of U.S. Army generals.[65]

Jenkins bid just over $12,000 and estimated that he bought about 80 percent of the basement.[66] The auctioneers had told him that there were 50,000 books down there, but the Jenkins staff ultimately counted 138,000 books, pamphlets, and broadsides from the Lowdermilk basement. Jenkins concluded that the "basement

grab-bag mystery turned out to be a genuine gold mine." After
the three-day February 1970 auction, Jenkins was proud to point
out that he didn't mind getting his hands dirty looking around in
Lowdermilk's basement, unlike most booksellers over sixty who
tried to act like "Edward VII and talk with an English accent."
Jenkins tried to project the image of a hard-working upstart
against the establishment to the reporter, but it was still a little
rich coming from the man who drove a Rolls-Royce around Austin when he was twenty-six years old.

A feature in the *Washington Star* touted Jenkins as a thirty-year-
old boy wonder from Texas with the nerve of Davy Crockett who
dared to take a plunge on the Lowdermilk inventory. The truth
was that the boy wonder was flummoxed by the actual mechanics
of transferring the inventory. First, one union brought thirty men
in to pack the books into boxes; then another union was required
to bring the boxes from the basement up to the street; finally, one
more union was required to pack the boxes into two semi-truck
trailers as well a large parcel post shipment.[67] Jenkins estimated
that the costs of shipping and of building new shelves for the
inventory exceeded the price of his purchases, but they were still
the "best buy" he had ever made.

There was another important lesson that Jenkins would remember from this purchase. The nationwide publicity from this transaction ran in Texas's leading newspapers, such as the *Austin
American-Statesman* and the *Dallas Times-Herald*, as well as many
other national newspapers. The news drew hundreds of letters
from curious customers and visits from more than one hundred
collectors and dealers to Austin to buy some of the legendary
inventory from the new boy-wonder bookseller.[68]

Just as important for Jenkins's image, the *Washington Star* feature described his purchase of Lowdermilk's inventory as that of
the man who was moving culture "from the East to the once-
wild West." Jenkins instantly grasped the power of that image
as a news hook for his business. He told the reporter that culture
was moving from the East to the West. The University of Texas,
for example, was the largest purchaser in the world of literature
and literary manuscripts.[69] At that time in 1970, Jenkins actually wasn't exaggerating about the appetite of oil-rich Texans for

culture. Years later when he finagled the coup of purchasing the multimillion-dollar rare book inventory of Edward Eberstadt and Sons, that hook of culture moving from the East to the West became the headline for the *New York Times* and the *Wall Street Journal*, among others.

———•———

Around this time, Jenkins acquired his most famous piece of office furniture, an eighteenth-century Black Forest chair carved with gargoyles and serpents. He spotted it at a second-hand consignment store on McKinney Avenue in Dallas and had to have it. The chair was enormous; one visiting rare book dealer thought that Jenkins had mounted a small platform under the new chair in his office so that he could look down on visitors. In fact the seat of the chair sat several inches higher than normal, and that alone was probably enough reason for Jenkins to love it. Of course, even though the height of the new chair gave Jenkins a dominating vantage point, it also meant that with his short stature he couldn't place his feet on the floor. Never bothered, Jenkins simply began sitting cross-legged at his desk.[70] "Buddha-style," he said later, which gave rise to his sobriquet for how he sat at the poker tables, "Austin Squatty."[71]

Later in 1970, Jenkins applied for membership in the prestigious Antiquarian Booksellers Association of America (ABAA). He was probably encouraged by the resounding national publicity of the Lowdermilk sale. To apply for membership, candidates had to be in business for a certain number of years (four or five), had to be recommended by several other current members of the association, and had to hand over bank statements to show good business practices. Membership in the association meant that Jenkins could exhibit at the prestigious book fairs in New York, California, and Boston and would serve as an endorsement of Jenkins for prospective customers.

Jenkins submitted his paperwork in November 1970. He was stunned to receive the news in January 1971 that his application was denied: "Your application for membership was not acted on favorably."[72] He must have wondered why they had denied him membership. The terse note fueled Jenkins's deep resentment against the more established dealers of the association.

Jenkins didn't dare complain to anyone about his rejection, but he thought that the older dealers in the association must have been behind it. He wrote an angry letter to the board about the more established dealers who opposed him. Robert Black, an autograph dealer from New Jersey and member of the board of governors, wrote in response that he would be the last person to put any objection in the way of a reliable dealer, and particularly a young dealer, who wished to join the ABAA, "for the future of the organization depends on them and not on old dealers like myself."[73]

The actual reason for Jenkins's rejection, though, was that some of dealers on the ABAA board of governors remembered the incident in Jenkins's Catalogue 3 of the secretarially signed Kennedy letters that were described as autographed by Kennedy. His correspondent Black was in fact the dealer who had sold him the secretarially signed Kennedy letters.

Jenkins took a different tack and tried to explain to the board that his cataloguing of those letters was a result of youthful naiveté, which happened while he was still "in college." He argued that it was a mistake that anyone without experience could make, especially since the book on Kennedy's autographs by Charles Hamilton, the leading autograph dealer, had not yet come out. Jenkins told them that this was before Mr. Hamilton's book was published, and before Jenkins clearly understood the differences between the technical descriptive terms used by dealers, such as ALS, TLS, and ANS (abbreviations used in the trade: Autograph Letter Signed, Typed Letter Signed, and Autograph Note Signed; "autograph" in this context means "in the hand of").[74]

This explanation sounds plausible, and Jenkins insisted that he had done everything possible to correct the situation at the time as soon as someone pointed it out to him, including mailing correction slips and not selling any of the letters as original signatures. Having made the mistake, and having admitted it, Jenkins didn't see what else he could have done. For good measure, Jenkins told the board that he had done all of this in good faith and cheerfully.[75]

Unfortunately for Jenkins, that was not what he had actually done, and the board knew it. Black replied that, besides the

Kennedy business, they had received several other objections about Jenkins's membership application, including complaints about his association with Dorman David, although the Kennedy business was the most serious one. Black told Jenkins that his memory of the Kennedy letters was not correct, reminding him that "you knew that these letters were secretarially signed or robot signed when you bought them" because "I sold them to you on the invoice that way."[76]

In some ways, Jenkins's experience with the secretarially signed Kennedy letters is similar to that with the many overgraded coins he sold, except that the buyers were trusting him more and were less able to see for themselves what was false about the letters. This practice of overgrading and misdescribing followed Jenkins to the very end of his life. I think it speaks to something else in his character, a bent for bluffing that he felt just as ungovernably in dealing with documents and books as he did in holding a hand of cards. As long as the hand is never called, Jenkins could act as though he had a royal flush and no one would ever be the wiser.

The resentment Jenkins felt about his membership application was a deeply held secret; even Michael Heaston, who managed the Jenkins rare book department for several years in the 1970s and was privy to many of Jenkins's private affairs, never knew about his ABAA rejection. But Jenkins did not believe in adding bad blood to bad luck, as he saw it; instead, he spent much of the early part of 1971 trying to find a way to improve his reputation dramatically among his fellow booksellers. Out of the blue, some rare book crooks suddenly presented him with the chance to show everyone he really wore a white hat.

3

The Audubon and Eberstadt Capers

A few months after Jenkins's 1970 application to the ABAA was rejected, he spied an opportunity to turn his reputation around. Newspapers around the country covered Jenkins's role in going undercover with the FBI to recover rare Audubon plates stolen from Union College. Jenkins promoted himself as a hero bookman, and nearly everyone in the country heard about his caper.

There is, however, one crucial hole in Jenkins's story. In the many times that he recounted his heroic episode, the crook comes to Austin, seemingly unexpected, and offers some rare "bird pictures." After he leaves, Jenkins is thumbing through an issue of the weekly trade magazine for antiquarian books when he happens to see the notices of the stolen plates and other rare books. The story sounds quite plausible until one wonders why the crooks picked an out-of-the-way bookseller in Austin, Texas. There were, after all, so many more booksellers on the East Coast, or for that matter on the West Coast, to choose from. Jenkins was not yet a member of the national trade association for antiquarian booksellers, and though he had achieved some publicity for the Lowdermilk purchase two years previously he was hardly a national brand. The hole in the Jenkins story he never told was that he had done a deal the previous year with the ringleader of the Audubon thefts, James S. Rizek.

Rizek was by all accounts a natural-born hustler. Walter Gold-water ran the University Place Book Shop on Fourth Avenue in New York for more than fifty years and was a founding member of the ABAA. He was well acquainted with Rizek and called him the most crooked person he knew in the book business. Gold-water said that if Rizek had been able to make more money being honest than dishonest "he still wouldn't have done it." Michael Ginsberg also knew Rizek by his reputation. "Rizek," he said, "was the consummate con man."[1]

In the 1950s, Rizek ran the Jabberwock, a high-end record and stereo store in New Brunswick, New Jersey. From there he masterminded a financial manipulation scheme encompassing nineteen corporations and netting him hundreds of thousands of dollars. He was convicted on December 11, 1957, of fourteen counts of embezzlement and two counts of forgery. Although Rizek was sentenced to five years in prison, because it was his first offense and he had some underlying medical issues, the sentence was suspended and he was given probation.[2]

Later, in the early 1960s, he defrauded the Scranton Public Library and Union College Library in Schenectady out of thousands of books and government documents in exchange for microfilms that never materialized. On May 5, 1965, Rizek was convicted, and after a lengthy appeals process he was finally sentenced to two years in Lewisburg Federal Prison, which he began serving in December 1969.[3]

Perhaps Rizek remembered Jenkins as the brash Texan who had swooped in to purchase the Lowdermilk stock the previous year. Just as likely, he heard the bookseller rumors that Jenkins had access to Texas oil money. In any event, sometime that fall of 1970 while Jenkins was finalizing his ABAA application, Rizek approached him about another bookseller's inventory. John E. Scopes ran a longtime book shop in Albany, New York, and specialized in Americana. Charles P. Everitt, an old-time antiquarian bookseller himself, recalled that Scopes was "one of the dozen greatest living Americana dealers."[4]

No doubt Jenkins thought the deal sounded like it would be right up his alley, and when Rizek made the offer Jenkins plunged in, eager to see what rarities Scopes's inventory would turn up. Unfortunately, Jenkins's gut instinct did not serve him well in this transaction. Scopes's inventory had been well culled of all rarities, and when the boxes were unpacked in Austin all that remained were standard and difficult-to-sell books of Americana, with no treasures among them.[5] The bad taste of this transaction, where Rizek had bluffed him, remained with Jenkins.[6]

While in Lewisburg prison Rizek reached out to two inmates who had connections to the Jewish mob in Philadelphia. Allen Rosenberg and Kenneth Paull were part of the same rough Jewish gang, and both had been convicted of robbing a Philadelphia bank of more than $100,000. Rizek asked why they went in for stealing "diamonds and stuff like that" when it was a whole lot easier to steal art?[7] Rizek remembered the valuable Audubons at Union College, and he no doubt also remembered that those college officials had helped to convict him on the earlier charges. He suggested the Audubon plates at Union College to Rosenberg and Paull as an "easy heist" after their release from prison.[8] Rizek had served only eight months of his sentence when he was released on parole August 1970.

Rizek called Jenkins again sometime in late June 1971, this time with a tale of real treasures. Jenkins still resented being taken by Rizek on the Scopes deal, and he would have remembered this transaction when Rizek first offered him one hundred Audubon double elephant folio plates from the *Birds of America*. Jenkins may not have known that the plates were stolen, though he would soon have figured it out. In addition, Rizek told him, no doubt in hushed tones, there were other very rare materials, including early manuscript books, all from the "not-to-be-named" estate. Rizek tried to get Jenkins to fly to New York to see the materials, but Jenkins demurred without giving a reason.[9] He may have suspected that the materials were stolen and was waiting to see if the thefts would be publicized. It would have been difficult for him to contact the authorities about the stolen goods until the thefts were widely known, without disclosing that he learned about them from Rizek.

The standard magazine for news and gossip in the book trade at this time was *AB Bookman's Weekly*, and every antiquarian bookseller watched for it eagerly in the mail. Besides advertising books wanted by dealers searching for out-of-print books for customers, it also had weekly listings of books for sale, some real treasures. Antiquarian booksellers were even known to complain if their copies of the magazine did not land in their mailboxes on Thursday, since they would then miss out on whatever prize might be lurking in that week's columns.

At the end of June 1971, *AB Bookman's Weekly* published a four-page advertisement listing 195 rare books and manuscripts stolen from Solomon R. Shapiro, president of Books for Libraries. Shapiro's shop at 29 East 10th Street, New York, had been robbed on a Monday night, June 7, and the Union College Audubon plates were stolen just under a week later, on June 13. The Shapiro robbery was in the June 28 issue, the Union College theft in the July 5 issue.

When Jenkins refused to fly to New York to look at the plates, the two burglars tried to get Rizek to take the materials to Austin. Rizek refused with the excuse that the FBI was closely watching him during his parole. Kenneth Paull agreed to travel to Austin, posing as jewel dealer "Carl Hoffman." Paull walked into the Jenkins Company offices on Thursday, July 8, at 11 A.M.[10]

As Jenkins told the story, the appointment had been made by his secretary, seemingly without his knowledge. In real life, Jenkins never took a meeting or even a phone call without being sure he knew whom he was speaking to.[11] He must have had a good idea from Rizek that Paull wanted to see him that morning about some rarities. Paull later confirmed that this was why they had met. "Oh absolutely. Absolutely," Paull said. "I was a professional thief. Do you honestly think I just flew down to Texas and looked around for somebody to buy stolen goods? We didn't do anything on spec. We had a customer."[12] That customer was John Jenkins.

Jenkins would certainly have seen the notice of the stolen Shapiro books by then, and possibly that of the stolen Audubons. Using the Carl Hoffman persona, Paull introduced himself to Jenkins as a dealer in jewels and stones who had come across a group of rare books, manuscripts, and old prints. He first showed Jenkins a sixteenth-century Persian manuscript of the Koran. This confirmed Jenkins's suspicion that the material Paull was offering was the same stolen from Shapiro. Then, "on a hunch," Jenkins asked the dealer if he had any old American bird prints, such as the ones by Audubon? Paull replied that yes, he had about a hundred of those. That was Jenkins's confirmation that all of the rare books and prints Paull was selling were stolen. Jenkins said he would very much like to buy the Audubons, and Paull promised to return in a week with all of the materials.[13]

A few moments after Paull left his office, Jenkins sent his secretary out to the parking lot to get Paull's license plate number, but the mobster had left. In the interim, Jenkins called Union College and Solomon Shapiro and confirmed the thefts. Jenkins took his secretary to the airport and look through the car rental lots, but they were unable to find the car Paull had been using. After that, Jenkins called the FBI, was put in contact with agent Bob Chapman, and waited for the next message from Paull. Jenkins did all this without telling either the FBI or Union College or Shapiro that he was well acquainted with the dealer, James Rizek, who had set up this deal.[14]

Just a few days later, on Tuesday, July 13, Jenkins received his second call from Paull. Worried that the thieves or their friends might see the notices that had been published about the stolen books, Jenkins offered to fly up to New York the next morning, and Paull said he would pick him up at JFK Airport. Jenkins then called the FBI and stressed the urgency of following Paull until they recovered the stolen books and prints. Since the East Coast federal agents had never met Jenkins, he agreed to deplane from the Texas flight smoking a bright orange University of Texas pipe in order to be spotted easily. Though Jenkins quickly found Paull, he was unsure whether the well-hidden FBI agents had, in fact, seen him. Paull took him out to his car, with Jenkins nervously noticing that the car "careened" out of the airport parking lot and took a number of U-turns. Paull was looking "continuously" at the rear-view mirror.[15]

When Paull was satisfied that they were not being followed, he took Jenkins to the Jade East Motel in Queens, just a short distance from the airport. The FBI agents would have been familiar with the Jade East; it was used in 1967 when Mafia-connected thieves and a prostitute gained access to a locked room at the Air

France terminal and stole nearly half a million dollars in cash. The Mafia-connected motel was later depicted in the 1990 Martin Scorsese film *Goodfellas*.

Before going inside the motel room, Jenkins looked around but did not see his FBI friends. Wary of being spotted, they had parked a block away from the known gangland rendezvous. Inside the room, he saw two short stacks of about twenty-five Audubon plates on a bed. Jenkins knew that there were more than one hundred stolen plates, so not everything was there. Paull showed him some other rare books and manuscripts that looked like the ones stolen from Shapiro. Jenkins had to spend a couple of hours alone in the room with the mobster, "which scared me to death." Finally, he and Paull agreed to a price of $30,000 for the Audubon plates and another $20,000 for the rest of the rare books. Jenkins insisted on examining all hundred Audubon plates before paying any money, so Paull drove him back to his hotel. Jenkins claimed he had to call his banker in Austin to arrange the funds transfer, but he promised to return with the money at 5:30 P.M. when all the "merchandise" would be in the room.[16]

Safely back in his own hotel room, Jenkins called the FBI agents, who quickly came over and debriefed him about the encounter. Once they were assured Paull had the stolen goods with him, the agents escorted Jenkins to the Jade East at the agreed-upon time. Jenkins knocked on the door, and when the mobster opened it the agents already had their weapons drawn and arrested him. Paull was carrying two loaded revolvers. To Jenkins's surprise, none of the stolen materials were in the motel room. The FBI found that Paull had already stashed the Audubon plates and the books and manuscripts stolen from Shapiro in a car, along with his own luggage. The getaway car was registered to another mobster who had just escaped from prison. Paull had apparently intended to rob Jenkins, without delivering any of the stolen goods. As Jenkins concluded in his own retelling, "We were, as in all dramatic detective thrillers, in the nick of time."[17]

There was a natural-born publicity hound just under Jenkins's skin. He lost no time making sure everyone heard of the derring-do of the rare bookseller who had foiled the mob. The coast-to-coast newspaper coverage of Jenkins going undercover fed his desires for attention and approval. Jenkins admitted that the FBI wanted him to hide out in a new hotel under an assumed name—lest the friends of the thug try to get retribution—but anonymity was pretty much a lost cause after the newspapers and television got the story of the bust from him.[18]

The public accolades were especially heartwarming to the young bookseller who had been denied membership in the antiquarian booksellers' organization only a few months earlier. After reading about the Jenkins caper, the president of American Airlines wrote to his congressman, "I wish they would make Mr. Jenkins the next head of the FBI." Longtime antiquarian bookseller Tal Luther, of Kansas City, Missouri, wrote admonishing Jenkins to keep up the good work and suggested that perhaps one day a Jenkins detective agency would be listed among his corporations. This may be the only corporation that Jenkins never formed. Luther concluded, "I had long suspected that you were one of the white hats and this proves it."[19]

In the midst of these praises, Jenkins still kept a mental tally of who should be writing him letters of gratitude. When more than a month went by with no word from Solomon R. Shapiro, whose books Jenkins had helped to recover, he wrote: "In all my thirty-one years, I have never been so astounded or disheartened as I have been at the failure to hear a single word from you. What kind of man are you?" As it happened, Shapiro had suffered a series of unfortunate accidents after the robbery of his rare book shop: "While in Paris, I was involved in a bad five car smashup which put me out of commission for a time with shoulder, hip and knee out of order. Still in bad shape, I returned to London, having cancelled my trip to Florence; shortly after returning to the Savoy Hotel, I came down with a severe streptococcic infection of the throat."[20] When he finally returned to New York, the FBI showed Shapiro that only twenty-six of his 240 looted items had been found and let him know that they were not optimistic about recovering the remainder. Jenkins, unfortunately, never found any empathy for Shapiro's misfortunes.

Texas congressman J. J. Pickle lauded Jenkins on the floor of the House with this headline in the *Congressional Record*: "John H. Jenkins, Author, Publisher, Crime-Stopper and Friend of Audubon Society."[21] Jenkins paid the postage and sent copies of this recognition to customers on his mailing list around the country. One antiquarian bookseller from Lexington, Kentucky, complained at the expense to the government of mailing out such a thing and that he personally found it offensive." Jenkins curtly wrote the bookseller that he had received one because he was on the Jenkins catalogue mailing list. Jenkins told him that if he felt their catalogues, which had also been mailed to him at no expense to himself or the government, were also a waste of time, then Jenkins would be delighted to delete his name from the mailing list.[22]

The goodwill from Jenkins's crime-fighting escapade lasted for years. In 1973, Union College had Jenkins deliver the groundbreaking address for their addition to the library and awarded him the Union College Founder's Medal.[23] A television screenwriter even wrote a spec script for an episode of *Kojak* about the bookseller's undercover adventure. Even though it was never produced, Jenkins was quick to make the script part of his mythology ("the only antiquarian bookseller to have a TV episode written about him").[24]

Later, Jenkins inscribed a copy of the *Kojak* spec script for a bookseller friend, adding a note of honesty: "This is not me as I am but certainly as I envision myself."[25] In that spirit, Jenkins once tried his hand at a private-eye novelization of the Audubon caper. Though his efforts lasted only a couple of pages, they reveal again how Jenkins would have loved to be seen, at least in a clichéd detective story: "Jenkins is small statured, compact and quick-moving. He wears glasses and a mustache but looks younger than his 31 years. He gives the impression of being an ardent but modest scholar, of being quiet, even shy. There is nothing in his manner or appearance that shows how gutsy he really is."[26] Fortunately, he was not gutsy enough to finish the novel about Jenkins the gumshoe.

———•———

Jenkins's about-face on document thefts came at a price to his own personal history with Dorman David. One of the secondary reasons that ABAA board members had given for rejecting Jenkins's membership application was his dealings and connections with David, and with good reason. David had a ring of thieves raiding Texas county archives and courthouses for valuable documents and rare books.

One of David's thief-scouts was Bill Gray, a twenty-one-year-old who had graduated from Port Arthur High School. Even though Gray sported long hair and preferred to spend his free time drinking beer at topless bars, he dressed the part of a graduate student researcher when he visited the archives, wearing a coat and tie and carrying a briefcase.[27] On a Monday morning in August 1971, Gray went into the Austin History Center and asked to see any old maps that they had. The librarian brought several out, but the assistant director of the historical collection, Audrey Bateman, became suspicious of the young man's vague request; most researchers have a good idea which old maps they need to investigate a historical question. Perhaps Gray sensed the librarian's suspicions. After a short time Gray put one map in his briefcase and left, but he was followed discreetly by the librarian, who got his license plate number and called the police.[28]

The police searched Gray's car and found five rare maps stolen from the University of Texas library; Gray had pocketed only a modern copy from the Austin History Center library. But one of the rare originals taken from the University of Texas was Stephen F. Austin's 1840 map of Texas. This map is one of the most important and detailed ever done about the young Republic of Texas (the most recent auction sale of that map, in 2013, brought $251,000).[29]

In Gray's car police also found a roadmap with sixteen county seats marked out to visit, along with typed instructions for stealing documents and maps. It is always more helpful when a master criminal, such as Dorman David, makes it clear what the thief should steal: "1. Get as much as you can! 2. Get maps in these county clerk's offices. 3. Get all the old books you can. 4. Keep different counties separated." A thief who couldn't tell the difference between a rare original map and a modern reproduction probably needed specific typed instructions, which weren't always enough. Dorman the master thief even included Gray's name in some of the instructions: "Bill, you know the deal on this place. Get all the stuff you can get in the District Clerk's and County Clerk's office."[30] Just four days after Gray's arrest, state police investigated a Waco dealer who was trying to sell three rare documents stolen from the Texas state archives. Suddenly, officials were realizing that stolen documents in Texas were a huge problem.

In light of these arrests, Jenkins's earlier decision to separate his business dealings from Dorman David seemed a canny one. Just a few weeks prior to Gray's arrest, David held an auction of seventy-seven crown jewels of historical Texana from his own collection at the posh Warwick Hotel in Houston.[31] Jenkins did not want to miss an event like David's, for several reasons. A dealer wanted to stay abreast of the auction of rare documents, with a self-interested eye toward watching prices at the sale and raising them on anything in his own inventory that was similar. Additionally, if a new collector were drawn into the buying pool at the sale, that was also valuable information for a dealer.

A published catalogue from the auction shows several historical letters that were stolen. For example, Lot 5, a letter from Stephen F. Austin, the "father" of Texas, written from Mexico City on October 14, 1834, actually belonged to the University of Texas Barker Texas History Center. The catalogue described this letter as "one of the most important" ever written on the subject of Texas by Austin; it depicts Austin's emotions at a low point in his life, when he was feeling betrayed by friends while he was imprisoned in Mexico.[32] Imagine Austin's feelings if he could have known that his historical memory was to be stolen as well.

Jenkins visited with Waco collector Roger Conger at David's sale. Conger said before the sale that he doubted that he would do any bidding, since the opening prices in the catalogue were so high. After the auction, Conger told Jenkins that even though the sales room was not packed it did not take two hundred or even one hundred people to have a successful auction, as long as the ones who turned up were serious about bidding.[33] There were some heavy hitters who showed up to bid at the sale, like collector Jim Grizzard of Houston, who bought well over half of the sale, spending $13,000 (the sale netted David $23,000).[34] For his money, Grizzard got original letters and documents from Stephen F. Austin, David Crockett, W. B. Travis, and James Bowie, as well as a beautiful two-page letter from Sam Houston. Nearly all of those documents had been stolen from state and university archival collections in Texas.[35]

After David's auction on June 22, Jenkins wrote him a letter that for all appearances was Texas friendly, but he had an ulterior motive. Jenkins supplied a copy of this letter with his reapplication to the ABAA board. In it he expressed his reservations with the cautiousness of a dealer who wanted everything to be aboveboard, and who had an eye to how a copy of this letter would enhance his ABAA application: "Dorman, I still have doubts about the provenance of this large group of documents that you have come up with. Ten or twelve of the items in your sale were listed in Binkley, Gammel or the Austin Papers" (all published editions of original Texas letters). Jenkins added that he hoped David would have the sense to check the letters' sources before selling them, though this was just for the ABAA board's benefit. Jenkins added this caveat, which was almost certainly intended for the board: "I personally do not care to buy any more of these items from you until you can convince me of their legitimacy of the sources." Jenkins and David had a long history of working together through the 1960s, so Jenkins concluded on a friendlier note, inviting David for home-cooked spare ribs the next time he was in Austin.[36]

A short time after this, Jenkins calculated the risk-versus-reward factors of a continued association with the one-time prince of Texana. He realized that turning in Dorman David to the authorities would solve two problems for him. First, he would get rid of a competitor in his specialized field of Texana; second and more important, he would discredit a dangerous former associate who knew a little too much about Jenkins's role in the thefts from the Texas state archives ten years earlier. It may have seemed like high time to Jenkins, since David's addiction to heroin and financial troubles were only getting worse. The dinner invitation in Jenkins's letter suggests that the two men had maintained some semblance of friendship even after their partnership ended. Left unsaid is how Jenkins felt about betraying his longtime friend. Jenkins discreetly contacted the Texas Rangers and told them that the mastermind behind the document thefts of the previous year (1971) was C. Dorman David of Houston.[37]

On the evening of June 14, 1972, the Texas Rangers went to David's Houston shop with a search warrant.[38] Finding it locked, they broke down the door. They did not find any of the real Texana treasures, but they did find enough stolen material to fill a fifty-page inventory of stolen books, mainly from Lamar University in Beaumont and the Rosenberg Library in Galveston. Dorman David was arrested and charged with receiving stolen goods.

It is not known whether his old partner knew about Jenkins turning him in to the Rangers, though that could have provided another motivation for David to let Jenkins handle his Texas forgeries. Even after David's arrest and well after Jenkins wrote the ABAA saying that he was discontinuing any association with Dorman David, Jenkins continued to buy from him, albeit more discreetly. A receipt from July 5, 1972 (just three weeks after the Ranger's raid), signed by Dorman David to Jenkins shows that he sold him seven books and letters, including an "incomplete" 1838 *Abstract of Texas Lands*—one of the rarest of Texas books.[39] David was sentenced to prison for his crime, but he never turned himself in and went on the lam for the next seven years using pseudonyms while he was fighting his heroin addiction.[40] Just the same, Jenkins continued to purchase from him.

In the summer of 1975, a young William Reese was visiting the Jenkins plant. Reese was introduced to Jenkins while still a teenager at the Western History Association meeting in New Haven, Connecticut, in October 1972. Jenkins had an exhibitor table, and Reese was a Yale history major who collected books about cattle and the West. Reese came by his love of the West naturally. His family raised cattle on their farm in Maryland, and his uncle, Henry W. Jackson, had the X9 Ranch, covering 140 square miles encircled by the Rincon Mountains southeast of Tucson, Arizona.[41] During a summer trip west, Reese met Fred White Jr. in Bryan, Texas. White was just out of the air force and energetic about getting into the book business. Like Reese, White entered the book business while still in college at Texas A&M in 1967 when his parents loaned him the money to buy out the antiquarian book inventory (and mailing list) of Price Daniel Jr. (who had just been elected to the Texas House of Representatives).[42] Fred was fond of checkered sports jackets and always toted a doctor's satchel, which doubled as a carrier for his rare Americana and for dinner reservations when the table for "Dr. White" would be announced.[43]

In 1975 one of Reese's mentors, Peter Decker, referred him to an old customer's book collection. Melvin J. Nichols (1893–1975) was an active member of the New York Posse of Westerners International and had collected not only books about Custer but also rare books that spanned American history. The family wanted $40,000 for the entire collection (mainly because they wanted it moved out of the mansion so it could be sold for a million dollars—a real fortune in 1975). Even then Reese knew the collection was worth far more than that. He partnered with White to form Frontier America booksellers and borrowed the $40,000 from his parents. Then he shipped twenty tons of books in a tractor-trailer to Bryan, Texas, and paid his parents back within a year.

Reese was at the Jenkins plant when he spotted Dorman David as he pulled up in the parking lot. Jenkins knew that there was still a warrant out for David's arrest and refused to let him in the building. Reese saw Jenkins buy some items from the trunk of David's car. Among them was a prayer rug supposed to have been used by Malcolm X, which Jenkins placed at the entrance to the vault.[44] No doubt it was from a source similar to the frequently offered Brooklyn Bridge. More important, it is evidence of Jenkins's continued relations with a criminal.

⸻

With his widespread publicity about the recovery of the stolen Audubon plates, together with other reassurances like a copy of his letter to Dorman David, Jenkins resubmitted his membership application to the ABAA. Additionally, he got new laudatory letters of recommendation from leading antiquarian booksellers like Jake Zeitlin in Los Angeles.[45] On January 19, 1972, Jenkins's membership application was accepted.

The attitude Jenkins took about finally being admitted to the ABAA is revealed in a letter to Kenneth Rendell, a close friend who had helped him. Jenkins said nothing about his own misdeeds that had hindered his application the first time. Instead, he told Rendell that they were setting a new pace far beyond most of the old-timers, and that was causing "jealousies." The older dealers had never been friends with each other anyway, Jenkins wrote, because they were always back-biting, catty, and ready to stab each other in the back at the first opportunity. Jenkins concluded with the hope that their friendship would always be a genuine one, without regard for pride or profit.[46]

Jenkins showed what he meant to Rendell when they cooperated in buying an important collection of Einstein's manuscripts. One of the largest archives of Albert Einstein's scientific notes had come up for auction in November 1972 at Sotheby Parke-Bernet in New York. There were 326 quarto-size sheets in the lot, showing the evolution of Einstein's scientific thought from the early 1950s. These manuscript notes contained Einstein's final thoughts on finding the "unitary" theory that would unite the laws of gravity (i.e., general relativity) with those of electromagnetism, as well as theories about gravitational waves.[47]

Jenkins and his friend Rendell decided to take the plunge together to buy the archive.[48] Usually dealers in a joint purchase situation own the entire set of papers together, and then when one or the other dealer is able to sell them they split the proceeds 50:50 with their partner. This helps to divide the risk when purchasing rare and expensive items and effectively doubles the marketing opportunities. Against stiff competition, they bought the lot for $12,500 (with an auction house estimate of $6,000–$8,000).

Sometime after Jenkins and Rendell bought the Einstein archive, Jenkins must have talked to Warren Roberts at the Humanities Research Center, who mentioned their disappointment at not having learned about the Einstein archive in advance of the sale. In any case, Jenkins told Rendell that he wanted to divide the papers 50:50 rather than own them jointly. Rendell was surprised but acceded to the unusual request, so each dealer got 163 pages of Einstein's manuscripts. Later Rendell learned that Jenkins had sold his half of the papers to the Humanities Research Center, representing that all 326 pages were included from the auction lot. Rendell asked Jenkins how he had been able to do that, since Rendell still owned the other half of the papers. Easy, Jenkins told him. He just had his staff tear each of the 163 Einstein manuscripts in half (making them octavo instead of quarto size), so that there were now 326 manuscripts, just as described in the auction catalogue. Rendell knew that Jenkins was a hustler, but this chicanery still took him by surprise.[49]

Once Jenkins was in the ABAA, he was in all the way. In 1973 he organized the first Southwest chapter of the ABAA and recruited numerous friends to join. At least one of them, Dick Bosse of Aldredge Books in Dallas, responded to the idea of a chapter with a good bit of Texas leg pulling. Bosse, writing under the pseudonym "Fauntleroy J. Effete," told Jenkins that his boredom threshold was fairly low and that he tended to run amok with a kris (a curved dagger from Indonesia) when confronted with parliamentary procedure. However, if the proposed meetings were infrequent enough, it might be a good idea to get together so they could fix fees, divvy up territories, and plot auction rigging, all completely tongue-in-cheek suggestions.[50]

The ABAA adventures continued the next year in 1974 when Steve Weissman of Ximenes Books in New York suggested that Jenkins run for a seat on the board of governors of the antiquarian bookseller's organization. Jenkins told him that it was fine to list his name as candidate but modestly added that he felt he would only come in last place. Jenkins added that he would soon be up that way and asked Weissman to take him to one of those games where they "hit the little ball around on the ice? I forget what it's called."[51] But that fall, Jenkins, to his delighted surprise, was elected to the board of governors, another dividend of the Audubon caper.

During the early 1970s, Jenkins hosted a weekly poker game on Tuesday nights. Depending on who Jenkins was telling the story to, his game was either the oldest in Texas, started by Sam Houston, or the most dangerous in Texas, begun by Austin's gunslinging marshal Ben Thompson in the 1880s.[52]

At this time the betting limit was usually fifty dollar a hand, unless an out-of-town bookseller was sitting in, when it would be lowered to ten dollars a hand. Sometimes Jenkins's friends' tempers got the best of them in course of the games. One regular sometimes got so mad at losing a hand that he would throw all the cards across the room, so Jenkins started buying playing cards by the gross—144 packs at a time.[53] And though Jenkins usually won, when he lost he had his own unique way of showing his good-natured pique. Jenkins once lost $5,000 on a large poker bluff that was called by a friend, and he promised to bring the money when they met again. The next week Jenkins paid his bet to his surprised friend with a paper grocery bag stuffed with a thousand loose and crumpled five-dollar bills.[54]

Jenkins was often self-promoting, but he also mocked himself at his local game of poker so that his friends would keep playing with him. Still, there was sometimes latent resentment at how he took advantage of players. Once he was hosting a group of poker friends at dinner at the Petroleum Club in Austin, and while Jenkins took a phone call his friends looked over the wine list. One of them asked whether they should order some of the expensive wines since Jenkins was paying the tab for the evening. The friend's wife looked straight at her husband, who had often lost to Jenkins in poker: "Soak him good."[55] They drank well that evening.

In the 1970s, Jenkins also began helping to host poker games during the antiquarian book fairs held in California, Boston, or New York. The games had five-dollar bet limits and were usually hosted at a hotel suite with two or three other dealers (e.g., Richard Mohr, of International Bookfinders in Pacific Palisades, California).[56] The Plaza hotel in New York provided a bar and bartender, and waiters with silver serving trays of hor d'oeuvres lined up outside the doors of the suite. The games began at 11 P.M., well after book fair closing hours, and would sometimes last all night—though Jenkins usually gave out around 2 A.M. The socializing and camaraderie were as important as anything else in these book fair poker games. At least as many dealers were gathered around the edge of the room, watching the game, trading gossip, and drinking, as were playing at the table.[57]

Beside poker, Jenkins became enthralled with the idea of card counting in blackjack games. He imagined that it was a nearly foolproof way to beat the house on a regular basis. Jenkins got a copy of Edward Thorp's book *Beat the Dealer* and studied his system for counting cards.[58] He even took personal lessons from Thorp, not only making careful notes about playing techniques

but also asking questions about the best casinos to use the counting system and how much to bet and tip during play without
arousing suspicions from the pit bosses.[59]

Thorp's ten-count system was revolutionary at the time, though
the casinos tried to counter it by no longer dealing to the last card
and by using multiple decks in the shuffle. The easiest way to use
Thorp's system was to keep count of all of the cards valued ten or
higher. When a majority of the remaining cards are ten or higher,
the player has the advantage; if a majority of the remaining cards
are less than ten, the house has the advantage.

Jenkins took to this card system like a lizard to a sunny rock.
Sometimes he and Maureen would travel to Las Vegas with their
bookselling friends, Michael and Gail Ginsberg, to play blackjack.[60] Gail remembered that Jenkins said she was his good luck
during the blackjack games and always had her sit next to him.
Maureen laughed when I told her this, because Gail would always
show Jenkins her cards to ask his advice before betting, which just
aided him in the counting system.[61]

Jenkins often won so steadily that Maureen would drop by his
table every couple of hours to clear off his chips (making it less
likely that Jenkins would garner undue suspicion for his winnings). Often she would cash them in and take the money to the
hotel room safe; other times she would tell Jenkins that she was
going shopping, leaving him torn between the desire to stop her
and the urge to keep playing and winning.[62]

Eventually the casinos caught on to Jenkins and banned him
from the blackjack tables, though that didn't deter Jenkins, who
merely tried to disguise himself with a hat, wig, and mustache.[63]
Once, after he had been banned from Caesars Palace for card
counting, he found himself on a plane to Las Vegas sitting next
to the owner's wife. Jenkins turned on the full-press charm until
she said, "Mr. Jenkins, I know what you're doing—you're counting
cards at the blackjack tables." Jenkins was taken aback, but she still
got him unbanned from Caesars Palace, at least for that trip.[64] The
stage magician Ricky Jay specialized in card tricks and collected
books. He knew that Jenkins counted cards in Las Vegas and wrote
him a wry inscription in 1977 in his first book, *Cards as Weapons:*
"To John Jenkins: Who knows the evil of playing cards."[65]

Later, in the early 1980s, when Jenkins was playing high-stakes poker in Las Vegas, he once decided to take a break by playing some blackjack; perhaps he thought the pit bosses wouldn't remember him from his blackjack card counting years earlier. The pit boss pulled him off the blackjack table. Jenkins protested, certain that they couldn't possibly remember him from a decade earlier. The pit boss had videos that proved he was counting cards back in the 1970s; they were well aware of him, and the casinos shared the names of known card counters with each other.[66]

Card playing was something that Jenkins's extended family could enjoy with him as well. A Bastrop cousin, Kenneth Kesselus, once suggested a rafting trip with the cousins down the Rio Grande in Big Bend National Park and enticed Jenkins by mentioning that low-stakes poker games with "a real poker player" would be exciting and memorable. They were all camped out one night by the Rio Grande on the Mexican side of the border at Boquillas. The cousins tried playing Texas hold'em around the campfire, but the game was a bust because everyone was too timid to bluff. Then his cousin Richard, who was Jenkins's age, challenged him to prove his skill at card counting. Jenkins gave him the deck and asked him to shuffle it. Then Jenkins asked him to keep turning over cards until he got to the last card, when he should stop. Everyone was watching when the Richard stopped at the last card. Jenkins said, "That's a ten." Richard turned over the card, showing a ten.[67]

Jenkins enjoyed the legitimacy conferred by his ABAA membership and prestige of his seat on the board of governors, but he could still be careless and combative in dealing with customers. When the occasional customer complained, Jenkins's first reaction was to jab back, even if the mistakes were made by his employees. The ultimate responsibility for such errors, of course, lay with the proprietor, but Jenkins was very much in the hands-off mode of management for his rare book firm.

One longtime customer, Everette DeGolyer, wrote to him from Dallas to express his intense displeasure with two recent transactions. He reminded Jenkins that the DeGolyers had been purchasing books from rare book dealers since 1912, but that two recent book purchases from the Jenkins firm put any future transactions with them in jeopardy. Both books had been misdescribed in catalogues. The two books were an 1849 edition of Emerson Bennet's *Prairie Flower* (a fictional account of an overland trip to Oregon) that was lacking the text on four leaves, and a biography of Christopher Columbus, published in Venice in 1571, also missing four leaves. The faults in both books were something that should have been described in catalogues before customers ordered them from the Jenkins Company. DeGolyer told Jenkins that, if the books were not returnable, he should no longer consider them his customers.[68]

Not surprisingly, Jenkins was taken aback by the stern tones in DeGolyer's complaint. He asked DeGolyer if it would not have been nicer to write a friendly letter first or to call Jenkins up and say that two books were defective and that he wanted to return them, instead of writing Jenkins "the nastiest letter I have ever received from anyone in my whole life?"[69] Jenkins refunded his money with the explanation that he had a young staff who still needed to be trained in cataloguing. Whether this was true or just an excuse, Jenkins had the habit of deleting condition descriptions for rare books before the catalogue was printed; he was especially likely to do this for books that had problems, like the ones sold to DeGolyer.[70]

The problem wasn't just with Jenkins's catalogue edits, but occasionally with his thin skin. In June 1975, Jenkins offered the Yale curator, Archibald Hanna, a copy of Robert Creuzbaur's rare overland account of travel through Texas to California (published in 1849 with five maps). Hanna, with his tongue only partially in his cheek, sportily replied that if Jenkins had bothered to check Wright Howes's bibliography of Americana before quoting the Cruezbaur book he would have seen that Yale already had one of the six located copies. Jenkins testily replied in a letter marked "Personal" that he had noticed a sarcastic tone in Hanna's recent letters, which he hoped was just friendly banter. But Jenkins reminded Hanna the he did not need to be told to look at Howes's bibliography more closely since he used it almost daily. Hanna, realizing that Jenkins had taken offense where none was intended, and eager to keep good relations with a valued bookseller, quickly apologized.[71]

When he wanted, Jenkins could charm rare book librarians with the ease of a snake oil salesman. After the curator from the University of Georgia library visited the Jenkins establishment and sent a recipe for mint julep, Jenkins gamely replied with a dash of Texan pride, "It is a shame that you were unaware that the mint julep was actually invented in Central Texas in the 1700s by the Tonkawa Indians, who had their own corn whiskey concoction (the recipe for which, alas, has been lost). I learned this from my grandfather who got it from a 96-year-old Tonk woman who lived with our family until her death in the 1890s."[72] This is one story that had some factual basis; his grandfather hired a Tonkawa woman who cooked for the family. She towered over the short Jenkins clan at 6 feet tall and was known as "Aunt Puss."

Jenkins was never one to back away from a fight, especially when the London *Times Literary Supplement* criticized his publishing firm. In 1973, Jenkins reprinted Merle Johnson's classic of book collecting, *High Spots of American Literature*. Johnson's guide was originally published in 1929 and reflected the popular collecting tastes of the 1920s, recommending such bygone authors as Sherwood Anderson (author of *Winesburg, Ohio*) and William Dean Howells (*The Rise of Silas Lapham*). Johnson's guide had no listings for such recognized literary giants of the 1920s as Ernest Hemingway and F. Scott Fitzgerald.

The *Times Literary Supplement* dismissed Jenkins's reprint of Johnson's collecting guide, calling it an "old war-horse" with no more than historical interest. Jenkins jumped to the defense by noting that, whereas his firm's reprint had sold more than 1,300 copies in the past two years, Yale University Press's bibliography of Ernest Hemingway had just remaindered more than six hundred of their copies.[73] Now whose book was only of historical interest?

Jenkins could stiffen his back just as quickly when a customer questioned whether a book he was peddling was actually a forgery. Jenkins had written to John Mayfield, a major collector of Swinburne, offering him a proof copy of Charles Wells's poetic drama, *Joseph and His Brethren* (originally published in 1839), with several hundred manuscript notations, some of which were thought to be in Swinburne's hand.[74] Wells (1796–1879) was an English romantic poet whose work was neglected until Dante Gabriel Rossetti and Algernon Charles Swinburne rediscovered him, after which his poetic work became a shibboleth for poetry lovers.

Mayfield normally would have jumped at the chance to acquire a book like this; after all, he authored *Swinburneiana: A Gallimaufry of Bits and Pieces about Algernon Charles Swinburne* (1975). But he wrote to Jenkins that he had been warned off of this book by an English dealer who said only, "Watch out. Don't be hasty." Mayfield said that another friend had warned him off the book as well, and though this was only hearsay he was not interested in purchasing the book.[75]

Jenkins chaffed at this accusation. "I bought them from a major English dealer out of a catalogue and they look highly unfaked to me." Besides, he told Mayfield, it would cost ten times more than they were worth to fake them.[76] In fact, though, Jenkins didn't buy the proof copy of *Joseph and His Brethren* from a major English dealer; that was just his attempt to bolster the provenance. Jenkins actually bought the Wells book from Charles Hamilton's autograph auction in 1974.[77] Perhaps the bargain price Jenkins paid, $65, should have tipped him off, or at least warned him off the book. What Jenkins didn't know, and probably the reason some of Mayfield's friends had warned him off, is that the proof copy had originally come from the auction of the library of H. Buxton Forman (1842–1917) in October 1920.[78] Forman was an antiquarian bookseller and friend of Swinburne who made his reputation with bibliographies of Percy Shelley and John Keats. What he is best remembered for now are his forgeries, with Thomas J. Wise, of literary ephemera (a deception outed by John Carter and Graham Pollard in 1934).[79] Jenkins was innocent in this episode and in all likelihood the proof copy of *Joseph and His Brethren* was genuine, since Forman was never known to forge manuscript material.

------·------

In the spring of 1975 an amazing new opportunity to acquire a collection of rare Texana and Western Americana presented itself to Jenkins. Lindley Eberstadt was the last remaining partner of his father's rare book firm, Edward Eberstadt and Sons.[80] Edward Eberstadt (1883–1958) had founded the firm in New York City in 1908, spurred on after his accidental discovery of a rare book in a mechanic's garage.

One day while crossing the Brooklyn Bridge, Eberstadt was overcome by the need for a service station restroom. The mechanics obliged him, and while there he saw that pages from old books were being used for toilet paper. One old book, printed in Spanish, intrigued him. Eberstadt knew some Spanish, having spent time in South America as a young mining engineer, and he asked the mechanics what they wanted for it. He paid their asking price of fifty cents and took it to the only librarian he knew could help figure out what he had purchased.

Wilberforce Eames (1855–1937) had worked for rare book sellers before taking a post as a rare book curator for the Lenox Library (which at the time held the only Gutenberg Bible in North America). After the Lenox consolidated with the Astor Library in 1895 to form the New York Public Library, Eames became chief of the American history division, and later bibliographer. The *New York Times* called Eames "the greatest living scholar of books in America."[81] Eames examined Eberstadt's book and told the delighted scout that he had found an incomplete but rare Mexican incunabulum (a book printed in Mexico before 1600). Librarians are loath to put retail prices on books, but Eames recommended that Eberstadt take the book to Lathrop Harper, a rare book dealer in Manhattan.

Eberstadt got a good price from Harper, found that he liked scouting for printed gold, and established his own rare book business. His sons, Lindley and Charles, joined him in the 1930s, and over the next forty years they became the leading rare book dealers in Western Americana. By the late 1960s the Eberstadts had stopped issuing catalogues, and frequently they did not even bother responding to collectors and librarians who wanted to visit their offices and look at the rarities. After Charles's death in 1974, Lindley Eberstadt needed to sell the inventory to help settle the estate with Charles's wife, Iris, and began looking first for a buyer for the entire collection.

Lindley had heard of the prodigious amounts of oil money that the University of Texas poured into rare book and manuscript acquisitions. He contacted the director of the Humanities Research Center, Warren Roberts, to offer him the chance to buy the collection. Roberts was interested but thought the asking price of $5 million too steep, and the collection too broad. He asked Eberstadt about purchasing just the Texas portion, but Eberstadt did not want to sell the collection piecemeal.

So far, very few booksellers had heard that the legendary Eberstadt collection was about to be sold. Now Roberts mentioned his dilemma to Jenkins, who immediately sprang into action. First, Jenkins contacted Lindley and got him to agree to a ninety-day period in which Eberstadt would receive no other offers; he would also pay a 5 percent finder's fee for Jenkins if their deal was completed. Then Roberts tried to get a group together to raise the money. But his potential donors were only interested in buying the Texas portion, not the remainder.

Jenkins wanted to get his business partner's thoughts on the deal.[82] He tracked down Bob Venable vacationing in Italy and called him long distance, telling him that here was an opportunity to buy $5–10 million worth of rare books for $3 million. Jenkins was hoping that Venable's oil money connections could be used to front the money for the collection. At first Venable thought that Jenkins should continue to encourage Roberts to raise the money and just collect his 5 percent commission on the deal, which would still be $150,000. Just before hanging up, Jenkins told him that every major university in the United States had been trying for years to buy portions of the Eberstadt collection, and so the two of them had a ninety-day advantage over any other buyers.

After Jenkins hung up, Bob told his wife Kris about the phone call and Jenkins's need for $3 million, and they laughed. They had been reeling from increased drilling pipe costs for oil exploration (inflation in 1975 ran about 9 percent). Sometime after their return from Italy, Venable began thinking about Jenkins's proposition again. To his way of thinking, he had nearly $500,000 invested with Jenkins in his rare book business, which had thrown off $20,000–$30,000 a year to the Venables. If the Jenkins firm had

$6 million worth of rare book inventory, Bob thought, he should be able to get $200,000–$300,000 a year in returns.

Venable called Jenkins and asked him if they could use their existing rare book assets for collateral with Eberstadt for the deal? Jenkins said no, Lindley wanted cash. Venable had almost resigned himself to not doing the deal when he remembered Art Haas, a friend from his days at Murchison Brothers. John and Clint Murchison were the Dallas heirs to an oil fortune that they leveraged into real estate and other investments, including the Dallas Cowboys football team.[83] Venable was a young attorney at Murchison when he met Haas and considered him a financial wizard. They met for lunch and Venable laid out the rare book deal. He asked Haas if a $2.5 million guaranty could be gotten for the deal, and if so how much it would cost? Haas paused only a moment before answering; he had, after all, helped structure far larger financing deals for the Murchison brothers. He told Venable it would be no problem. Now came Venable's crucial question: how much would the financing cost? Haas said half of all the profits. Venable was taken aback and told Haas he needed to think it over.

Venable began to wonder if he could provide the guaranty for the financing himself. He had the necessary net worth of nearly $3 million, but he was already badly extended financially in land deals and high pipe costs, and this rare book investment would have meant going all in on a field in which he had little experience. Meanwhile, Venable told Jenkins to go ahead and fly up to inspect the collection in New Jersey while he continued to explore financing options. After all, if the collection's value didn't meet expectations, there would be no reason to continue looking for financing.

Jenkins called in his old friend and Americana expert, Michael Ginsberg, so they could look at the collection together. When they got to Lindley's office, he welcomed them and gave them a quick walk-through of the nineteen offices, each of which was filled with shelves of the rare book inventory. Neither of the booksellers had ever seen an accumulation of so many rare books in one place. Then Lindley took them to the vault and let them loose. Ginsberg was an old-school book scout. His practiced eye scanned titles one by one, quickly determining whether a book should be pulled out for further examination or whether to move on to the next book. The shelves were full of rarely seen treasures of Americana, and he anticipated taking several days to examine the Eberstadt inventory fully.[84]

Jenkins went directly to one of the vault file drawers; when he pulled it open he found rare Texas manuscripts and documents of such value that he murmured in surprise, "Oh my God." He leafed through some more papers and again said, "Oh my God." This continued for a few more minutes. Ginsberg also expressed his surprise as he discovered one rare book after another on the shelves, many times seeing rarities he had only read about in bibliographies. Then suddenly Jenkins closed the drawer and turned to Ginsberg and said that he had seen enough. He was going to buy the collection. Before they left the Eberstadt offices that day, Jenkins had Lindley put a wax seal on the vault door, then called his partner, Venable, to see how they could possibly do this deal. That night Jenkins was unable to sleep. He told a sleepy Ginsberg, "I have to own this."[85]

The possibility of such an enormous deal weighed on Jenkins and made regular business affairs difficult for him. In July 1975, Rice University Library had duplicates of some Republic of Texas rare books that they wished to sell or exchange for trade credit with the Jenkins Company. When Jenkins was slow to make an offer, they pressed him again. This time he told them that he had spent most of the last three months negotiating for a huge "upwards of $5 million" collection of rare Texana and Western Americana, which included several copies of each of the rare books that Rice was offering in trade. Jenkins told the library he could not make a decision until early August, when he would know for sure whether he would be buying the Eberstadt collection.[86]

The complexity of the Eberstadt financial negotiations appealed to Venable's problem-solving nature. He soon learned that if he and Jenkins could show enough collateral, and if they let his friend Art Haas have a small piece of the action, Haas would use his connections from the Murchison brothers to convince Wall Street investment banker Charles Allen Jr. to provide irrevocable letters of credit to secure the $2.5 million deal.

Though Charles Allen (1903–94) was one of the wealthiest men on Wall Street, he had been raised in a rented apartment on New York's Upper West Side (long before it was fashionable) and dropped out of high school after two years to become a Wall Street runner and then as a boy bond trader. He chafed at working for others, and in 1928 when he was nineteen years old he opened his own one-room trading office with only a thousand dollars of capital. One year later he was worth nearly a million dollars, but he lost it all in the stock market crash of 1929. He worked shrewdly to recover, and one of his bigger plays in 1938 was buying 150,000 shares of Missouri Pacific Railway stock at 22 cents a share (for a total of $33,000) when it was tied up in bankruptcy. He sold it a short while later for ten dollars a share, for a profit of nearly $1.5 million. By the 1950s, Allen had achieved such lasting success that in 1954 *Fortune* magazine had a feature article on him (Jenkins kept a copy of this article in his files). Despite his riches, Allen was a careful spender who did not draw unnecessary attention to himself. Instead of having a limousine and chauffeur, he bought a cab medallion and had his own full-time taxi driver.[87]

An irrevocable letter of credit guarantees payment and is generally used in international trade. In this case, if Allen were convinced of the value of the collateral, he would issue letters to Lindley and Iris (Charles's widow) Eberstadt guarantying the payment. The cost of the letters of credit to Venable and Jenkins would be around 1 percent of the value of the deal per year, payable in advance, roughly $175,000.

With that possible guaranty, Venable first asked Jenkins to get an appraisal of all of their holdings in Austin. Jenkins reported that the publishing company, the rare book business and inventory, the offices and land, and Jenkins's share of other investments, including the Country Store Art Gallery, came in at around $2.5 million in value. Haas decided that those assets, with the stated retail value of the Eberstadt collection of $5 million, would be enough to get irrevocable letters of credit from Charles Allen for the deal.

As in every complicated contract, there were devilish details. Once Allen was involved, Lindley and Iris Eberstadt had to sign a purchase agreement locking in the price for the collection for ninety days. This did not stop competitors from trying to buy the

collection out from under Jenkins. One highly respected antiquarian bookseller, Warren Howell of John Howell–Books in
San Francisco, had been trying to get Lindley Eberstadt to come
down a little bit more on his price of $2.5 million; now he offered
to top Jenkins's price by $250,000.[88]

Lindley preferred to deal with Howell, a bookman he had
known and worked with closely for years. After all, he and Warren and another dealer had worked behind the scenes in the final
few sales of the Streeter collection in the late 1960s, trying to
ensure they would not compete against each other (and unneces-
sarily run up prices at the auction). The final sales, where Streeter's
maps were sold, were poorly attended and Lindley and Warren
were able to purchase the maps. One leading dealer later thought
the two men had ringed the sale. This is an auction strategy quite
common in the United Kingdom (where it is not illegal) in which
the members of a group, or "ring," of dealers agree not to compete with each other and then later sort out the purchases they
made. Unfortunately, in the United States dealers who "ring" an
auction risk running afoul of the Sherman Anti-Trust Act (which
is enforced by the Justice Department, not the Securities and
Exchange Commission, and with penalties including prison).

The final sales were poorly attended, so Howell and Eberstadt
did not have to resort to ringing. The auction results still show the
much lower than normal retail prices.[89] It was hardly surprising that
Lindley would prefer to work with the devil he knew. He called
Jenkins to break the bad news. It was a nice try, kid, but Lindley
had a higher offer from another dealer whom he knew well.

Jenkins rose to the fight. He reminded Lindley that he had
already signed an ironclad purchase contract backed by attorneys
for the richest investment bank on Wall Street, Allen and Company. John told Lindley that if he reneged, Jenkins and the Allen
Company attorneys would tie him and his estate up in litigation
for the rest of their lives. Lindley knew Charlie Allen, even if by
reputation only, so he wisely reconsidered and told Howell that
his higher offer could not be accepted after all.

The day of the deal, August 7, 1975, Michael Ginsberg went
to New York and met Jenkins at the luxurious Carlyle Hotel on
Madison Avenue. Jenkins told him that the banker, Charles Allen,

would be by to pick them up in his car and warned Ginsberg not to talk politics, since he was not an "Austin Democrat" like they were.[90] In fact, Allen was a staunch Republican and supported Gerald Ford in the upcoming presidential election, whereas Jenkins was equally active in Democratic state politics in Texas.[91]

Allen picked up the booksellers and tried to get a conversation on politics going by asking Jenkins what he thought of the governor's race in Texas. When Jenkins was noncommittal, Allen tried to draw him out by asking whom he liked for president in the upcoming 1976 election. Again Jenkins refused to bite, saying there were good candidates on both sides. Finally Allen turned to Ginsberg, who wore his hair over his ears: "I won't even ask you about politics because you're from Massachusetts and they are all liberals."[92]

They met at the Eberstadt offices in New Jersey with a gaggle of attorneys, and after the deal was signed both Lindley and Jenkins lit up Cuban cigars. The final Eberstadt purchase price was $2.5 million (less $125,000 for Jenkins's 5 percent finder's fee), with $250,000 cash as a down payment ($200,000 from Venable/Jenkins and $50,000 from Haas), and a seven-year note (at 7.5 percent interest) for the remaining $2,250,000 that would be carried by Lindley and Iris Eberstadt. The payments would be $250,000 per year (plus interest) for five years, with $500,000 payments (plus interest) in the sixth and seventh years. There was no early prepayment permitted, so basically the Eberstadts earned almost an additional one million dollars in interest from the sale, for a total payment of about $3.25 million.

The ink on the contract was hardly dry before Jenkins, Ginsberg, and a crew began packing up the collection into 670 boxes, and then into the Allied Moving Van freight trailer.[93] Lloyds of London insisted that they would insure the collection only if non-union truckers were used. This requirement seems to have been intended to prevent the possibility of an inside heist.[94] The other terms of the insurance coverage from Lloyds meant that Jenkins and Ginsberg had to drive to Texas behind the tractor-trailer, calling and reporting their locations to the insurance company along the way. Though they did not stay at any hotels, because of rules governing team drivers they still had to stop for a couple of hours each day.[95]

In practice this meant that Jenkins, Ginsberg, and a retired sheriff's deputy friend took shifts driving the station wagon behind
the tractor-trailer, with one of them sleeping on a mattress pad in
the back. Once Ginsberg and the sheriff's deputy stopped for gas,
coffee, and to check in with Lloyds on a pay phone. Jenkins was
sleeping in the back, so after refueling they headed back out to
the interstate. While driving onto the ramp, Ginsberg happened
to look in the rearview mirror. He saw a small figure running to
catch up with them and waving his arms. Jenkins had gone to use
the restroom without telling anyone.[96]

The magnitude of the work began after they got back to Austin.
Jenkins wanted to get a large part of the purchase price back,
and the quickest way would be to sell the Texas portion of the
collection to the University of Texas. The director of the Humanities Research Center, Warren Roberts, wanted to buy the Texas
portion, but he needed to get some faculty members behind the
purchase as well as the board of regents. Roberts turned to William H. Goetzmann, who ten years earlier had won the Pulitzer
Prize in history for his *Exploration and Empire: The Explorer and
Scientist in the Winning of the American West* and who was rumored
to be the highest-paid humanities professor at the University of
Texas. Goetzmann wrote a strong letter for Roberts in support of
the purchase, noting that nothing comparable to it was likely to
ever come on the market again, and its acquisition by the University of Texas would place them in the top rank of institutions.[97]

There was a more important heavyweight in Roberts's corner
for the Eberstadt purchase. Former governor Allan Shivers was
chair of the university's board of regents and remembered that the
university had lost out to Yale two decades earlier when Thomas
W. Streeter's Texas collection was for sale. Shivers was so popular
in Texas that in the 1952 election both the Democrats and Repub-
licans nominated him for governor, making him the only Texas
candidate ever to run against himself. Democrat Shivers won 75
percent of the vote against Republican Shivers, who garnered 25
percent—still twice as many votes as any other Republican guber-
natorial candidate in Texas in the 1940s and 1950s. Shivers called in
chits and IOUs for the Eberstadt purchase from his many years in
politics, as well as relying on some homegrown Texas patriotism.

One of the regents who supported Shivers was Edward A. Clark, a University of Texas law school alum who had been legal counsel to Lyndon Johnson for his Senate races, president of the Texas Commerce Bank in Austin, and ambassador to Australia. In 1953, *Reader's Digest* called Clark the "Secret Boss of Texas," and in 1982 he was still named as one of the twenty most powerful Texans.[98] Once Clark was in favor of the Eberstadt purchase, Shivers had nothing to worry about. Shivers told these heavy hitters that the Eberstadt acquisition, with its Texas history holdings, meant that the University of Texas would finally eclipse Yale in importance.[99] Legend had it that Colonel Travis at the Alamo drew a line in the sand so the defenders could demonstrate their allegiance for independence; for Shivers, the prestigous collections of the University of Texas would be a line in the sand too, and the regents joined him.

The support of Shivers, Clark, and the other regents for the Eberstadt purchase was a big relief to Jenkins and Venable. They had some major payments to the Eberstadts coming up soon, and they were hoping for a quick sale to the university of between $1.2 and $1.5 million; Venable thought that they could nearly cover the total purchase price with the UT sale and then they could take their time and sell the rest of the collection at retail prices to get the highest return. In theory, this was a great plan for maximizing the return on a rare book inventory; in practice, with an impulsive gambler like Jenkins at the helm, it was much harder to carry out.

The University of Texas agreed to the purchase of the Texas and Southwest portion of the Eberstadt collection for $1.4 million (in three payments over two years—$500,000 down, $468,000 at the end of the first year, and $434,000 at the end of the second year). The Jenkins Company delivered nearly nine thousand high spots in 154 boxes in October 1975, including a collection of Texana ($475,000), a manuscript collection ($400,000), a Mexican War collection ($60,000), a Southwest collection ($350,000), a history of Mexico collection ($90,000), and a map collection ($25,000).[100]

Nearly the first dealers to visit Austin to see what they could buy from Jenkins's new inventory were Warren Howell, the San Francisco bookseller, and another bookseller who had bid

unsuccessfully with him for the Eberstadt collection. Howell, a
tall man of patrician mien, was described by one of his rivals as
the "snowy-thatched dean" of booksellers—though others mock-
ingly called him "The Emperor," both for his regal ways and dis-
dain of other dealers.[101] Warren proudly told new customers that
his firm was founded by his father in 1912 and was "one of the
biggest in the nation."

Howell preferred to make an imperial entrance. At the auction of Adrian Gladstone's library of detective and mystery fiction
in 1981, the auctioneer stopped the bidding on the most expensive lot of the auction, Arthur Conan Doyle's first book about
Sherlock Holmes, *A Study in Scarlet*, because the emperor had not
yet arrived. A shouting match from angry bidders was underway
when Howell walked in wearing a three-piece pinstripe suit. He
pretended to be unaware of the shouts of protest at his arrival and
bid "with seemingly disdainful flicks of his perfectly cuffed wrist,"
buying the book for the highest price at the auction, $15,000.[102]
Earlier, before the deal was done, Jenkins had reached out to see
if Howell and his colleague would be willing to commit to buying
a large portion of the inventory.[103] As much as anything, this was
probably a way of reassuring Jenkins's investors that he had purchasers for the immense inventory.

To help with pricing the Americana, Jenkins hired Ginsberg,
giving him a $2,500 monthly retainer and a credit card for travel
expenses. During Howell's visit both Jenkins and Ginsberg felt
that the big dealers were treating them like rubes. When Ginsberg took them to the vault room to look around, Jenkins told him
to discreetly turn on the two-way intercom so they could listen to
the visitors. Back in Jenkins's office they both sat listening while
Howell and the other dealer examined rarity after rarity. Howell
kept asking his bookselling colleague, "Do you think he knows
what this is? Do you think he knows what it is worth?"[104]

When the two visiting dealers emerged from the vault with their
selections, they waited for Ginsberg to price each of the rarities.
They started in with their bargaining tactic on the most expensive set: "Two thousand for this book seems awfully high." Ginsberg, prompted by Jenkins, responded, "$2,250." The two dealers
were surprised, "Oh, come on." Ginsberg, again encouraged by

Jenkins, said, "Fine, $2,500." Though Howell and his colleague still grumbled, they paid the $2,500 asking price.

Jenkins resented dealers he considered to be "blue blood," those who had inherited position or money in the rare book trade. The old Boston Brahmin and rare book dealer George Goodspeed had never shown Jenkins any hospitality, much less respect. After the Eberstadt purchase, Goodspeed's Americana buyer, Bailey Bishop, came down to Austin to shop the stock. Jenkins insisted on taking Bishop to lunch and the Boston dealer happily obliged (probably thinking that Jenkins was trying to impress him). Jenkins pulled up at the most blue-collar restaurant in Austin, the Hoffbrau, and parked right alongside the pickups and dump trucks. The Hoffbrau had been serving steak lunches on West Sixth Avenue in Austin since 1932. If Bishop had any reservations, he kept them to himself, until the waitress brought his order of soup and he found a hair in it. Bishop called the waitress back over and pointed the hair out to her. "Yep, you're sure right, darling," she said, and walked away.[105] Jenkins loved every minute of it.

The Eberstadt deal inflated Jenkins's already healthy ego. He told Ginsberg that the older prices for books weren't valid any longer. With this quantity of inventory, he was the market maker in the field and would raise the prices on Americana.[106] However self-important Jenkins seemed, dozens of dealers suddenly wanting to come to Austin to have a chance to pick through the Eberstadt treasures verified his judgment.

Jenkins took the opportunity to ham it up for a picture. He posed in front of the vault holding the Eberstadt collection with his father, Holmes, and Michael Ginsberg. Holmes had a six-shooter tucked in his belt and Ginsberg held a lever-action rifle. Jenkins, though, wore his .38 Special revolver holstered by his side (the same one he had used to chase out the home invader).[107] They clearly delighted in casting themselves as three tough Americana booksellers protecting the rarities with their guns.

———•———

Jenkins's already oversized ego got some further inflating in the mid-1970s. First, his mentor at the Texas state archives, Dorman

Winfrey, nominated him for membership in the elite and scholarly Texas Institute of Letters. Jenkins was grateful and thanked
Winfrey for being a good friend through the years.[108]

But the real and nearly unbelievable gratification for Jenkins
came in 1976 when Union College presented him with an honorary doctorate. This was in part for his efforts in recovering
the stolen Audubon plates, in part for his establishment of the
John H. Jenkins Award in Bibliography at the college, and to
recognize his distinction as a "bibliophile and collector."[109] Jenkins's other honorary doctorate corecipients that weekend were
persons widely recognized for their achievements: Academy
Award–winning filmmaker John Houseman and celebrated African American historian John Hope Franklin.[110] Union College
probably knew that Jenkins's accomplishments were not up to the
level of the other recipients, and they had their own tongue-in-
cheek comments for his presentation: "John Holmes Jenkins III,
self-styled Texas bookmaker, by your account, your ancestors
suffered a most un-Texan deafness to opportunity's knock, but
they left you a rich legacy of other Texan virtues, including the
yarn-spinner's way with a good story."[111] Jenkins must have been
uniquely honored to receive a doctorate for his ability to tell tall
tales. He was positively giddy when he accepted, declaring that
he had never been so excited and pleased in his life and adding
for modesty's sake that he certainly "did not deserve all of their
kindnesses."[112]

Jenkins returned to his office after receiving the honorary
degree, and he wanted the staff to begin using his new title. He
had hired Sheri Tomasulo as his secretary earlier that summer.
Now he instructed her to begin calling him "Dr." Jenkins. His
new secretary had been raised on the Texas prairie, where folks
were naturally suspicious of anyone who used titles to lift themselves above others. Tomasulo looked Jenkins right in the eye and
said, "That'll be fine, as soon as you start addressing me as Mrs.
Tomasulo instead of Sheri."[113] She never heard another word about
"Dr." Jenkins.

Jenkins did not waste any time broadcasting his new status as
the market maker in Americana. He went to a Sotheby's auction
in New York in 1976 to bid on the first printed copy of the U.S.

Constitution ever to appear in a newspaper. The *Pennsylvania Packet and Daily Advertiser* was the official printer for the Constitutional Convention in 1787, and the text appeared in their September 19 edition (an issue wholly devoted to the text of the new document). The bidding opened at $300, but Jenkins bid aggressively and finally purchased the newspaper for $2,000.

What price would the newest market maker in Americana list it for in his catalogue? That same year Jenkins issued a special *Americana Celebration* catalogue and priced the special newspaper for $85,000. How far off was Jenkins in terms of the test of time? His imagination may have been running way ahead of other booksellers in 1976, but his audacity has been vindicated. Two other copies of that same newspaper have sold at auction in the intervening years; one at Sotheby's in 2001 brought $148,550, and another in 2005 at Freeman's in Philadelphia brought $207,225.

When the Grolier Club came to Austin in 1976 after the Eberstadt purchase, Jenkins took everyone to dinner.[114] Among the esteemed guests was H. P. Kraus (1907–88), easily the most important rare book dealer of the late twentieth century. Hans Peter Kraus was born in Austria, the son of a doctor at the University of Vienna. At sixteen he was in the attic of an old house in the mountains rummaging through a sixteenth-century chest for stamps when he came across a mouse-chewed atlas. The owner gave it to him, and the boy later found he had stumbled on a treasure—a 1578 Mercator atlas.[115]

Kraus established a thriving bookstore in Vienna, but as a Jew he was imperiled by the Nazis. He spent several months in Dachau and Buchenwald before being released. The Nazis expelled him from Austria in 1939, and he was forced to abandon his rare book shop and nearly 100,000 volumes. He managed to take a few rarities with him, and he arrived in America, on Columbus Day 1939, with an original copy of the first printed account of the discovery of the New World, known in the antiquarian trade as the Columbus letter. Kraus always had a keen eye for publicity, and the story ran in the *New York Times*. Eventually he restarted his rare book business in New York. Among many other rarities, he handled a Gutenberg Bible and sold it to the Morgan Library for $2.5 million.

Kraus was curious about the young dealer who had managed such a large acquisition. He asked Jenkins what he was looking to buy for inventory. Jenkins, on the heels of having made the largest purchase of a rare book dealer's inventory in the twentieth century, looked right across the dinner table at the most important rare book dealer in the world and, in front of everyone, said, "I want to buy you." Another guest noticed that Kraus looked out of sorts for the rest of the evening; perhaps he wondered how much more oil money Jenkins had up his sleeve.[116] If nothing else, it was a collision between old-world manners and the swagger of a young, brash Texan.

The autograph dealer Kenneth Rendell loved finding gag gifts for his dealer friends. After the Eberstadt purchase, he found a dartboard to give to Jenkins but marked it with different prices instead of points. Jenkins loved the joke and the sly teasing about his post-Eberstadt pricing methods. Thereafter Jenkins would tell people that his pricing system was based on the best practices given to him by the finest dealers on the East Coast, all the while looking over his shoulder at his dart board.[117]

With his newfound status as the market maker in Americana, Jenkins eagerly signed up the firm to exhibit at book fairs. One that would have been better avoided was the Chicago Antiquarian Book Fair in the summer of 1976. Jenkins wanted to go all out, purchased a silver travel trailer, gutted it, and filled it with books. He dubbed it Parnassus II (in honor of the fictional book trailer in Christopher Morley's 1917 novel *Parnassus on Wheels*). He planned to park the trailer in front of the convention hotel, the better to grab customers before they went into the book fair. Jenkins even distributed advertising fliers touting the innovation. But the hotel management refused to let him park it on the street, and Jenkins had to park his gleaming innovation on the lowest level of the parking garage, dooming dutiful employees to take shifts remaining with it.

The failure of Parnassus II was only one aspect of the unmitigated disaster of the Chicago Book Fair that year. The exhibition floor was devoid of customers, and the only people chatting in the aisles were bored booksellers. One esteemed bookseller, Norman

Storey, whose bookshop on Charing Cross Road in London was never as vacant as those aisles in Chicago, finally had too much. Storey had survived twenty-eight aerial bombing missions as the rear gunner on a Lancaster during World War II, but now he looked over the empty fair aisles, put a bag over his head, and ran blind up and down the aisles waving his arms and yelling at the top of his voice.[118] No one even paid him any attention.

The Eberstadt success and sales gave Jenkins a vastly increased cash flow and the opportunity to expand into books and fields about which he knew little. Somewhere he acquired the very rare true first edition of Herman Melville's *Moby Dick, or, the Whale*, which was published in London four weeks before the New York edition. As was typical of British novels at the time, it was published in three volumes (known in the trade as "triple-deckers"); the volumes had blue covers and cream-colored spines decorated with gilt whales. The spines of Jenkins's set were apparently soiled, and he probably assumed that they were faded. Rather than consult Jacob Blanck's *Bibliography of American Literature*, which would easily have explained the two-colored bindings, he fixed the "problem" himself by coloring the spines to match the boards with a blue sharpie.

At a New York Antiquarian Book Fair in the late 1970s, Jenkins sold that *Moby Dick* set (along with a 1786 Kilmarnock edition of Robert Burns's *Poems, Chiefly in the Scottish Dialect*) to a collector named Carolyn Manovill (1919–2001). Manovill had been a naval lieutenant at Pearl Harbor; now she was an executive who lived in midtown Manhattan and a customer of John F. Fleming Rare Books.[119] Shortly after her book fair acquisition, she had Fleming over for drinks and proudly showed him her new set of *The Whale*. Though Fleming's reaction is not recorded, his shock was enough that she insisted Jenkins retrieve the sharpie-colored books and refund her money.[120] For good measure she had him take back the Kilmarnock Burns too. Jenkins never lost his proclivity for finding solutions to nonexistent problems.

It is either the triumph of Jenkins's folly or the nadir of his hypocrisy that he composed a bit of doggerel about forgers for his vanity

volume, *Audubon and Other Capers*. Referring to the Thomas J.
Wise forgery of Elizabeth Browning's *Sonnets from the Portuguese*,
which was exposed by John Carter and Graham Pollard in the
1930s, Jenkins wrote:

> The worldly wise
> Did Sonnets devise
> Then Carter and Pollard
> Hollared![121]

The rare book dealer Tom Taylor was the first to uncover the
Texas fakes and "hollar" about them in the late 1980s. How did
the forgeries begin? Innocently enough, according to their per-
petrator, Dorman David. In 1970 he had been working on some
expert reproductions of important documents of early Texas history: "I had considered offering a portfolio of facsimile printed
Texana items to my customers and had printing plates made."
David remembered that he had made about five different ones,
including the Texas Declaration of Independence, the Declaration of Causes, and the Travis "Victory or Death" broadside.[122]

Dorman David sold some of these forgeries as authentic at this
time too, though he later denied it. At least one of David's forgeries was consigned to Parke-Bernet (later Sotheby's) in New York
by an associate of Dorman David's. The consigned fake was one
of the rarest imprints listed in Streeter's *Bibliography of Texas*, Lt.
Col. William Travis's "Victory or Death" broadside written from
the Alamo. Travis had left a failed newspaper in Alabama before
coming to Texas to escape debtor's prison in 1831. He may not
have been much of a soldier, since the overwhelming majority of
soldiers first elected James Bowie rather than Travis to lead them.
Bowie fell ill, and Travis took command and penned the letter the
same day, February 24, 1836. The newspaperman in him minced
no words: "I am besieged by a thousand or more of the Mexicans
under Santa Anna." The enemy demanded surrender, and Travis
answered them with a cannon shot and reported that the flag of
Texas still flew over the Alamo. Travis called upon Texans in the
name of liberty to come to his aid as soon as possible, and signed
his letter "Victory or Death." Travis's penned letter escaped the
Alamo siege and became the printed plea for help a few days later.

Before the New York auction, only two copies of the Travis letter had ever been located, and both were in the Texas state library. In 1953 the state library traded Thomas W. Streeter for a rare Texas imprint they did not have, but by sometime in the 1960s the library's only original had been stolen—which was the copy Dorman David used to make his forgery.[123]

One passionate collector who heard about the Travis letter in the auction was John Peace, a San Antonio attorney and regent of the University of Texas.[124] Peace did not find out about the Travis letter in the auction from his usual agent, Jenkins. Instead, he heard about it from another Austin rare book dealer, Ray Walton, and at the last minute sent him to New York with an unlimited buy bid. Walton had retired from working in the post office in San Antonio and devoted himself to selling rare Texana and cultivating Jenkins as a friend. Walton played in Jenkins's weekly poker games, and later Jenkins gave him first choice of any rarities in the Eberstadt collection.[125] Walton got the Travis letter for $5,000—the second-highest price ever paid at auction for printed Texana up to that time.

Although Peace was elated at his acquisition, he was disappointed that Jenkins had not told him about it. The day after the auction, he wrote to Jenkins complaining about not getting advance copies of auction catalogues that had rare Streeter Texas items listed in them. Peace warned him that, "if we are to continue our relationship as we have in the past," Jenkins had better become more responsive.[126]

Jenkins may have apologized to Peace for not telling him about the Travis broadside, but in all likelihood he did not bid (and did not want to encourage other potential customers to bid) because he already had a few copies of the forged Travis broadside. The Travis broadside at Parke-Bernet was consigned by one of Dorman David's associates in his theft ring. David had to use an associate because by 1973 he had been arrested by the Texas State Rangers for theft and so could not consign it under his own name.[127] When I mentioned the consignor's name to Houston collector J. P. Bryan Jr., he confirmed that that person had approached Bryan with stolen documents in the early 1970s. Bryan turned down the suspicious documents and remembered that the fellow was associated with Dorman David.

David's spendthrift problems with his inheritance were compounded by his heroin addiction, and he decided to sell off what he could. David sold a large quantity of his remaining inventory to William Simpson's auction gallery in Houston, but he was still short of money. He decided to sell off the printing plates he had made for the reproductions along with his remaining facsimile broadsides to Jenkins, as well as his remaining lots of old paper. "I got down to the last three boxes I had, and John Jenkins bought them." This was in the late autumn of 1970. Jenkins said, "Well, it is the last things I'm going to buy from you," and Dorman replied, "Yes, they're the last things I have."[128]

What did Jenkins do with the forgeries? Jenkins sold Peace a forged Texas Declaration of Independence, a forged Spanish Declaration of Causes, and a forged copy of Sam Houston's army orders. He did, however, sell Peace the genuine English Declaration of Causes—the one from the Eberstadt collection that the University of Texas did not get. Peace's collection eventually went to the University of Texas at San Antonio.[129]

Unfortunately for the University of Texas, Jenkins substituted several Texas forgeries for the real items in the Eberstadt collection sold to the university in 1975. The forgeries included Sam Houston's army orders, a broadside issued on March 2, 1836, while the Alamo was still under siege by the Mexican forces: "The citizens of Texas must rally to our army, or it will perish" (the forgery of this broadside was reproduced as an illustration in the prospectus announcing the acquisition of the Eberstadt collection by the university).[130] Jenkins also substituted a forged Texas Declaration of Independence for the real one in the Eberstadt collection; the authentic one he sold to his Austin dealer and friend, Ray Walton, in 1975, who sold it to a private collector.

Some of Jenkins forgeries were completely fabricated. Archibald Hanna, the curator of Western Americana at Yale, bought a Columbia Jockey Club broadside advertising a horse race in Texas in 1835, which would be a very rare and early Texas imprint, except that no such broadside ever existed. Glen Dawson, a Los Angeles rare book dealer, spotted it in a Parke-Bernet's auction in 1975. He bid for Yale and bought the fake for them for $375 plus his commission (though he later said that he could not remember from

whom he purchased it).[131] Although the consignor of that fabricated broadside is unknown, the only two other copies of it found
both came from Jenkins.

The Columbia Jockey Club broadside was one of at least three
fabrications of Texas broadsides that never existed. Either Jenkins or Dorman David fabricated these, though my money is on
Jenkins; after all, he owned a printing plant, had access to the
equipment for typesetting, and had layout experience from his
father Holmes's graphic design business. These fabrications, all of
which can be traced back to Jenkins, were the Columbia Jockey
Club (1835) broadside; a broadside announcing the Texas victory at
San Jacinto, "Glorious News!" (1836); and a broadside promoting
the city of Houston (1836).[132] More crucial, each of the fabrications
shows some signs of Jenkins's slapdash approach to fabrications.
Rather than research typefaces actually used by the early printers
in Texas, he simply used easily available fonts and typefaces—
such as Linotype Century for the Columbia Jockey Club broadside—a typeface that was not invented until 1896.

Once Jenkins sold through the copies of the better-crafted
David forgeries, he simply resorted to photocopying ones on old
Mexican and Texas paper (Jenkins kept a supply of old blank
paper). To the untrained eye, they could be easily passed off. His
rare book manager in the late 1970s remembered seeing Jenkins
make photocopies of the Spanish version of the Texas Declaration
of Causes on old paper.[133] The only reason Jenkins didn't make
photocopies of the Texas Declaration of Independence on old
paper was that it was too big for the machine. Ginsberg remembered that one of Jenkins's employees told him that Jenkins kept
all the forgeries at his home, bringing them to ship at his shop
only when they were sold.[134]

Jenkins later emphatically denied ever buying the printing
plates or forged broadsides in the fall of 1970 from David: "The
idea that I would have bought any plates like that from a drug
addict, a man like Dorman David, is just preposterous. I certainly deny the charge."[135] Denial or not, there are two check
stubs that still survive in the archives showing payments from
Jenkins to Dorman David that fall (October 27, 1970, for $2,500,
and November 25, 1970, for $1,800).[136] The check stubs from

Jenkins to David do not list what was purchased, but they are proof of the transactions.

Why did Jenkins sell these forgeries as authentic documents? His dishonesty of substituting forgeries in the Eberstadt purchase is even harder to understand than his early thefts from the Texas state archives. A young man with no stake in adult life might have difficulty resisting an easy temptation to steal or even understanding the long-term consequences of his thefts. But by the early 1970s Jenkins had vaulted into the highest ranks of his profession. The Eberstadt collection coup, properly handled, should have created the foundation for a prosperous rare book business.

What "imp of the perverse," to use Edgar Allan Poe's phrase, prompted Jenkins to substitute forgeries in place of the true rarities, and so risk destroying everything he had built up? Somehow he convinced himself that the difference between authentic printed documents and fakes ones didn't matter, as long as the customer believed the fakes were real. Or perhaps it was Jenkins's experience with poker, where an unrevealed card in the hand could be whatever he could bluff someone into believing.

John Holmes Jenkins III, age four, playing poker
with a Kesselus cousin, Beaumont, Texas,
ca. 1944. Collection of the author.

Wedding day of Maureen Mooney and
John Holmes Jenkins III, June 5, 1962,
Dallas, Texas. Collection of the author.

Signing the papers for the purchase of the Eberstadt
collection, August 8, 1975, Montclair, New Jersey.
Jenkins is in the back with a cigar, and Lindley Eberstadt
is to his left. The brunette in the foreground is Iris
Eberstadt (Charles Eberstadt's widow and half-owner
of the inventory). Collection of the author.

"Standing guard"
at the vault door
after the Eberstadt
purchase. (*From left*)
Holmes Jenkins
(known as "Mr.
Jay") with a six-
shooter in his belt,
Michael Ginsberg
(*kneeling, with rifle*),
and Jenkins with
his holstered .38
revolver. Collection
of the author.

Jenkins (*left*) in gown for his honorary doctorate,
June 13, 1976, Union College, Schenectady,
New York. Collection of the author.

Jenkins sitting cross-legged at the Austin Book Show,
ca. mid-1980s. Collection of the author.

Jenkins and "Amarillo Slim" (Thomas Preston Jr.) at the Super
Bowl of Poker, Las Vegas, ca. 1980s. Collection of the author.

"Austin Squatty" Jenkins at a Las Vegas poker table,
ca. 1980s. Collection of the author.

Jenkins Company warehouse in Manchaca, Texas,
after the September 1987 fire. Collection of the author.

Interior of the Jenkins Company office warehouse.
Collection of the author.

4

Double or Nothing

Jenkins didn't just bet at the blackjack and poker tables; wagering infused his book life too. When a dealer bought a book from him, Jenkins often proposed a coin toss for double or nothing on the invoice. Michael Thompson was a bookseller who specialized in early printed editions of scholarly works. He was at the London Book Fair in the early 1980s when he spied a first English edition of one of the ancient Greek classics at Jenkins's stand. He inquired about the price and was told it was £750. Thompson asked about a trade discount, and Jenkins said in manner of a dare from the old West, "Let's flip a coin for the volume—double or nothing." Thompson was feeling game and agreed. Jenkins took out a pound coin, flipped it, and Thompson won the toss and got the book for free.[1] I noticed in the course of soliciting stories about the coin toss from dealers that only those who beat Jenkins shared their stories with me; none of the losers did.

Longtime rare book dealer William Reese gamely took Jenkins up each time on one of his double or nothing rare book bets. To Reese the wagers felt more like the opening of Tom Stoppard's play *Rosencrantz and Guildenstern Are Dead*. Rosencrantz and Guildenstern are two minor characters in Shakespeare's *Hamlet* who are entrusted to carry a secret message to the king of England ordering Hamlet's death. Stoppard's take on that theme of fate and probability opens with Guildenstern tossing a coin that always come up heads, ultimately 157 times in a row. Guildenstern is first puzzled, then worried, then finally wondering whether they have entered some space where alternate logic applies. Reese won the coin toss at least a dozen different times in a row over different expensive rare books. Jenkins, ever the resolute gambler, must have finally been convinced that some alternate luck applied and stopped offering to flip a coin with him.[2]

Jenkins's rough and ready attitudes applied to his treatment of his books too. In the summer of 1981, Stuart Bennet was a young bookseller, fresh from England, visiting Jenkins at the plant in Austin. Jenkins offered to let him spend the night in the guest apartment at the offices, and his father cooked up hamburgers and gave him a gin-and-tonic to help him cope with the heat. Bennett was looking at a copy of the 1759 translation of Plato's *Republic* by Spens when he noticed a later eighteenth-century tipped-in advertisement for Thomas Taylor's translation of Plato in the back of the Spens book. When Jenkins came by to see how he was doing, Bennett showed him the tipped-in broadside, with the lament that it was too bad it was part of the book, as he would have liked to purchase it. Jenkins pulled a utility knife out of his pocket and, quick as that, handed the broadside to a very surprised Bennett with the comment, "Now it isn't."[3]

The same optimism that Johnny the teenager showed by singing in the shower stayed with Jenkins the rare book gambler. The last manager of the Jenkins Company, Michael Parrish, thought his employer was one of the most optimistic and energetic people he'd ever known. One morning Parrish walked into his office and saw Jenkins sitting in his big chair smoking a cigar and staring into space. When Parrish asked him what he was doing, he said, "I'm thinking about having a great day. How are you?"[4] Jenkins buoyant trust in his luck had carried him far by the 1980s and, so far, despite occasional setbacks, his luck showed no signs of slowing.

The success of the Eberstadt deal, and the subsequent sales of that collection, meant that Jenkins had money to burn. As William Reese pointed out, all he would have had to do after the Eberstadt deal was to let his employees sell the rare books and use the proceeds for select future rare book acquisitions. Jenkins would have been well set for the rest of his life.[5] The disadvantage of attaining a great find like the Eberstadt collection at a relatively young age (thirty-five years old) is that Jenkins thought that opportunities like this would come along every five or ten years, instead of only once in a lifetime. Jenkins probably figured that when the cash flow and sales of Eberstadt inventory slowed he would just get the next big collection.

Instead of reinvesting the money, Jenkins the visionary used the cash flow to be noticed. He always wore his white Stetson with the high sides, which real Texas wranglers called a "politicians' cowboy hat," and cowboy boots that made him an inch or two taller. He was a dandy who loved to preen. The biggest skill Jenkins brought to his rare book business was knowing when his story could catch popular and national attention.

In the early 1980s, Jenkins graced the cover of regional magazines such as *Southwest Airlines Magazine*, which featured him with the headline "So Rare: Antiquarian Book Dealer John Jenkins" and showed him piously holding a seventeenth-century vellum-bound book.[6] He published a guide for rare books as financial investments that was quoted in *Time* magazine: "Concludes Jenkins: 'All an investor needs is patience, a good adviser, and a collection worth more than the sum of its parts.'" Jenkins had two collections ready to sell to any potential investors reading this article: a complete library of imprints by Iowa publishers and all of Charles Schulz's *Peanuts* publications with Snoopy.[7] These collections, easily stocked with less expensive books as fillers, exemplified Jenkins's antiquarian book sense.[8]

The easy cash flow from Eberstadt sales enabled Jenkins to invest in nearly every scheme except his own rare book business. He chased dreams of investing in movies, of starting his own conference center by buying the campus of a defunct college not too far from the Dallas–Fort Worth metroplex, and of having the first printing press in space. Jenkins freely admitted that the rare book business provided the funds that he "invested or squandered" in these projects.[9]

The largest boondoggle Jenkins ever undertook was his dream of a "Jenkins University," or conference center. In the summer of 1977, Jenkins learned that the campus of the former Westminster University at Tehuacana (approximately forty miles northeast of Waco in Central Texas) was for sale. He jumped on the purchase.[10] The campus, such as it was, consisted of seventeen acres of land, one decrepit 42,000-square-foot limestone building in serious need of repair, and a few other unused buildings.[11] Jenkins could see in his mind's eye what an excellent conference center it would make—even if it was remote and needed serious repairs. The project became a money pit. Later Jenkins leveraged the mortgage on the campus, and the new debt became an additional financial demand on the business.

The dream of space travel held a deep allure for Jenkins, and the Eberstadt cash flow provided funds for another plunge. When NASA announced that they would sell small cargo spaces on future space shuttle missions, Jenkins jumped at the chance. The cargo space was the size of a large plastic storage container, dubbed the "Getaway Special." It was intended for university and student researchers as well as entrepreneurial small businesses. Jenkins reserved his space on a future shuttle flight in the late 1970s, and his cargo would be the first zero-gravity printing press in space. When asked by a reporter how much he was spending on the project, Jenkins said, "There's no point in me talking about how much I'm blowing on it." So far, the zero-gravity press was just an engineer's three-dimensional plot on a computer screen at the world-famous Heidelberg Press in Germany, and Jenkins figured to have a test model of the press ready by 1984.[12] The zero-gravity press never made it off the ground, but the reserved cargo space on the shuttle became more valuable by the end of the 1980s, and Jenkins's estate was able to sell it at a profit.

The movie investments first came by accident in the 1960s, but Jenkins enjoyed the experience. His store on Congress Avenue had a medieval suit of armor in the window, and some students making a short film asked for permission to use it. They made a slapstick horror movie that played at a film festival in San Francisco, and in exchange for loaning the armor Jenkins got his first film credit as a set designer.[13]

His film credit inspired Jenkins's next foray into movies. He had coauthored a book about Frank Hamer, the Texas Ranger who killed the outlaws Bonnie and Clyde. H. Gordon Frost, a high school teacher in El Paso, had gathered the research materials for writing a biography of Hamer and took the project to Jenkins's publishing company, Pemberton Press. Jenkins was excited about the project. In return for some editorial and historical insights (and probably for his commitment to publish the book), Frost added Jenkins as a coauthor.

Shortly before publishing *I'm Frank Hamer*, Jenkins said he "foolishly" sent the manuscript to every studio in Hollywood but did not hear back from any of them.[14] The next year, Warner Brothers released *Bonnie and Clyde* to popular and critical acclaim, including a nomination for the Academy Award for Best Picture. Jenkins said that he sued Warner Brothers over the script because there were a number of details in the movie that could have only come from his book. Actually, the Hamer family descendants sued Warner Brothers for defamation of character because the film depicted Hamer as a bumbler who was captured by Bonnie and Clyde. In that pre–Supreme Court ruling era (which eventually decreed that dead persons could not be defamed) Jenkins financially supported the family's suit.[15] After a lengthy process, the studio eventually settled, and the Hamers and Jenkins "received a nice settlement out of court."

Flush with this taste of victory, or at least the settlement money, Jenkins next invested in a docudrama narrated by Burl Ives. *The Other Side of Bonnie and Clyde* played on the success of the Warner Brothers film and was written and directed by Larry Buchanan, best known for directing movies for drive-in exploitation specialist American International Pictures. Some of Buchanan's other celluloid masterpieces were *Attack of the Eye Creatures* (1965) and his crowning glory, *Mars Needs Women* (1967). The *New York Times* obituary said that one quality united all Buchanan's films: "They were deeply, dazzlingly, unrepentantly, bad."[16] *The Other Side of Bonnie and Clyde* played in drive-in theaters alongside *Hells Angels on Wheels*. Jenkins appeared in the film as an authority on Hamer and received a cast credit. His only regret on this film was that he "never found out where his share of the proceeds went."[17]

William Witliff, best known for writing the screenplay for *Lonesome Dove*, suggested the next movie investment to Jenkins and a few other friends during a poker game. He told them about a new horror movie that needed investors. What impressed Jenkins, who called Witliff "the tightest man who ever lived bar none," was that Witliff had actually invested his own money in the project. That was enough for Jenkins and the others, and together they put up $300,000 to finance *The Texas Chainsaw Massacre*—with the proviso by Jenkins that he never have to watch it.

The Texas Chainsaw Massacre was a smash hit upon its release in October 1974. The movie was enormously popular at local box offices and revered worldwide. In the decades since, it has consistently been listed as one of the best horror movies of all time. Just over two months later the investors received $500,000 back on their $300,000 investment. Once the financial success of the film became evident, Jenkins eventually won each of his other partners' shares of the film in his weekly poker games.[18] When two more years went by with no additional royalty payments, Jenkins and his friends hired attorneys to go after the distributors, who had disappeared to South America, leaving a vacant office and warehouse. Eventually Jenkins received two hundred prints of the movie and some subsidiary rights, and as recently as 2018 royalty checks were still being received from the movie.[19]

The easy success of *The Texas Chainsaw Massacre* led Jenkins into other movie investments, none of which, however, came close to returning his money like the slasher flick. He sponsored a black-and-white comedy filmed in Austin, *The Whole Shootin' Match*, which was shown at the New York Film Festival but never achieved any success after its release at the box office in 1978. Jenkins also invested in another horror film and got a producer credit on *Mongrel*, a 1982 release about an out-of-control ghost pet, which, needless to say, was a dog. Jenkins sought out John Steinbeck's heir and bought the movie rights to his novel *Cannery Row* for $15,000 in 1978.[20] The movie starring Nick Nolte and Debra Winger was eventually released in 1982 by MGM and achieved some critical and box office success.

———◆———

Austin could not contain Jenkins's rare book ambitions any longer; he wanted a worldwide empire of rare books under his name. Jenkins began by buying the Aldredge Book Store in Dallas in the late 1970s. Sawnie Aldredge Jr. (son of a Dallas mayor) had founded the antiquarian store in 1947, and his wife sold the store to Jenkins a couple of years after his death.

Jenkins used the newfound Eberstadt cachet to expand to California too. He began by luring away two young booksellers, Ron Randall and John Swingle, from Warren Howell in San Francisco. Howell, the same dealer who had lost out on the Eberstadt purchase, was angered that Jenkins had raided his help. In a fit of pique he wrote Jenkins, calling Randall "dumb and ungrateful" and Swingle "a scoundrel." When Jenkins advised the two young booksellers of Howell's comments, he also recommended that they avoid saying anything bad of Howell, so that he would look like the one with "sour grapes." Randall wrote back, taking umbrage at the insult of "dumb," which was just a word like "Jane" or "Smith" with nothing unusual to recommend it. More frustrating, Randall said, was that Swingle refused to trade appellations with him. Wouldn't Jenkins agree that "scoundrel" carried romantic connotations that brought to mind visions of Errol Flynn—a swashbuckler or raconteur?[21] Jenkins's reactions to these pseudo-complaints is not known, but if he wanted a worldwide presence he would have to put up with the personnel egos and problems from partners that came with it.

Of course, actually having rare book stores all around the world would have involved a substantial investment of money and time, so Jenkins did the next best thing. He consigned materials from the Eberstadt collection to select dealers in California, New York, London, and Frankfurt, Germany, with the proviso that Jenkins could list their stores on his letterhead as branches of the Jenkins Company.

One such arrangement was made with Tobias Rodgers of Quevedo Rare Books in London. Jenkins approached Rodgers at the Düsseldorf Book Fair in 1977 with his proposal to have a London office of the Jenkins Company by taking a consignment of Eberstadt books. Jenkins in turn, would promote and advertise the London rare book store as a branch of the Jenkins Company. The advantage for Jenkins was that he could expand his name and prestige by leveraging access to the Eberstadt collection. Rodgers took him up on the offer in a letter, noting only that he wanted travels and voyages, Latin Americana, and perhaps a little of that

Eastern Americana—but none of those "obscure rarities of Western Americana," please. Rodgers added that he had just finished reading Jenkins's *Audubon and Other Capers;* this letter represented the first step in what Rodgers would undoubtedly refer to in his dotage as "the Jenkins Caper."[22]

When the inventory of the venerable London bookshop of Henry Stevens, Son and Stiles (which by then was in Guilford, England) came up for sale, Jenkins jumped at the chance to purchase it. The legendary bookstore had accumulated thousands of books on travel and the Americas, including many that were incomplete and were housed in a separate back room. Such incomplete books carry the politically incorrect book trade designation "cripples," because they lack a map, a plate, a frontispiece, or perhaps a page or more of text. The closet or shelf where they are kept in the book shop is known as the "hospital."

After the Henry Stevens, Son and Stiles inventory purchase, there were plenty of incomplete books on the Jenkins Company shelves. Ken Rendell bought a pair of crutches for Jenkins's fortieth birthday party (March 22, 1980) "to help with all the cripples" he now had in the book shop. The next time Rendell came to visit, he noticed that Jenkins had placed the crutches on either side of the door to the vault—a wry insider's joke about the condition of his "hospital-like" inventory.[23]

Jenkins parlayed his success with the Eberstadt collection into a stint as ABAA president from 1980 to 1982.[24] The most important issue he faced during his tenure was how to coordinate an organized response to the problem of book theft in the antiquarian trade. This was motivated in part by his experiences with the Audubon thieves, and more recently by a young collector who had stolen from him.

Ron Whittington was a beginning book collector with a Ph.D. from the University of Texas. After the Eberstadt acquisition he became a frequent customer and often paid for his purchases with monthly installments. Unfortunately, he also took advantage of the lax atmosphere and trust given to visitors at the Jenkins offices, stealing a large number of rare items of Americana, including the rare first newspaper issue of the U.S. Constitution. The Clovis, New Mexico, police department, acting on a tip from Jenkins, found the

Constitution folded into a copy of *Playboy* at Whittington's home.[25] Jenkins's testimony helped send Whittington to prison.

The problem of rare book thefts motivated Jenkins to work actively with the FBI while he was president of the ABAA. He wrote a pamphlet on how to report rare book thefts for dealers nationwide.[26] He also instituted a rare book theft reporting system with the FBI and told the association that in the past year they had the organization hooked into the FBI computer system, and that every book theft reported to the FBI would now be passed on to the association. Since instituting the reporting system the association had already been instrumental in catching three thieves and recovering stolen books.[27]

The other problems of running a national organization of booksellers were of much less interest to Jenkins. Trying to convince a group of booksellers who largely consider themselves to be the Continental descendants of an erudite métier to agree with your particular viewpoint, is, as the French would say, *à fouetter les chats.*[28]

There were a few female booksellers entering the male-dominated ranks at this time who encountered some prejudice. Victoria Dailey was on the ABAA board of governors when Jenkins was president. When one member's application for membership came up before the board, she nixed it based on her prior experience with that person's dishonest business practices. The applicant's friend who had sponsored him heard about what she did and confronted and threatened her at a Boston book fair. Dailey went to Jenkins to complain about the threats, and Jenkins couldn't have cared less: "Honey, that's just life in the big city."[29] He was far more interested in his title as president, or in dealing with more prestigious issues such as national thefts, than in handling members' personal problems in the organization.

Jenkins wasn't only bored by the messy problems in a national organization. When the monotony of running his business overcame him, Jenkins sometimes escaped by coming out of his office to the center of the showroom. He would loudly proclaim for all the staff to hear, "I have absolutely nothing to do!" Everyone would look at him, and Michael Parrish, who catalogued rare books for the firm, was sometimes tempted to say, "Well, I have a stack of Americana pamphlets on my desk that need to be catalogued."[30]

Jenkins never developed the skills and knowledge needed by rare booksellers, so he was uncomfortable buying rare Americana. Despite his own knowledge of Texana, by and large he did not spend his time looking for rare books to purchase from other dealers. The rare book game is at its essence a game of wits, enhanced by knowledge and experience. Many collectors might assume, for example, that the first edition of George Wilkins Kendall's *Santa Fe Expedition*, published in 1841, which contains a great account of a small group of Texans who set out after independence to seize New Mexico from the Mexicans, might be the best. Actually, any specialty bookseller worth his salt knows that the seventh edition published in 1856 is much rarer, for it was the first to include the diary of Thomas Falconer, an English spy who accompanied the Texans. Jenkins was the first to admit his lack of skill: "I can't buy Americana books. They all sound alike."[31]

After years of association, William Reese, a master bookseller of Americana, had his own judgments about Jenkins's rare book abilities. Reese did consider him not a particularly brilliant or even smart rare book seller. By this Reese did not mean that Jenkins did not ever purchase valuable books in fields such as Texana; he simply meant that Jenkins was much more comfortable buying scarce, not-so-scarce, and even common books to build a collection that could be foisted on some new unsuspecting collector. Jenkins would drop in on Reese's New Haven store and say, "I'm here to buy some big, fat books," which Reese at first thought was a joke but then Jenkins really would buy a lot of big, fat books.[32] One of Jenkins's employees remembered that at the Boston Antiquarian Book Fair in the fall of 1977 Jenkins roamed the floor looking for "puffers," books that could fill out collections he was building. He bought twenty-five boxes of mostly less desirable books and dumped them on his employees to figure out how to ship home.[33]

Jenkins never grasped the difference between acquiring an outstanding inventory like the Eberstadts' versus building up a collection of fairly common and relatively easy-to-find books. Just after purchasing the Eberstadt collection in 1975, Jenkins was elated to find a new customer for Wagner-Camp overland narratives. This was the abbreviated bookseller moniker for the bibliography of rare overland narratives and guidebooks to the West printed between 1800 and 1865, which was compiled by Henry R. Wagner and Charles L. Camp and published in 1953.[34]

The new client was Klaus W. Werner (1928–2018), who immigrated to San Francisco from Germany in the 1950s to work at the Franklin Savings and Loan. Part of the reason Werner came West was that he had a friend in Germany, Rüdeger Lorenz, who collected rare Western Americana and who had helped Werner develop an interest in the West. Since Werner was in San Francisco, Lorenz sent him a list of books he was looking for and asked Werner to check in the city's leading antiquarian bookstore, John Howell–Books. Werner didn't find any of the books on his friend's list, but he was tempted to buy his own first rare book—Frank Soule's *Annals of San Francisco*, an early history of the city published in 1855. The price was sixty dollars. Werner remembered that he "reluctantly spent the money," and that he felt terribly guilty over spending so much on the book. One day in 1971 he went into the bookstore and Warren Howell, a savvy bookseller, persuaded him to purchase a copy of the Wagner-Camp bibliography for thirty-five dollars. This is a time-honored bookseller entrapment technique for new collectors. Werner later remembered that purchase as the best buy he had ever made. His collecting course was decided, and from that time on he decided to collect only "Wagner-Camps."

Then in 1974 Werner was browsing in a used bookstore on Golden Gate Avenue in San Francisco when he found a couple of copies of Jenkins Company catalogues for sale. Werner ordered some antiquarian books, and the company gladly sent him some more recent catalogues as well. Victoria Mattison, who filled his orders at the Jenkins Company, mentioned in passing that John had just purchased the largest collection of Western Americana in the world. Werner wasted no time. He flew to Austin in September 1975.

Among the rarities Jenkins happily tossed to the new collector was the notoriously rare account by James O. Pattie of his travels through New Mexico and the Southwest to California in the 1820s. The book was printed in 1831 but sold only a very few copies. In 1833 the publisher's son opened a bookstore in Cincinnati and printed a new title page with the 1833 date for the remaining copies (probably attempting to make it appear as a new book on the market). The 1833 Patties are moderately rare, but the 1831 Patties are the black tulips of Western Americana. At the Streeter sale just seven years earlier, the 1831 Pattie fetched a record price of $3,900. Jenkins was either too preoccupied or too lazy to check the prices in the Streeter sale, and he sold his 1831 Pattie to Werner for just $1,200. Years later he told a friend, "I am still buying books from this remarkable collection."[35]

In the rare book business one has to gamble one's own wits and knowledge about the price and rarity and salability of each potential expensive plunge. In a land of diamond dealers who examined jewels looking for natural color, exquisite cut, and intense brilliance, Jenkins was the merchant of brightly colored gems and baubles who had an affinity for quantity—even if some of the gems, like the 1831 Pattie, were actually among the rarest of diamonds.[36]

Jenkins felt much more comfortable gambling his wits and money against other card players and the casino house than in betting his knowledge against other booksellers. Reese, whose own rare book business grew to multimillion-dollar annual sales, acknowledged this with a big grin: "I gamble buying antiquarian books. And I am the house."[37]

Although Jenkins was most comfortable as a generalist in his rare book business, at least he was a visionary one. His customers' response to his *Americana Celebration* catalogue issued in 1976 was astounding, even to Jenkins. He had organized the catalogue with items from each year of American history. The catalogue's most overwhelming response came from the items printed since 1940, such as the Atlantic Charter, the United Nations Charter, the McCarthy Commission witchhunt reports, wanted posters featuring Patty Hearst, and anti–Vietnam War underground guides to making Molotov cocktails for protests.[38]

Jenkins didn't stop building collections with that catalogue. He began purchasing every space report published by NASA (usually at a dollar or so each), and he tried to encourage other curators and librarians to do the same. Jenkins remembered that during the Vietnam War protests he urged the librarian at the University of Texas to step outside each day and gather up copies of the handbills being passed out about the war. "What a part of our history they were! And now they are mostly lost."[39]

Jenkins was most successful in building and selling collections of Texas books. John Hill was the attorney general of Texas in the 1970s. Jenkins actively supported his political campaign for governor in 1977 and even spoke at a fundraiser, lambasting the current governor, Dolph Briscoe, for his "ostrich attitude and siesta style."[40] Even though Hill was unsuccessful in his campaign, he bought a collection of nearly six hundred Texas books from Jenkins in 1979 for around $40,000.[41]

Jenkins occasionally chased a high spot from a famous author. At an auction in London he bought a typescript carbon of Henry Miller's famous second novel, *Tropic of Capricorn*, for £1,100 (approximately $2,750 in 1972). Jenkins wrote to Miller, then living in California, that he had been a fan for many years and would very much like to purchase the manuscript of *Tropic of Cancer* to go with the other one he now owned. Miller knew that *Tropic of Cancer* was his most important novel and wrote back that he would ask a "staggering price" for it, for he knew its importance to collectors. Therefore, he was saving it for a rainy day. Regrettably, he had no other manuscripts to sell; he seemed to have given most of his manuscripts away. Jenkins was undeterred and told Miller what he had paid for the *Capricorn* typescript. "Why not sell it to me, and save the money for a rainy day?"[42]

To my way of thinking, Jenkins overplayed his hand with Miller by disclosing the price he had paid; Miller probably had a higher price in mind and now would not be interested in selling the *Tropic of Cancer* manuscript for a price similar to what Jenkins had paid for the *Capricorn*. Jenkins would have done far better by letting Miller name a price, no matter how outlandish it might have seemed, and then working from that point. This is aptly summed up in the old trading aphorism that the first one to name a price loses.

Miller, however, did offer Jenkins a tantalizing consolation prize. "Do you want to buy letters (by me)—not to be published till after my death?" They were written to Miller's Japanese wife, Hoki, but many were unopened and some had never been mailed. Miller added in a postscript, "We no longer live together."[43]

Unfortunately, Jenkins never followed up to purchase the love letters to Miller's estranged wife, which were published in 1986.[44]

One of Jenkins's greatest fears was the public exposure of a gaffe. In 1981 the influential curator and customer Archibald Hanna was retiring from Yale. Jenkins dedicated Catalogue 137 (which contained items from Howes's bibliography, *U.S.iana*) to Hanna. The catalogue was ready to be distributed at the Boston Book Fair that fall when someone found a glaring error in the introduction. After praising Hanna for his contributions, Jenkins had made a passing reference to Streeter's *Bibliography of Texas;* the only problem was, Jenkins mistakenly called him "Frank Streeter" instead of Thomas W. Streeter (Frank was Thomas's son). It was a small error, but Jenkins was mortified. He refused to allow any of the catalogues to be distributed at the fair and had a new edition printed up with the name corrected to "T.W."—since there was no room (without retypesetting the page) for the full name when the wrong name, "Frank," was taken out.[45]

Always in pursuit of the next deal, Jenkins often sailed close to the wind when it came to professional ethics for curators and librarians. One scandal involved F. Warren Roberts (1916–88) at the Humanities Research Center (HRC) at the University of Texas. Roberts was a student and protégé of Harry Ransom, the University of Texas chancellor who became the driving force behind the research collections at the HRC. After Roberts became director in 1962, he and Ransom actively built the literature collections by modern writers, including D. H. Lawrence. Roberts wrote his dissertation on the bibliography of Lawrence, collected Lawrence, and even found a major manuscript archive of Lawrence materials at his publisher's estate in Italy.[46] Roberts decided that his personal collections would be better placed in the HRC. His lapse of personal judgment came when he consigned the materials to Jenkins to sell, and then he purchased his own collections with the HRC's funds. The final straw for many HRC staff members came with the major purchase ($7,500—over $30,000 in 2018 dollars) of another of Roberts's collections, sold to the HRC through the Jenkins Company in late December 1977.[47]

The higher-ups at the University of Texas decided that an audit was needed. Kenneth Rendell, the manuscript and autograph dealer from Massachusetts, was brought in to examine the purchases and review Roberts's dealings with Jenkins. Rendell was friends with Jenkins and hated coming to Austin without telling him, especially under those circumstances. But Rendell knew that he would give Jenkins a fair shake, and if someone else had done the audit Jenkins might have come out far worse.[48]

A few years earlier, on Rendell's first visit to the HRC, Roberts imperiously told him how the game of selling to the HRC was played, with the clear insinuation that if Rendell played along he could be rewarded too. Roberts told him at that time that all purchases for the institution were made only through the New York City rare book dealer Lew David Feldman. The House of El Dieff (a play on Feldman's initials "LDF") was Feldman's rare book palace on East 63rd Street. Feldman issued lavish and handsomely printed catalogues and carried a gold-headed cane. More important, he was nearly the exclusive rare book seller to the University of Texas (and the New York Public Library).[49] Rendell, who thought Feldman was obnoxious, was not so eager for a sale that he would work with the House of El Dieff.[50]

The scathing report of Roberts's practices pulled no punches. Before the audit was made public, one of the regents, Edward Clark, called Roberts on the carpet in a meeting of higher-ups about the audit and other problems: "Goddam it, Warren! You can fuck your office help, you can spend money you don't have, you can steal, you can lie, but not all at once!"[51] When the report was released, the *Austin American-Statesman* headline read "Chaos Charged: UT Audit Blasts HRC Operations." Roberts and his staff resigned. There were few lasting repercussions for Jenkins besides the negative news story accusing him of improper and "questionable dealings" with the HRC.[52] Besides, Rendell said with a grin, "Johnny was the first to admit he was a huckster."[53]

Jenkins continued his work on Texas scholarship, with one eye open to other possible angles of selling Texas books. As early as 1970 he had considered the idea of compiling a guide to the best

Texas books for collectors. He reached out to book people and scholars for suggestions. Dorman Winfrey, his former boss and director of the Texas state library, wrote that he would be pleased to look over the list of Jenkins's suggested titles and thought it was a commendable undertaking.[54] If the truth were told, this project was motivated less by Jenkins's love of Texas than by his desire to have an easy guide for collectors, with purchases from the Jenkins Company, of course.

Jenkins was justifiably proud when *Basic Texas Books: A Guide for Research Libraries* was published in 1983. There were many accolades from collectors and scholars. Senator Ralph Yarborough said, "Each time I open this Jenkins book about the books of Texas, I find new dimensions of learning about Texas. If I had to reduce my Texas library to one book, this might be it."[55]

What Jenkins actually wanted was effulgent praise for his book from fellow booksellers and bibliophiles who might use it on a daily basis. Jenkins sent early drafts of the manuscript to fellow Americana specialists, ostensibly for their critiques and comments. William Reese took the time to read and annotate Jenkins's draft extensively, adding suggestions for clarity and organization as well as pointing out bibliographic errors. When Jenkins got Reese's annotations and corrections back, he never looked at them. It can be difficult for authors to accept criticism of their infant masterpiece, especially if what they were actually fishing for were compliments.[56]

Reese reviewed Jenkins's book in the leading bibliographic journal. He didn't quite damn Jenkins with faint praise, but it certainly fell far short of the adulation Jenkins deeply wanted. Reese said that, since booksellers were independent minded, they often developed bibliographic systems to fit their own needs. As a result, their bibliographies can be both useful and idiosyncratic. "That describes *Basic Texas Books* by John Jenkins very well."[57]

Reese's review stung Jenkins. According to one employee, Jenkins erupted in anger at the plant when he read this review, "Damn him and damn his money!"[58] But a bad review did not deter Jenkins. He simply supplied his own extravagant praise about his book whenever he could. Sometime after that review was published, Robert Rubin, an antiquarian bookseller, saw

Jenkins at the Boston Book Fair and asked him to inscribe a copy of *Basic Texas Books*. Jenkins took a long time to write it out, and Rubin wondered what Jenkins was writing about him. He wasn't, as it happens. Instead Jenkins's inscription celebrated his book and himself: "What is simply the best and greatest and most wonderful book about Texas ever written. John H. Jenkins."[59]

Jenkins didn't just consider his bibliography to be the greatest book on Texas. He wanted to use it to launch himself as the president of the Texas State Historical Association (TSHA). In March 1982, at the annual board meeting of the TSHA, the choice came down to two candidates for president—John H. Jenkins or George R. Woolfolk, a leading African American scholar of business history at Prairie View A&M University. Woolfolk had been second vice-president of the organization, but Jenkins wanted to be chosen president. Just minutes after Woolfolk was chosen in the board meeting, an employee of Jenkins's firm (Michael Parrish) walked into the meeting and handed the board Jenkins's resignation from the organization (which had been prepared ahead of time). Jenkins's overreaction and resignation certainly cost him his shot at the TSHA presidency. As it was, Woolfolk resigned later that month from the TSHA as well, citing "personal difficulties and health."[60] Just as likely was the resistance he experienced as the first African American president of the TSHA and the imbroglio caused by Jenkins.

Jenkins's ambition wasn't limited to writing a guide for the best Texas books. He had long dreamed of writing the definitive history of the Texas Revolution. In 1979 he gave a talk on the revolution and the need for new research and a new interpretation. He noted that forty years earlier William C. Binkley, former chair of the Department of History at Vanderbilt and editor of the *Mississippi Valley Historical Review*, had called for a new synthesis. Jenkins said in his talk that for his own selfish reasons he hated to bring up this topic, since writing such a synthesis had been his "great personal dream" for more than twenty years, and he harbored a secret fear that someone else might write it first. He told the historians that his research files were overflowing with notes for his book, and that as far as topics went "the Texas Revolution was the ripest field for the plucking."[61]

Jenkins admitted to them that sometimes the task of writing such a history seemed overwhelming. He was reminded of other historians who had procrastinated on their projects, such as Harriet Smither with her intended biography of early Texas pioneer Ashbel Smith. Smither gathered information for nearly fifty years without ever publishing the book, and her files fell to Texas state librarian Dorman Winfrey. Over the past fifteen years, Jenkins said, Winfrey had told him about fifteen times that he was ready to begin that biography. So, Jenkins confessed, he had nothing but the same excuses that had kept previous historians from completing their magnum opus. But with any luck, this year or the next, he would take that sabbatical and write that "astonishingly erudite, Pulitzer-Prize winning History of the Texas Revolution in two thick volumes." He hoped that it would find a place on historical shelves between Bolton's multivolume work on the Spanish Southwest and Walter Prescott Webb's history of Texas and the Great Plains.

Because Jenkins had resigned in his fit of pique from the TSHA, he was unaware that the Texas Sesquicentennial Commission had begun looking for a historian to write a new official history of the Texas Revolution (the 150th anniversary would be celebrated in 1986). By 1982 the Sesquicentennial Commission intended to give the assignment to Archie P. McDonald, a historian at Stephen F. Austin State University. Before giving McDonald the final contract, the Sesquicentennial project director decided to call specialists with expertise in the field, just to be sure that "no stone was left unturned." The last person he called to review the proposal was John Jenkins. There was a prolonged pause, then Jenkins told him that he was already writing a new history of the Texas Revolution and was spending 50 percent of his time on the project.[62] Additionally, he had acquired two times the source materials in the original ten-volume *Papers of the Texas Revolution*, and two-thirds of that material had never been used by historians. Jenkins stressed that he had been working on this book since 1965, and that two years earlier (1980) he had spent most of the summer working on his new book. He anticipated having the history ready for publication by the end of 1984.[63]

Unfortunately, although Jenkins almost certainly had large files on the subject, everything else he told the project director about the book was just another Texas-size bluff. Still, the Texas Sesquicentennial Commission gave the book assignment to Jenkins. The director, for one, had no doubt that Jenkins's book would be of "superb quality."

The next year, David Weber, chair of the History Department at Southern Methodist University, followed up to see if Jenkins was still writing a history of the Texas Revolution. Indeed he was, he replied, as he continued his bluff. Jenkins said that he planned to cover the social, political, and military events of 1835 and 1836 in a two-volume work, one of text and the second of annotations and source materials. This would enable the text volume to have some bookstore and popular sales, though he modestly "hoped to God" his book would not be compared to T. R. Fehrenbach's *Lone Star: A History of Texas and the Texans* or James Michener's best-selling *Texas*. Then Jenkins grew honest with Weber about one of his deepest hopes: "If I am ever to be considered a serious scholar rather than a compiler, it will derive from this work."[64]

Jenkins never finished his landmark history. It is even doubtful that he ever wrote any of it before his death; I found no draft in his archives. The episode is a reminder not just of how convincingly Jenkins could spin a story but how compulsively he did, even in situations where he could not make good on his promises.

As for the historian that Jenkins got pushed off the Sesquicentennial project, Archie P. McDonald continued to work in Texas history and eventually did a couple of side projects on the Texas Revolution (including a children's book and a history of New Orleans in the Texas Revolution). McDonald's historical contributions were eventually recognized in a biography published by Texas A&M University Press, but without the Commission's support McDonald was never able to write that seminal history of the Texas Revolution.[65]

While Jenkins dreamed to be recognized as an author instead of a compiler, another dream of being a professional poker player began to dominate his life. Perhaps Jenkins thought that the poker winnings would replace the dissipating sales from the Eberstadt collection. From one point of view, perhaps this was a natural evolution. He often won in his home games, and years earlier, once he had learned to count cards, he profited handsomely from the Las Vegas gaming tables. Now, professional poker playing came to dominate his life, and Jenkins began staying out in Vegas for weeks at a time in rooms given complimentarily by the casinos to frequent players.

The first professional tournament to tempt Jenkins was Amarillo Slim's Super Bowl of Poker. Long before sports franchises began trademarking the names of their championship playoffs, poker promoters simply lifted them. Thus, there was also Benny Binion's more famous World Series of Poker tournament as well as the America's Cup of Poker, the Grand Prix of Poker, and the Triple Crown of Poker.

Amarillo Slim (Thomas Preston Jr.) had five World Series of Poker titles to his name when he conceived his idea of a competing tournament, the Super Bowl of Poker. Slim had honed his gambling skills as a pool hall hustler and illegal bookmaker in Amarillo in the 1950s and had begun playing poker in the smoke-filled back rooms of Las Vegas casinos in the 1960s. His folksy persona made him hard to forget: "With his cowboy hat and boots, Texas drawl and country wit, he became the public face of poker." Slim was elected to at least four gambling halls of fame and played poker with presidents Lyndon B. Johnson and Richard M. Nixon and the drug lord Pablo Escobar.[66] Slim used his Nevada connections to host the Super Bowl of Poker at different hotels in Reno, Lake Tahoe, and finally Caesars Palace in Las Vegas over a dozen years starting in 1979. Slim's tournament was always smaller than Binion's World Series of Poker, but it drew many more professional players of poker than amateurs.

Slim gave Jenkins his gambling sobriquet after Jenkins's first win in the February 1983 Super Bowl of Poker. Slim had watched the diminutive Texan sit cross-legged at the poker tables, and when he gave him the second-place prize money from the seven-card hi/lo stud game, the 6 foot 4 inch host stood next to the new 5 foot 5 inch winner and in his native Texan cornpone patois dubbed him "Austin Squatty."[67] In the best tradition of nicknames, Austin Squatty was a dual reference to both his short stature and how he sat at the tables. Jenkins thereafter claimed in every interview with a reporter that other players had given him the nickname after watching him "squat" like a Buddha at the tables. The advantage to Jenkins was that his explanation said nothing about his being short.

In that first year, 1983, Jenkins took $18,000 from his first win and $16,000 when he placed third in another Super Bowl of Poker event. Jenkins didn't go home from the Super Bowl of Poker with $34,000 in winnings, though, since he also paid $10,000 to enter the no-limit Texas hold'em championship, which he lost by not placing.

That May he flew back out to Las Vegas for Binion's World Series of Poker. Benny Binion (1904–89) was a former mob boss in Dallas who was notorious for killing rivals. In 1951 he left Texas (ahead of the law) and went to Las Vegas, where he opened Binion's Horseshoe Casino.[68] In 1971 he hosted the first World Series of Poker, which soon became the most popular and prestigious poker tournament. Jenkins won the $1,000 ace-to-five draw limit game in May 1983, collecting $9,900. The highest he ever finished in the most important game, the World Series of Poker $10,000 Championship, was also that May, when he placed seventh and won $21,600. "I thought I'd found a birds-nest on the ground," he drawled, chuckling at his early naiveté. "I figured I could just give up everything else and win $40,000 a day at poker."[69] Jenkins actually only ever won more than that in one day of his life, near the end. But he wanted to believe it about himself.

Jenkins played professional poker the same way he conducted his rare book business; he was far better at publicizing that he played than he was at actually winning tournaments. Throughout the 1980s he managed to have features on the novelty of a rare book dealer who played poker written about him in local gaming publications as well as national magazines like the *Village Voice*. He told Richard Cornett from the *Las Vegas Review-Journal* that, even though he owned the largest rare book store in the world, he had to be a detective scouting out treasures that others had overlooked, such as when he bought a Spanish Peruvian manuscript map for $1,000 in a dusty bookshop and then found that it was an Incan treasure map for buried gold, which he sold for $125,000. All of this sounded wonderful to any newspaper reporter looking for something out of the ordinary in the poker tournament, though the wise reader will take Jenkins's story with the same grain of salt as when he claimed in an interview that he won $150,000 in his first poker tournament. Jenkins told Cornett, "I have to use a great deal of detective ability to go and find the books I sell. Isn't it the same in poker to know when someone's bluffing?"[70]

The rare book business at first easily supported his poker betting in the 1980s. When Jenkins began staying six to seven weeks a year in Las Vegas, the business was selling around $750,000–$1,000,000 annually (with sales of $500,000–$700,000 coming from the literature department and the remainder coming from the Americana department). Unfortunately, Jenkins was not reinvesting those profits in rare books; instead, the money was being siphoned off into poker bets. His employees began picking up on his clues of financial distress when he occasionally came out into the middle of his offices and announced that no one should buy books for the firm unless they could make six, eight, or ten times the amount paid for the book (depending on how strapped for cash Jenkins was feeling at the moment).[71]

For the public face of the rare book business, Jenkins stressed the miraculous nature of the Eberstadt collection, which even ten years later he painted as some Aladdin's cave of rare book treasures: "My bankers, to whom I am perpetually in hock, have always tried to get me to give them a monetary value to stick on books. All I can say, quite truthfully, what is left of the collection, at the end of each year after selling from it, is worth more than what it was worth at the beginning of the year." What was still left in 1984, or 1985, or 1986, when he repeated this pitch, "is worth more than the whole collection was worth in 1975."[72] This was piling it on pretty deep, even for Jenkins.

In 1984 it seemed like Lady Luck was still watching over his poker playing, even if she was not asking him for the last dance at the championship. Jenkins might have wondered where she was when he lost all of the early Super Bowl of Poker games that February, but he felt vindicated when he took sixth place in the Texas hold'em championship (and finally won a purse of just slightly more than twice what he had paid to enter, $27,500). Lady Luck deserted him at the cards after that. Jenkins won no more major tournaments during the rest of the year and had to arrange lines of credit to keep entering and playing the high-stakes games.

A financial reprieve for Jenkins came with a major new collector of Texana. L. R. "Bob" French Jr. (1926–2013) had worked his whole life in the oil patch out in the Permian Basin of West Texas. At the height of the oil boom in the early 1980s he sold his wells to Saxon Energy for the then staggering sum of $20 million (just over $50 million in 2018).[73] French had collected coins with the help of a longtime Dallas dealer, John Rowe. Now Rowe brought him to Austin in August 1984 and introduced him to Jenkins. French asked Jenkins about the possibility of building a great collection of Texas books.

Jenkins could hardly restrain his delight. He explained to French that the current market situation for very rare Texas books and materials meant that the best ones went out of state to institutions with large endowments. If French would commit to building one last spectacular Texas research collection, Jenkins could keep the best materials in Texas. Jenkins said he went home that day with "tears in my eyes."[74]

Jenkins plied him with stacks of rare Texana from his inventory and promised to hold the books safely until French got his own library built in Midland. After French left for home, Jenkins and Rowe did a little celebratory jig in the center of the offices.[75] Who wouldn't, after all? Jenkins got a new big customer—a "whale" in casino (and antiquarian bookselling) parlance—and Rowe was to get a 10 percent referral commission of everything Jenkins sold to French.

Collecting is a strange passion to those who do feel the itch. Some understanding of their desire is seen in a friendly letter from the law school acquaintance who became one of Jenkins's oldest friends and customers. J. P. Bryan Jr. once wrote to Jenkins, not quite entirely tongue-in-cheek, "Now my children have no shoes and we're cutting back our employees at a rapid rate. I'm book poor, forever plagued with the insatiable desire to own yet another valuable piece of Texana. Rather than a respected book dealer, I view you more as my drug dealer."[76]

During that first visit at Jenkins's offices, French bought a "basic Texas books" collection for $27,600 and another large group of rare Texana for over $36,000—together nearly $64,000 worth of inventory. More ominous, at that first visit with an excited and important new collector, Jenkins sold him a forgery of the Travis "Victory or Death" broadside for $5,500. After the visit, he wrote to French to tell him how delighted he was to be building one of the great Texas book collections and promised him that "doing so will be one of the high points of my career and I will work hard to give you no cause to ever regret our association."[77] It is difficult to give Jenkins the benefit of the doubt when he immediately sold French an expensive forgery. Why did Jenkins risk sabotaging himself by selling a forgery to his most important customer right from the very beginning?

During the rest of 1984, French's purchases helped to subsidize Jenkins's forays to the Las Vegas poker tables. French, a University of Texas alumnus, told Jenkins that he would stop by when he came to town for a football game; he wound up dropping nearly an additional $50,000 for rare books.[78] Lady Luck smiled on Jenkins there and didn't exactly shut him out in his card wagering, but the rewards were quite small by comparison with the stakes he wagered. Jenkins won $3,900 in the $200 lowball game at the America's Cup of Poker in September, and he won $1,850 in the $500 limit Omaha game in November.[79] He showed no signs of slowing down. Jenkins told one reporter that playing high-stakes poker in Vegas had him completely hooked: "I will be coming back here forever."[80]

Jenkins always believed that each person had a fixed amount of luck that they could use to their advantage, if they had enough courage to bet on it. He explained his philosophy on fortune this way: "Over a period of time you get the same amount of luck allotted to you as everyone else does."[81] Like many poker players, Jenkins liked to believe that he didn't let the money at the table affect him. He had a good grasp of the mathematics of poker, enhanced by his years of card counting at the blackjack tables. The thing that surprised him the most was how many of the best players went on "tilt," letting their agitated emotions affect their strategy.[82]

Of course, Jenkins shrugged, poker wasn't just about your skill at card math and controlling your emotions about the money: "It's how you make use of the luck allotted to you that makes you win or lose."[83] The belief that one's luck is bound to turn is just another version of the gambler's fallacy. This is the common but mistaken belief that if something happens more often than normal in a given period, it will happen less often in the future.

Perhaps the most famous example of the gambler's fallacy occurred in a game of roulette at a Monte Carlo casino on August 18, 1913, when the ball fell in black twenty-six times in a row. This was an extremely uncommon occurrence, with a probability of around 1 in 136.8 million. Gamblers lost millions of francs betting against black, reasoning incorrectly that the streak was causing an imbalance in the randomness of the wheel, and that it had to be followed by a long streak of red.[84] Jenkins never lacked in the quality of spirit that enabled him to wager one more time. The danger lay in amassing more and more casino debt while clinging to the mistaken belief that his allotted share of luck would show up again.

At the beginning of 1985, Jenkins's luck seemed to improve when it turned out to be a banner year for selling to French. Jenkins wrote in January that he had another great group of rare Texana for French's collection. While French's items were being stored at the company, Jenkins's bindery also benefited by making leather cases for many of the rare books. Jenkins reassured him that his collection would not only look spiffy when the cases were done but would be "the most spectacular Texas collection in private hands without any doubt."[85]

At this point Jenkins made a strategic mistake by missing a golden opportunity to reinvest his profits back into his rare book business. As early as 1978, Lindley Eberstadt had been trying to get Jenkins to buy his personal collection of Western Americana. In addition to the business inventory that Jenkins had purchased, each of the Eberstadt brothers had also kept personal collections of rare Western Americana. Jenkins wrote to Lindley that he had been having the time of his life with the Eberstadt collection and that Lindley would "never know how many times I have thanked you in my heart for letting me purchase it." More important, however, "I have been waiting patiently (and you know how hard that is for me!) to receive the list and prices for your books. Do you think it will be ready any time soon?" Lindley replied that he was sorry for the delay but had been feeling lousy. However, if Jenkins got up that way, he should drop in for a visit and they could talk about Jenkins purchasing the collection.[86] That is one lead Jenkins should have followed up on, but he did not. Lindley Eberstadt died in October 1984, and his collection of Western Americana was sold at auction by Sotheby's on May 1, 1985. Many of Lindley's rare high spots of Western Americana went for stunning bargain prices at the auction.[87]

In retrospect, the sale was an uncommon opportunity for Jenkins, in part because he had a great positive cash flow from his new customer, Bob French. Instead, though, Jenkins largely sat out the sale while his dealer friends, William Reese and a couple of other Americana specialists, proceeded to buy rarity after rarity.[88] For example, one lot they purchased (177) about Kansas and Nebraska actually dealt with the Colorado Pike's Peak gold rush of 1859. Almost any guidebook dealing with the 1859 Colorado gold rush is incredibly rare; no doubt the Sotheby's cataloguer could not find auction records for some of the extreme rarities and so just unknowingly put many in the same lot together. The lot had four identified books and six more that were designated only as "others," and Reese and his partners got them all for just $1,200 (some of the individual volumes in that lot later sold for more than the entire lot price). Reese and the others were relatively young dealers at this time; instead of jointly owning and marketing the volumes, they put all of the books on the floor of their hotel room and drew numbers to pick out rarities for their own inventory one at a time.[89] Jenkins should have used this opportunity to increase his rare book inventory. Instead, he used the profits from French to compete in poker tournaments in Las Vegas.

There were other signs that the Jenkins rare book empire was declining. The Aldredge Book Store never became the cash cow that Jenkins envisioned in Dallas, and he sold it to Dick Bosse, who had been running the store for a few years. Jenkins wanted to keep the Aldredge name, but Bosse refused to do the deal without it, since the store would have been useless without the name recognition in Dallas. Bosse had known Jenkins long enough to be wary of any deal, so he carefully stashed all of the inventory not on consignment from Jenkins in storage units, and probably some books that belonged to Jenkins.[90] When Jenkins's employees arrived one day to pack up the inventory, they found half of the Aldredge shelves empty, so they just packed up everything left there. Later, when a longtime customer came into the Aldredge Book Store after Bosse had repurchased it, he noticed the half-empty shelves and remarked that he must have had a hell of a sale. Bosse smiled while telling him the story of stashing his books off-site before Jenkins came.[91]

Though French eventually went on to spend nearly $250,000 with Jenkins just in 1985, his collection suffered by being stored at the company. After selling the books to French, Jenkins constantly and perversely removed complete copies of rare books and replaced them with inferior or incomplete copies (which were in lesser condition or lacked maps or plates). On one occasion Jenkins replaced a beautiful copy of *Sam Houston Displayed*—a rare pamphlet printed in 1837 he had sold to French about the significant battle of San Jacinto, where Santa Anna was captured—with a $35 facsimile reprint.[92] Jenkins impulsive behavior probably reflected his desire for an additional risk in the transaction. He substituted forgeries and inferior copies to sophisticated collections and scholars just as readily as he did to a beginning collector like French. The risk of a daring and unethical impulse seemed to drive him more than anything else.

The substitution of inferior books for better ones was a pattern of behavior that Jenkins was unable to resist over the years. His former rare book manager recalled that Jenkins once had an order for a $15,000 rare book with a map. Before Jenkins had it shipped to the customer, he saw a $1,500 copy in another bookseller's catalogue; the book was cheaper because it had a facsimile map. Jenkins ordered the copy with the facsimile map and had that shipped to the $15,000 customer, keeping the more expensive and genuine copy for himself.[93]

The unjustified conviction of invincibility that launched Jenkins into dishonest transactions also carried him into Las Vegas poker tournaments even when the entry fees were ruinously high. In January 1985 he placed seventh in the no-limit hold'em game at the Grand Prix of Poker, taking $21,300 in prize money—not the big money, but still twice his entry fee. Then in February Jenkins placed first in one of the preliminary games at Amarillo Slim's Super Bowl of Poker, taking $42,500. He must have been feeling confident when he went to Binion's World Series of Poker in May, but despite his frequent plays he won money only once, when he placed eighth in a preliminary game, taking $2,200. Despite his frequent returns to Las Vegas, Jenkins never won again for the rest of 1985. As the year came to a close, it seems likely that his poker debts at the casinos were becoming overwhelming.

A source of cash offering a temporary way out for Jenkins appeared just when gifts are most anticipated, the night before Christmas. A devastating warehouse fire struck the Jenkins Company on Christmas Eve 1985. According to the insurance report, the fire started when some heavy metal doors rubbed the insulation off an extension cord for a portable electric heater (about a third of the way back in the offices by a dividing wall). The resulting electric arc sparked a fire in a nearby stack of trash, spreading to a wicker chair, and then to the wooden bookshelves and the books on the dividing wall. The fire spread more rapidly to the south part of the warehouse where Jenkins stored most of the firm's publishing and rare book inventory. The books all suffered heavy fire, heat, and smoke damage. The north part of the building, where the offices and the vaults were, was spared from the flames, but the inventory and reference books not in the vault still suffered severe smoke, heat, and water damage. Jenkins told the fire investigator that the damages to the inventory and the 20,000-square-foot building would total at least $5 million.[94]

Jenkins said that he was the only one working in his office complex that day; everyone else had the day off. He had been working in the south part of the building that afternoon, not in his offices, and had left the portable heater on. This is one part of the story that seems a bit shaky; winters in Austin are quite mild, and the historical weather records show that the afternoon temperature that day was 60 degrees. The fire investigator asked Jenkins if he had any disgruntled employees who might have had a motivation to burn the building. Jenkins said that all of the employees had gotten a Christmas bonus and he wasn't aware of anyone who was unhappy.

Kent Biffle accompanied Jenkins the day after the fire and watched him slog through the warehouse's inky puddles in dripping cowboy boots. In the smoke-filled building Jenkins slumped down in a scorched chair still damp from the firefighters' hoses. Behind a cigar he managed one of those "smiles that is a semicolon this side of tears." Jenkins told the journalist that he would never go back to publishing books again after this fire, and the journalist thought that was a terrible loss for Texas culture.[95] Jenkins kept his upbeat sense of humor, later telling customers about his smoke-damaged inventory, "We now not only deal in books that are rare, but also in those that are medium-well and well-done."[96]

The fire investigators never pressed Jenkins to find out about his gambling debts or other motivations to pursue an insurance payout. Jenkins eventually collected just $2 million dollars from this fire.[97] His reference and regular inventory books were badly smoke damaged, which gave his employees years of practice at using art erasers to scrub and clean books. But most of the rarest and most valuable part of Jenkins's inventory had been stored in a fireproof vault at the offices and so was completely undamaged.[98] A month before the fire, Jenkins had been telling the employees to be sure to put any expensive consignments in the small vault before going home for the day. The vault had the doors closed every night. Even better, French's Texana collection had fortunately been taken to Jenkins's home before the fire, and so it was completely safe too.

After the fire, Ben Pingenot, who catalogued Texana and Americana for the rare book department, told Jenkins that an expensive presentation copy of the Kennedy *Texas* book had been left in the bindery for work. The set of books, published in London in 1841, is rare, and this presentation copy from the author had a unique three-quarter calf binding.[99] Such presentation copies are nearly unknown in the trade. When Pingenot told him the spines had burned off the Kennedy set in the fire, Jenkins somewhat strangely said, "I wish I had known that set was in the bindery."[100]

The evidence is far from conclusive, but the strange circumstances of this fire strongly suggest that Jenkins, under the pressure of his poker losses and casino debts, set fire to his own warehouse. There is no doubt that he had sold multiple forgeries and incomplete books by this stage of his career, but if he crossed the line into arson, it would show a fair amount of desperation. Perhaps he justified the fire by reasoning that, if the books were his to sell, they were also his to burn.

French nearly stopped buying rare books from Jenkins in 1986. Because of the slump in his oil and agricultural businesses, French said he wanted to "place a moratorium on buying for the collection until things improve or at least we can see some light at the end of this tunnel." He fully intended to resume the building of the collection as soon as the oil economy returned to normal. Later that year French had his library at his offices finished, and Jenkins began shipping the books to the Midland oilman.[101]

Jenkins's business suffered another blow when Kevin MacDonnell, the manager of his literature department, left at the end of 1986 to start his own rare book business. MacDonnell left with the blessing of his boss. Jenkins even allowed him to publicize the new business in the Jenkins Company Rare Literature Catalogue 195 in December 1986. MacDonnell's departure meant a sharp reduction in the rare book department's literature sales, which had been averaging half a million dollars annually in the 1980s.

Nevertheless, Jenkins continued his jaunts to Las Vegas through 1986 and early 1987, perhaps hoping to recoup the lost sales by trying his luck at the poker tables. He continued to spend forty to fifty days a year there, by his own estimation, gambling and taking advantage of the casino's generosity with hotel rooms.[102] Jenkins's betting was enabled by easy credit; at one point he had lines of credit for poker tables at more than twenty different casinos.

Jenkins's poker winnings seemed to desert him, though. Perhaps as his money troubles worsened, the poker player's "tilt," which he had once found hard to understand, began to affect him. He won a few small tournaments at the Triple Crown and Grand Prix of

Poker events in January 1986, but nothing at Amarillo Slim's Super Bowl of Poker, nor did he place in the money at Binion's World Series of Poker in 1986. The next year (1987) he managed to place eighteenth in one of the preliminary events of the Super Bowl of Poker, winning $2,500, and in June he flew to Atlantic City for a poker tournament and managed to win $4,200. Almost certainly Jenkins's lack of any big wins during 1986 and the first half of 1987 meant that his casino debts had dramatically increased.

———•———

Rare book sales took a disastrous turn for Jenkins in the late spring of 1987. His biggest customer, Bob French, threw a party to show off his collection of Texana at his oil production offices in Midland.[103] One of the scholars he invited was J. Evetts Haley, a respected historian and collector of Texana. Haley had authored books such as *The XIT Ranch* and a biography of famed Texas cattleman Charles Goodnight, which were collectible in their own right.

Haley and Jenkins were political opposites. Haley wore his Republican views like hard leather boots and had little patience for Jenkins's Democratic soft-shoeing. Haley even wrote a book attacking Lyndon Baines Johnson called *A Texan Looks at Lyndon*. One smart-aleck bookseller described the condition of a copy in his sales catalogue as "spine and neck rubbed red." Jenkins once said, "I've never had a friendly word with Evetts Haley in 25 years. Our politics are completely reverse." Aside from their political differences, Haley never cared for Jenkins's way of dealing. The antagonism wasn't helped a couple of years previously when Jenkins called Haley a "pompous ass" in a newspaper interview.[104]

Haley had heard about a forged Travis broadside offered to H. Ross Perot through the booksellers' grapevine. In late 1985 an Arkansas dealer offered a Travis "Victory or Death" broadside to Perot, who did not rely on trust for his purchases. Perot had the document examined by experts at Yale University in early 1986. George Miles, the curator of Western Americana, along with another curator, Don Etherington from the Library of Congress, compared Perot's copy to the authentic copy at the Beinecke Library, and they discovered that Perot's was a facsimile (largely through a broken typeset letter in the original, which was clumsily repaired in the forgery). The Arkansas dealer returned the broadside to the dealer from whom he had bought it: John Jenkins.[105]

When French showed his "Victory or Death" broadside, it was with no small degree of pleasure that Haley told him it was fake. "Bob," Haley said, "Jenkins stuck you in a squeeze chute like a bull does a cow."[106] French was raised in West Texas and knew what the cowboy slang meant; a squeeze chute was a narrow steel bar enclosure to hold cows for artificial insemination. French was not only embarrassed in front of his guests; he was angry at Jenkins for taking advantage of him. Up to the time of the reception, he had spent over $550,000 (nearly $1.5 million in 2019 dollars) with Jenkins, making him the Jenkins Company's most important customer during the 1980s.[107]

Now French decided to call on another dealer to examine his library and find out how badly Jenkins had stuck him. French's son, Fuller, had bought some first editions from Kevin Mac-Donnell, and he knew that MacDonnell had managed Jenkins's rare literature department for six years. Fuller also remembered that MacDonnell had recently gone out on his own. French hired him to examine and collate his library of Texana. Collation is a technical term used by rare book dealers which simply means counting the number of pages, illustrations (or plates), and maps in a book and comparing it to described copies in bibliographies to be sure it is complete. Of course, one of the bibliographies that MacDonnell used to collate the French collection was written by Jenkins himself, *Basic Texas Books*.

Eventually the comparison of French's copies of Texas books to known copies in bibliographies showed that nearly 60 percent of his Texas collection (around $327,000) was misdescribed or incomplete.[108] In addition, they found three other Texas forgeries that Jenkins had sold him (for a total of four forgeries).[109] French remembered that Jenkins had given him a standing guarantee of being able to return for credit any book from his collection.

French devised a plan to return the books to Jenkins and make good on that warranty without tipping his hand. Additionally, he would hold back the forgeries in case he decided to take legal action against Jenkins. MacDonnell tapped his old friend Ben

Pingenot, who still worked at the Jenkins Company. Pingenot was a historian who authored books and had been TSHA president. He had the advantage of knowing where much of the valuable Texana inventory was stashed in the firm's offices, and using the Jenkins Company catalogues he and French were able to compile a list of rare Texana at the Jenkins Company totaling around $300,000 retail value.[110]

French had locked horns with the best oilmen in Texas and figured he could take on Jenkins's penny-ante games. He put on his best poker face in late June 1987 for his visit with Jenkins in Austin and proceeded to select rare Texas book after rare book. Jenkins was elated to think that he had just sold over $300,000 worth of his rare Texana. Jenkins offered to ship the books to French in Midland, perhaps hoping to play his old trick of substituting incomplete or facsimile volumes for the more valuable books. French appeared to think it over for a minute and then said, "Ah hell, wrap them up and I'll take them with me now." Even with so many of his very best materials gone, Jenkins must have been positively glowing at the thought of that French invoice receivable driving off to Midland.[111]

Three days later a UPS truck delivered ten boxes of rare books *from* Midland, all from Bob French. The puzzled employees showed Jenkins the large shipment and he also wondered what was going on, since French had left his premises less than a week earlier with a large group of new Texana. He called French, who told him exactly what he had done and why. Jenkins's response survives in the form of a lengthy seven-page single-spaced letter, which French later said was the longest letter he had ever received in his life.[112] The theme of Jenkins's pleading was his innocence: "I have never been so astounded as when I talked to you yesterday."[113]

In the letter Jenkins began by revisiting their conversation. First Jenkins asked him if he had had a change of interest in his collecting. French was frank and honest. No, instead he was completely dissatisfied with the Texas books Jenkins had sold him and felt that Jenkins had taken advantage of his trust and that was why he had returned them. Jenkins told him he was completely crushed by that accusation. He told French it was beyond belief that he would jeopardize the continued building of his collection by "mistreating it or you in any manner." It is hard to reconcile Jenkins's assertion with his having replaced the authentic editions that French purchased with forgeries, facsimiles, and incomplete books.

Jenkins admitted that there was one returned book "which completely befuddles me, and that is the Woodman." David Woodman's *Guide to Texas Emigrants* was published in Boston in 1835 and is especially valued for the rare map; copies at auction have brought more than $20,000. The October 1984 invoice from the Jenkins Company shows that French paid $850 for a first edition for the Woodman. The returned Woodman "which definitely came from us" (as Jenkins acknowledged) had the unusual feature of being a facsimile reprint with binding work intended to make it look as though it were in the original cloth covers. Of course, there would be no reason to do this because the reprints are worth far less than the binding work, unless one were trying to deceive someone. Jenkins maintained that "this is not the book I put in your collection." Jenkins insisted that how it got there was a complete mystery to him.

Jenkins stressed his stellar reputation to French. After all, he had stared down a mafia pistol while working with the FBI to capture book thieves, he had been elected president of the ABAA, and the TSHA was going to reprint his *Basic Texas Books* to help him recover from the fire. Jenkins said that misdescribing rare Texas books in his catalogues would be "suicidal" because his catalogues were reference works. He avoided pointing out that no competitor, or for that matter reader of the catalogues, would ever know the book was misdescribed without having the copy in hand next to the catalogue entry. Jenkins wondered if "jealous" competitors (many of whom had trained with him) were to blame or possibly someone in Midland. "The only person out there with whom I don't get along is old J. Evetts Haley, and our antagonism runs back to the 1960s."

Finally, Jenkins stressed his integrity: "I am an honest man." Groucho Marx understood what such a statement said about someone: "There's one way to find out if a man is honest. Ask him. If he says yes, you know he is crooked."[114] And this particular honest man, like every abuser who tries to convince a partner to stay in a harmful relationship, said that he actually loved French's collection: "I would no more consciously mistreat your collection than I would a member of my own family."

The loss of French as his major customer of Texana was a punishing twofold blow for Jenkins: French never bought another book from him again and, more damaging, Jenkins had lost the most valuable part of his inventory to French and instead had it replaced with unsellable and incomplete books that were worth far less. The poker tables were equally unkind to Jenkins for the rest of 1987, and it is likely that while wrestling with the French crisis he was also adding substantially to his casino debts.

It is a damaging thing to lose your best customer; it is a devastating thing to lose your most valuable inventory at the same time, with nearly no hope of collecting anything for it—unless by some fate another fire struck your rare book business. This is exactly what happened, and Jenkins's main hope was that, as with the first fire, no one would look too closely at the claimed insurance losses.

Late on a Monday afternoon in September 1987, the Manchaca (pronounced "man-shack" in Texas) Volunteer Fire Department received a fire alarm call for an office-warehouse complex at around 5:32 P.M.[115] Jenkins had moved his business to the 6,000-square-foot complex after the previous fire; he was leasing the building, which was in a rural office-warehouse park on Regal Row.

The fire department was located less than a mile away and Jenkins and his employees were well known there because they ate nearly every week at the Fire Hall Kitchen, a nonprofit intended to help fund the volunteer fire department. The Fire Hall Kitchen served all-you-can-eat catfish buffets as well as chicken-fried steak. The fire department responded with eight trucks, but some firefighters were surprised to pass Jenkins in his gold Mercedes-Benz speeding away from the smoking building. The volunteers worked quickly and had the fire under control about ten minutes after arriving. Jenkins told a reporter that "it did more damage to me psychologically than anything else." He said the previous fire had damaged about 500,000 volumes of rare Texas history, and that they couldn't have taken another big trauma of fire or smoke damage. Fortunately, Jenkins added, "I can't say for sure, but it doesn't look like our book inventory was damaged." Fire captain Jeff Reeves said the fire "was good and hot." More ominous for

Jenkins, the fire captain also said that, without clear evidence of an accidental cause, he would be contacting the state fire marshal's office and asking them to investigate the fire as a possible arson.[116]

———•———

The first Jenkins Company fire in 1985 came just two years after Jenkins started wagering large bets in tournament poker games. The insurance payout of more than $2 million should have been enough to pay off his business loans and gambling debts. If Jenkins had been able to stop the mad race of his life, this would have been the right time. But he didn't. When he lost his major customer and the poker windfalls never materialized, Jenkins looked to another fire. The second Jenkins Company fire, coming less than two years after the previous one, raised suspicions of arson. This fire was too soon after the earlier one, and was less carefully planned, with no artfully frayed extension cord or strategically placed stacks of burnable trash. Instead of his candid admission about working in the warehouse on the day of the first fire, Jenkins had raced from the scene of the second fire.

Why was Jenkins so self-destructive? He had been ticketed for speeding many times when he was a college student. When he bought a newer Chrysler Plymouth in 1959, he took it on the highway to see how fast it could go. Jenkins's new car's speed was mouthwatering, and he was "proud" that when he sped between 135 and 145 mph the front tires came up off the road.[117] Most people never take their cars over 100 mph, much less keep flooring the gas pedal when the car is no longer steerable.

Jenkins the mad driver relentlessly floored the accelerator of his life. He raced off to the Las Vegas gambling tables as fast as he sold forgeries and crippled books. He put the pedal to the metal right into the second fire and the hope of another huge payoff. Young Jenkins loved the thrill of going fast enough to lift his front tires off the highway; Jenkins the adult got his thrills pressing the gas pedal all the way to the floorboards, even as his steering tires lifted up and he fishtailed wildly out of control. In NASCAR, officials wave a black flag to order a dangerous racer off the track. Jenkins ignored every black flag waved at him.

5

The Final Hand

The savings-and-loan crisis that hurt Texas in the late 1980s nearly bankrupted Jenkins. He had used the easy credit to leverage almost everything he owned, including his inventory, his office warehouse in Austin (for $600,000), and his college campus at Tehuacana (perhaps as much as $1 million in loans). Additionally, he had personal lines of credit, including one for $20,000 to Texas American Bank, and he personally guaranteed some oil investments (for over $250,000).[1] Jenkins used business checking accounts the same way as the inexpensive books he bought as fillers for his collections. Besides being able to say that he was a major depositor at multiple banks, more accounts meant check kiting was easier too.

Access to credit was easier for Jenkins than most business owners because of his poker and old boy networks. He sat on the board of directors of North Austin State Bank because an old buddy and a cousin of LBJ, Huff Baines, had vouched for him.[2] Jenkins used that position and his connections to secure seats on the boards of several other regional banks and savings and loans.

Jenkins avoided confrontations with loan collectors by cultivating the ability to be nearly invisible. There was a large Persian rug in the entry to Jenkins's office that had been custom made for the King Ranch but for some reason had never been claimed from the U.S. Customs office in Houston. Jenkins bought it from Simpson's Auction Galleries in 1976.[3] He noticed after buying the rug that the threads were faded, so he sometimes sat on the rug with felt tip markers and recolored it (just as he had with his first edition of *The Whale*). Once, before the first fire, Jenkins was squatting on the rug coloring the threads when a group of bankers who did not know him came by the Jenkins Company offices demanding payment on a note. They had tried to get him to come to the bank but had been unsuccessful, so they had decided to visit him. Jenkins sat in plain sight while the employees sheepishly explained that the boss could not be found. The bankers left without noticing the short, smiling man coloring the rug.[4]

———•———

At first, the investigators of Jenkins's Regal Row office fire had no more luck in finding him than did his bankers. Joseph "Joey" Porter had worked at the state fire marshal's office for nearly ten years when he got the referral from the Manchaca Volunteer Fire Department. Porter visited the burned-out offices and gathered some burned samples in one-gallon cans. Then he tried repeatedly to question Jenkins about the fire, but Jenkins never returned Porter's calls and refused to make an appointment. Porter had dealt with suspicious characters before in fires, but he was also preoccupied with the investigation of a fatal fire and did not have time to chase the rare book dealer. He concluded that more manpower was needed in the Jenkins investigation and called on the Federal Bureau of Alcohol, Tobacco, and Firearms (ATF) to assist.

ATF special agent Charles Meyer got assigned to the case. He placed the burn samples that Porter had collected in the ATF evidence vault, and together the two men examined the fire and collected photographs as evidence. It was clear to both of them that the fire had started in the mail room, and they looked for pour patterns on the concrete floor of a "probable" flammable liquid. Their initial investigation showed that "no sources of possible accidental or equipment ignition" were found in the building. They believed that the fire was set intentionally.[5] The Jenkins Company remained open, but the owner remained as elusive as ever.

———•———

While the arson detectives looked for Jenkins, Tom Taylor was about to begin the investigation into Texas forgeries that would implicate Jenkins. Tom Taylor's interest in books came naturally. His great-grandfather built a library in the literary tastes of the 1920s, so he grew up surrounded by fine press books and modern first editions.⁶ In 1972, Taylor was twenty years old and a sophomore at the University of Texas when he heard about a campus book-collecting association, so one afternoon after classes he went to his first meeting of the club at Ray Walton's home. Walton was a local bookseller who had retired from the post office in San Antonio to pursue his avocation of rare Texas books. Walton's love of eating was the only thing that surpassed his love of rare book storytelling. Walton settled his large body into his mahogany Barcalounger and enthralled Taylor so that he stayed all night listening to him.⁷ Taylor found a purpose that spoke to him more deeply than college. He dropped out of school and started selling books from his great-grandfather's collection. "It was an act of utter folly that I never regretted," he said.⁸

A bookseller's training is ad hoc. Taylor benefited by getting acquainted with local booksellers, such as Jenkins, and special collection librarians. Decherd Turner was the director of the Bridwell Rare Book Library at Southern Methodist University in Dallas. One morning on a visit, Turner took the fledging bookseller down the library hall to the vault. While Taylor looked away, Turner spun the combination, opened the door, and took Taylor's coat. "Enjoy yourself," Turner said. "I will come get you for lunch."⁹

On subsequent visits Turner would let the young bookseller roam the special collections vault so that Taylor could develop a "feel" for rare books. This intuitive sense is finely honed in the best booksellers and accounts for how they can recognize a rare book that they may never have heard of; because of their experience examining thousands of other different but similar books, they can recognize a rarity when it shows itself. It's not just the bibliographic information that counts in the case of a rarity. Charles Everitt, an old-time New York bookseller, put it this way: "It's imagination, not bibliography, that makes money."¹⁰ I think Everitt meant that the best bookseller is not the one who has looked at the largest number of rare books but the one who can imagine where a particular volume fits in the pantheon and why it would be important for a collector.

Thanks to the kindness of Turner in allowing Taylor to roam the vault, he began to build the type of experience that teaches a bookseller why some books are much more valuable than others. Turner also benefited from Taylor's inexperience. Once during setup at a Los Angeles book fair, Taylor found one of the rarest items of Americana, the original 1494 Basel, Switzerland, Columbus letter, the pamphlet announcing the discovery of America. Even though Taylor had never seen one, he figured that buying the pamphlet for $3,000 should still leave room for money to be made, though he was a little unsure of his judgment. When the fair opened and Decherd Turner arrived at his stand, Taylor eagerly pulled the Columbus pamphlet out of his briefcase. The special collections librarian kept his poker face while asking Taylor the price of the rare pamphlet. Taylor hadn't thought about it yet, but he quickly figured that he needed a new roof on his home in Austin, and that would cost $5,000. On the basis of that shaky calculus, Taylor blurted out, "$8,000." "Oh," said Turner, "I'll take that, Mr. Taylor." Taylor asked if he wanted the pamphlet shipped to the library with an invoice and began to suspect that maybe he had priced it too low when Turner said, "Oh, no, why don't you just write it up now and I'll take it with me."[11] How badly did Taylor miss on the price? Ten years earlier in the Streeter sale of Americana, the Columbus letter sold for $30,000; the most recent auction price in 2017 was for over $750,000.[12] Not too bad a return to a library for letting a young bookseller roam its vault.

———•———

Poker kept drawing Jenkins to Las Vegas. The gaudy night life of the neon city probably felt like an escape into a different world, one where so many people were not looking for him. Michael Kaplan left a description of Jenkins in a professional poker game in 1988. Kaplan described the cigar-smoke-filled room at Binion's Horseshoe Casino as a pit "teeming with snakes." Here Jenkins chomped a cigar, wore his trademark white Stetson, brim just above his eyebrows, and sported a pair of ostrich-skin cowboy boots.[13] Jenkins carried a wad of cash, just like the other players, and he intended to make it grow.

This Jenkins game was no-limit Texas hold'em, all the chips on the table were worth $10,000, and everyone in the game except Jenkins and his opponent had been eliminated. Jenkins had the habit when he was sitting at the poker table of rolling and restacking the plastic chips in front of him while he contemplated his next move. Kaplan watched Jenkins take off his Stetson, wipe the sweat off his brow, and do a slow shuffle with his two hole cards, fanning and unfanning as he looked at the flop in the center of the table. The flop showed five cards (to be used by both players)—an ace, jack, ten, three, and queen. Jenkins had been playing his conservative game, but now he decided to pounce and pushed all of his chips (around $5,000) into the center of the table.

His opponent looked at his cards, then counted his chips. He called, and Jenkins flopped his two cards on the table with a hopeful look on his face. Jenkins had an ace and a queen, good for two pair—aces and queens. The other player darted his eyes around the table "like a cornered possum looking for quarter." He found none and looked at his cards one last time before slipping them face down to the dealer. Jenkins suppressed a grin of victory as he raked in his chips to the sound of cards being shuffled at the next table.

The arson investigators kept trying to interview Jenkins. While they waited, they spoke to the employees who were there on the day of the fire. Michael Parrish had started working at the Jenkins Company in 1976, and in 1981 he became the general manager of the rare book firm. The investigators noticed that Parrish was cooperative until the interview concentrated on the fire, John Jenkins, and the financial condition of the company. At that point they thought Parrish was giving somewhat "evasive and defensive answers," though they did not suspect him of anything other than loyalty to Jenkins.[14]

Parrish told the investigators that he had arrived for work later in the morning on the day of the fire, and that it seemed to be a fairly normal business day. At the end of the day the bindery personnel left at 5 P.M. and the firm's secretary left just a little later.

Parrish said he left around 5:15 or 5:20 and noticed that Jenkins's car was the only one still in the parking lot, though he had not seen Jenkins before leaving.[15]

The investigators still had one more Jenkins employee to account for during the time of the fire. Where had Jose Alvarez, the night watchman who lived in an apartment at the offices, been? When the investigators interviewed him, they learned that in the weeks before the fire Jenkins had asked him to move a large number of rare books from the offices to Jenkins's home. Alvarez said that on the afternoon of the fire he had picked up the firm's mail at the post office and brought it to the office. At about 4:45 P.M. Jenkins asked him to go out and get a box of his favorite cigars. They were sold only at Highland Mall in Austin, which was nearly a forty-mile round trip from Manchaca. The errand would take even longer than normal during rush hour, so even though Alvarez had been notified by his beeper to return to the office he did not get there until the fire was already extinguished.[16]

The ATF investigators also eliminated any other suspects in the arson at this time. They administered a lie detector test to Alvarez and cleared him of any involvement in the fire.[17] The investigators continued trying to contact Jenkins while continuing to go through the remains of the fire. Could they find proof that Jenkins had set the fire?

———•———

The book dealer Ray Walton had become a good friend to Taylor by the late 1970s.[18] One day Walton offered him a copy of the Texas Declaration of Independence, and Taylor experienced the same frisson as when he had bought his Columbus letter. "My family has been here a long time," he said, "and I have a sufficient amount of chauvinism to get worked up about a Texas Declaration of Independence if I see one."

For a Texan, the state's Declaration of Independence is the ultimate collectible. Texans printed the one-page document in 1836 when they were fighting to break away from Mexico. It was an act of faith and bluster, because shortly after the document was printed General Santa Anna defeated and executed the

Texans at the Alamo in San Antonio. The news of the Alamo's fall on March 6, only four days after the declaration, and General Santa Anna's subsequent execution of over four hundred captured Texans at Goliad on March 27 was all the motivation the remaining Texans needed to flee for their lives across the Sabine River to Louisiana (and the presumed safety of the U.S. Army). This episode of Texas history became known as the Runaway Scrape.

Because so many Texans fled, the Texas Declaration of Independence was almost little more than a bibliographic footnote, just as the California Declaration of Independence would be a decade later. In California in 1846 a small band of Americans overwhelmed a remote Mexican government outpost in Sonoma County. The "rebellion" lasted just long enough to issue a manuscript proclamation declaring independence for California and to sew a banner for the Bear Flag Republic. Three weeks later Capt. John C. Fremont took California for the United States, and the copies of the California proclamation became nothing more than a historical curiosity. A few manuscript copies were made to circulate the news before Fremont claimed California; the last copy of one of these sold at auction in 2005 for $11,500.[19]

There were no waiting U.S. troops in Texas to help the settlers, and the outcome was in serious doubt. But less than a month after the Goliad massacre, a small force of Texan soldiers surprised and captured Santa Anna and his larger band of Mexican troops, and a myth was born. The Texas Declaration of Independence became the sacred relic and printed incarnation of that myth. Even though Taylor knew "zip" about the Texas Declaration, he was certain that he wasn't making a mistake and gladly paid Walton's $11,000 asking price in late 1977.

Taylor's gutsy purchase was rewarded by a stroke of luck. Shortly after buying the document, his car broke down in Dallas. While he waited in the repair shop he saw in the newspaper that a group of Dallas businessmen had raised enough money to buy a printed copy of the U.S. Declaration of Independence and present it to the city of Dallas. Taylor called the lead businessman, Jack Stroube, and sold him on the idea that a Texas Declaration would make the perfect companion piece. Jack Stroube was a successful oilman from Corsicana and by the late 1970s was a founding member of the Preston Trail Golf Club in Dallas. He was best known for delighting club members with his stories. If they complained about his East Texas dawdling drawl, he had a ready comeback: "I'm telling the truth as fast as I can make it up!"[20]

Stroube traveled to Austin to compare the condition of Taylor's copy of the Texas Declaration with other copies. It never occurred to either of them to question the authenticity of the document. The two of them took Taylor's copy to the Texas state library and then to the University of Texas, each time comparing it to a known genuine copy. The copy for sale seemed to match those at the rare book libraries, even though the printing was a tiny bit blurrier on Taylor's. Neither man found that too troubling. After all, the printers themselves apologized for errors in the Declaration in their newspaper, explaining that they had printed it "in too much haste and chiefly in the night."[21]

The Dallas group approved the purchase for $20,000 and gave the Texas Declaration to the city of Dallas. About a year later, Ray Walton turned up another copy of the Texas Declaration (which he had bought from Jenkins), at a slightly advanced price. Taylor bought it for $15,000 this time and sold it to the San Jacinto Museum of History for $30,000. By now Taylor felt like he knew what the condition of a Texas broadside should look like, so he didn't bother to compare it to the institutional copies.

Two years after selling his second copy of the Declaration, Taylor went to see Dr. Paul Burns, an Austin specialist, about an obscure neck ailment. When Taylor filled out the new patient form, there was a line for his occupation. "Rare book dealer?" Dr. Burns said. "I collect Texana." Taylor was soon tracking down a copy of the Texas Declaration of Independence for Dr. Burns.

He found a copy at the H. P. Kraus bookshop in New York and offered to buy it for the doctor at the Kraus price of $30,000 plus a 10 percent commission. Taylor flew to New York and felt a little intimidated when he walked into H. P. Kraus Rare Books, which occupied an entire building on West 46th Street. The Kraus Company was easily the largest rare book dealer in the world in 1981. It was customary to be seated at one of a number of mahogany side tables and to look through a card catalogue in order to request the book you wished to examine for purchase; God forbid you should ask to browse their vast library of rarities.

Taylor found the card for the Texas Declaration of Independence and noticed that it showed evidence of several price changes, including some with references to Taylor's own rare book catalogues and prices for his copies of the document. Being forced to swallow your own medicine, or prices, is tough. Taylor sat down with the short German dealer to examine the Kraus copy and figured that, since Kraus had raised the price several times, he had a little room to bargain. The customary dealer discount made the price $27,000; Taylor offered Kraus a check for $26,000. Kraus lowered his glasses slightly on his nose and gave Taylor a bored look. He informed Taylor that business was very, very good right now: "If you talk to me about spending three or four hundred thousand dollars, perhaps I could do something. But this? This is so little." Taylor had no choice except to meet Kraus's asking price. The satisfaction he got from Burns's pleasure at the purchase almost made up for the indignity he had suffered at the hands of the imperious dealer. The one thing Taylor didn't think to ask Kraus was who the owner of that document had been before he bought it.

The bluff in poker is central to the game. It is an act both of faith and of transubstantiation.[22] Until the cards are shown, they are whatever the player chooses to believe, and especially what the player can make others believe. The historian John Lukacs captured this sentiment in an essay on poker and the American character. He called it the game closest to a Western conception of life, in which the most important part is not what happens in poker but "what people think happens."[23]

Jenkins was in a high-stakes Omaha game where he and former 1973 World Series of Poker champion Puggy Pearson were going for the pot.[24] Pearson was born in Kentucky and cultivated his poker skills with three stints in the navy, from which he emerged $20,000 richer than he entered. Pearson's poker philosophy was simple: "Fear is the basis of all mankind." To win in poker, you simply had to psyche out your opponent and put the fear of losing into them.[25]

You also had to judge your opponent's willingness to do the same to you. Jenkins had cultivated an image as a tight player—one, in other words, who hardly ever bluffed. In the poker game of Omaha, each player is dealt four cards, which they never show; two of these "hole" cards must be used in their hand. Then the dealer shows five community cards face up, and each player can choose three to combine with their two hole cards.

In this hand, after Jenkins had bet Puggy raised the pot (increasing the amount of the bet). Then, before the flop (when the five common cards are revealed), Jenkins reraised the stakes and got everyone's attention. The dealer played out the flop—a queen, then a four, then another four. Johnny bet the size of the pot, and Puggy called (matching his bet). The next card shown by the dealer, "fourth street," was another queen. Jenkins bet the size of the pot again, and Puggy decided that enough was enough. He had a pair of fours in his hand; with the two fours on the table that made four of a kind. Puggy assumed that Jenkins had at least two queens in his hand, which with the two queens on the table would have been a higher-ranking four of a kind. Puggy threw his cards on the table saying, "This guy never bluffs."

Jenkins won the pot, but another player who had folded earlier said, "He didn't have you beat, Puggy." He grabbed his discards and showed Puggy that he had had one of the queens in his hand, which meant that Jenkins couldn't have had the fourth queen. Johnny couldn't resist any longer. He tossed his cards at Puggy, showing him that he'd bluffed with only an ace high (meaning that Jenkins had no combinations in his hand, and his high card was a solitary ace). Austin Squatty must have figured that some of that same bluff, bluster, and luck could only help him in the arson investigation.

The fire investigators found more evidence that someone had deliberately set fire to Jenkins's office. First they found a box of cotton twine of the type used to wrap packages. The box had a heavy odor of solvent, but amid the fire debris the investigators could find no remains for such a container of solvent anywhere in the office. They sent the rolls of string to the ATF laboratories for testing.[26]

Next, they decided to see if they could find the fire's burn patterns on the floor. This would help them figure out if the fire had been set intentionally. They began by removing all the burned debris from the office; then they cleaned the concrete floor with water and let it stand and dry naturally. The standing water would show any uneven areas in the floor. The puddled water exactly matched the burn marks on the concrete floor, "consistent with the pouring of a flammable liquid to create a fire trail." The investigators photographed the pour patterns for evidence. Clearly, someone had poured a flammable liquid on the floor, starting at the base of the north and west walls of the office, then going to the east wall of the room (where there was a work table), and finally stopping at the doors. The investigators had carefully examined the wiring, circuitry, and machinery in the room and had found no possible cause of accidental ignition.

Based on the pour patterns of the flammable liquid, they concluded that the fire was incendiary—a term that in investigator's parlance means the criminal and deliberate setting of property on fire. The investigators knew that Jenkins played high-stakes poker in Las Vegas; had his gambling debts motivated the fire?

Tom Taylor met one of his printer friends, Bill Holman, at their favorite Chinese restaurant for lunch.[27] The restaurant was close to Holman's son's printing press (Wind River Press) on the east side of Austin, so it was a natural stopping place. Holman had been the chief librarian of the Rosenberg Library in Galveston, the head of the San Antonio Public Library, and finally the head of the San Francisco Public Library for seven years. In 1967 he was recruited by Harry Ransom to come to the Humanities Research Center in Austin to help in the acquisition of rare books and manuscripts.[28] He had also won awards for his book design and fine printing, and the previous year he had published Stewart and

Scott Gentling's folio book *Of Birds and Texas*, which has been described as "stunning and magnificent."[29]

Holman wanted to pick Tom Taylor's brain. A collector in Dallas interested in selling his copy of the Texas Declaration of Independence had contacted an antiquarian bookseller in Austin. Something in this copy of the Declaration disturbed the bookseller. He knew about Holman's experience with fine printing and asked him to look at the document.[30] There are a few evidentiary tests to help determine whether a printed document is forged. For example, if the forgery is printed on paper made after the time period of the document, that would be evidence that it is faked. There are nearly no scientific tests though, so Holman took the Declaration to the University of Texas to compare it to their authentic copy.[31]

At first in a casual comparison everything looked fine. Then Holman placed the university's copy on top of the Dallas collector's copy and noticed that the columns in the collector's copy were just slightly smaller. Frames of type used in printing do not uniformly contract while being used on the press. The only logical explanation seemed to be that someone had made a photographic negative of an original Declaration, and when they had a printing plate made from the photographic negative they had not noticed that it was smaller than the original document. Was the collector's copy a forgery?

Taylor was not enjoying his lunch, and at that moment he lost his appetite for his egg roll and twice-cooked pork. He had harbored nagging doubts over the increasing numbers of rare Texas historical printed documents that had come on the market over the previous two decades. "At that moment I knew," he said. "I didn't know all the details, but I was sure of the basics." The doubts had started as Taylor began noticing more copies of the Texas Declaration on his travels in Texas.

"I would be on trips around the state and I'd wander over to the Washington-on-the-Brazos Museum with my kids and say, Oh, the Declaration of Independence, how interesting," he said. "And then I'd go somewhere else and there would be a Texas Declaration of Independence. And I'd say, Oh, how interesting. The numbers were starting to add up." Previously the standard source on early printing in Texas had located only five copies of the Texas Declaration, but Taylor knew of at least twenty copies in museums and private collections. He himself had sold three of the Texas documents in his bookselling career. Now, Holman's finding brought all those nagging doubts to the surface. Had any of Taylor's copies been forgeries? Who had been doing this to history-loving Texans?

———————•———————

Amarillo Slim knew Jenkins well from years of tournament poker, and his remarks about Jenkins's playing style at Binion's World Series of Poker were only slightly tongue in cheek: "He's a sneaky, clever rat, and that's not a put-down; John Jenkins is as fine a man as ever put gun-powder on a safe."[32]

The opening day of Binion's 1988 poker tournament proved disastrous for many previous world champions, including Stu Unger, Jack Straus, and Doyle Brunson. After seven hours of play they were out, though 104 players remained, including Jenkins, who had had to play more aggressively than normal to stay alive. He told Michael Kaplan over a cheeseburger that he got crappy hands early in the day: "Anytime that I made a hand, nobody else had anything, while every time I saw a flop it flopped nowhere close to what I needed." Kaplan noted that after two days of play Jenkins was down nearly $8,000, with $2,000 left. Said Jenkins, "I've never been emotional about poker. Besides, I've never seen the point of getting mad at bad fortune. When you do that you add bad blood to bad luck."

Jenkins's style of play earned a grudging admiration from his opponents. That he was able to stay in with poor hands was in part a tribute to his skill with very little luck. One of the other players at the tournament said, "Squatty's strength is his short stack game. With the cards he was getting yesterday, though, there are a lot of players who wouldn't have lasted." Jenkins knew that the next round of play would be one where he would not have the luxury of waiting for better cards. Kaplan watched Jenkins as he stretched a bit before he headed up to the room for an afternoon of playing cards under the halo of cigar smoke and bright TV lights. Jenkins told him that, this time, "I've gotten myself into a position where I have to move in everything in the first four or five hands unless the cards absolutely won't let me. I have to move in and cross my fingers."

When Jenkins sat down at the table, the loudest sound in the poker room was his nervous tapping of plastic chips against the felt table. Benny Binion's son, Jack, was the master of ceremonies and announced the start of play. True to his word to Kaplan, Jenkins went all in on the first few hands, scaring out the other players and winning a few small pots that boosted his stake. Several rounds into this game, Jenkins decided to go all in again after only the first two cards had been dealt. The only player willing to see his larger pot was Seymour Leibowitz, a retired garment district scion. Both players turned their first two cards up (since no more betting on the hand was possible). Jenkins had an ace/ten to Leibowitz's pair of fives. Jenkins jumped to his feet as the flop revealed an ace, a ten, a six, and a two. Jenkins now had two pairs in his hand. He was about to sit down when he thought better of it; if the last card shown was a five, Leibowitz would have three of a kind, beating his two pair. Jenkins told the reporter, "I'd better not sit down yet." Then Kaplan heard him whisper, "Trey" (the poker term for three), as the fifth card came up a three and locked the hand for Jenkins. He pulled in the chips and let out a big sigh.

After watching the action at the table, Binion put the microphone to his mouth and said, "Austin Squatty drew out again, ladies and gentlemen." "Drew out?" Jenkins balked in mock annoyance. "Why don't we talk about skill?" "We'll talk about skill when you have $50,000 in front of you," Binion jabbed back.

Tom Taylor knew that his next task had to be making himself an expert on the Texas Declaration of Independence.[33] He made a form showing the measurements of each copy that he examined, plus a list of former owners. Provenance is a genealogy for objects; the farther back you can trace the owners of a particular copy of the Declaration, the more likely that it is genuine.

Eventually Taylor found twelve genuine copies of the Texas Declaration, and at least twelve forgeries. The genuine copies were a few millimeters wider than the forgeries, and the print quality of the genuine copies differed too. The genuine copies had crisp, clearly printed letters, whereas the fakes had a slightly fuzzy tone in the printing. The final, most important difference between the two groups was that each of the genuine copies had a provenance, a history that showed its passage from owner to owner. None of the forgeries could be traced to an owner before 1970.

Now that Taylor knew he could spot a forged Texas Declaration, he had the uncomfortable job of contacting his customers to examine their copies. As soon as he examined the copies at the San Jacinto Museum and the Dallas Public Library, the forger's errors were glaringly obvious. "I didn't see any problem when I sold them because I didn't want to see a problem," Taylor said. "This has to do with life as well as forgeries. You don't find the problem you're not looking for."

A repayment arrangement was worked out with each institution, but one daunting examination remained of the most expensive copy he had sold, the copy for $33,000 to Paul Burns. After Burns brought his copy from the vault, Taylor opened it with a silent wish that he would not have to make another cash refund. As he examined it, Taylor let out a sigh of relief. The printing was clear and dark, and the Burns copy had all of the broken type found in the originals and none of the inked-in corrections of the forgeries. But the document was the wrong size. Instead of being slightly larger like each of the other genuine copies, the Burns copy of the Declaration matched the size of each of the forgeries.

The puzzle of why the Burns copy matched each identifying feature of the genuine copies, except their size, stymied Taylor at first. But a thorough examination revealed a pattern that he had missed before. The type letters that had been corrected on the forgeries formed a grid, as if someone had folded the paper in thirds, like a business letter. The forgeries themselves showed no signs of folding. But the Burns copy did have those folds, and they corresponded exactly to the corrected letters in the forgeries. If the forger had used the Burns copy to make the facsimiles, he would have had to correct each of the blurry letters that had been distorted from the folding.

But why was the Burns copy different in size from the other original declarations? Taylor finally found another genuine copy to compare in the Daughters of the Republic of Texas exhibit at the Alamo. It matched the Burns copy in clarity of printing and in size. Taylor theorized that when Baker and Borden printed the Declaration in March 1836, they first printed one batch, and then unlocked the bed of type from the press, setting it aside for more urgent business until they could return to the job for the Republic of Texas. In fact, the printer's bill showed that they had first printed one hundred copies, then unlocked the type, keeping it for use a few days later when they printed the final nine hundred copies.[34] The Burns and the Alamo copies were from each of these later printings, when the type had been relocked and slightly compressed from the earlier printings.

Taylor concluded that the Burns copy was the one the forger had originally used to make his facsimiles. So, who had owned it before he purchased it from H. P. Kraus? The company told him they had purchased it for $5,000 in 1973 from Dorman David, the original fabricator of all the fake broadsides.[35] Jenkins had not been the only rare book dealer willing to buy from Dorman David after his raid by the Texas Rangers made him persona non grata.

After Taylor exposed the forgeries, David spoke openly about his method of making them. He had first photographed the original broadsides and then blown up the negatives, sometimes as much as ten times larger. Next he either touched them up or sometimes altered them, according to his whimsy. Then he reduced the negatives and had a zinc plate made, and finally he printed the documents on pages of old paper that he had purchased from Jenkins (presumably including the Republic of Texas facsimile paper he had ordered from England in the previous decade).[36]

David later said, "I was still experimenting, but I didn't have a good finished product."[37] This rings a little hollow, because David had been practicing and working with his own printing press since 1963, when he noted in the introduction to his Catalogue 2 that "this is our second catalogue, our second venture in printing on our own press."[38] Later he even bragged to Lisa

Belkin from the *New York Times*, "I'm an artist. I believe in my heart that if I wanted to I could make something no one could detect."[39] David's lack of satisfaction with his reproductions may actually have been due to their being uncovered as fakes. Perhaps one of David's original motivations for the forgeries was to one-up Jenkins, the dealer who had taken advantage of him in so many trades. David certainly knew that Jenkins had turned him in to the Texas Rangers for the document thefts, and that would have been additional motivation for revenge.[40]

David later added some fanciful details about his printing process, saying that he made "old ink" by collecting carbon from candle smoke in a bag. He also fabricated a story that he "inked" the facsimiles by tapping the paper on the printing plates letter by letter with a wooden mallet. As Taylor noted, this technique would "inevitably produce printing that looked like smeared lipstick," which was not the case with the fake Texas documents.[41]

Lloyds of London was not about to pay up on Jenkins's fire insurance claims without a thorough investigation of their own. They hired a claims adjuster from Houston, William Buck, but he wanted a rare book expert to look at the damaged inventory. Jenkins was happy to recommend a couple of booksellers (who were also close friends), but Buck reached out instead to William Reese Rare Books in Connecticut. Reese recommended that Buck hire Jennifer Larson of Yerba Buena Books in San Francisco.[42]

Larson came into rare books with the natural grace of an English major who had always loved reading. She helped put herself through school by working in the college library acquisitions department, but a chance temporary reassignment to the college library rare book room fixed her course. The lovely leather-bound volumes in the glass cases swept her away, and after graduating she got her master's degree from the University of California, Berkeley, with a specialty in rare books . She took a job in 1978 at John Howell–Books, thinking it would be temporary until she found a rare book library position. The proprietor, Warren Howell, was a "sensational teacher" and her ambitions for a librarian position did not last long. She worked for several years with Howell, and after he died in 1984 Larson opened her own rare book business, Yerba Buena Books.

William Buck hired Larson, satisfied that she came recommended by a leading antiquarian bookseller. He already harbored deep suspicions about Jenkins and prided himself on being able to detect the manure in any story, no matter how strongly perfumed. When Buck spoke to her by phone, Larson was naturally curious about what he had found so far. She didn't expect to find anything amiss, since Jenkins was one of the most respected dealers in the country.[43] Buck said he didn't want to influence her, except for this: "I've got my opinions. After you get here, I think you'll have yours." When she arrived at Austin's Bergstrom Airport, Buck met her and drove her to the hotel. They had a couple of drinks that evening as they got acquainted, but Buck was careful not to divulge anything. The next morning at 9:30 they met Jenkins at the burned-out offices in Manchaca. Jenkins greeted them warmly, if with some caution.

Jenkins tried the friendly approach on Larson first, telling her with all the aplomb of a late-night tippler hitting on a single woman, "You look like someone I could easily be doing $10,000 a month in business with." Upon Larson's refusal to take his baited offer, he next tried a not-so-subtle threat in the guise of an off-hand story: "Do you know the story of the rare book dealer who threatened a colleague?" Larson shook her head, not really caring, but Jenkins went ahead: "The dealer told them that he could spend a million dollars in lawsuits making their life miserable." The threat was opaque but the implication was real: Jenkins could spend a vast amount of money tying her up in litigation for years. Larson was undeterred in her investigation.

Buck's gut hunch was correct. That evening Larson tried to describe to him exactly what was wrong with some of the Texas broadsides she had looked at that day. It was obvious to her that several of them looked like reprints (from photoengraved plates) done on old paper. To the inexperienced eye the broadsides might have appeared fine, but to someone who had looked at thousands of examples of nineteenth-century printing it was immediately clear that they were poorly done fakes. However, the problem of explaining why they were fake was a different one than she had faced before. In the trade, if you see a broadside that looks questionable, you simply decline to buy it. Now, she would have to explain her reasoning to a nonexpert, and every term she could come up with was subjective.

The next day (January 22, 1988) Buck and Larson met with the ATF investigator and the Texas state fire marshal's investigator. Larson could already determine after a cursory examination of the fire damages that "several of the books were misrepresented as to type and condition." The most important outcome of their meeting was Larson's disclosure that she had "found one document valued at $22,000 that was a fake."[44] When the investigators pressed her to show them how she identified the fakes, the best analogy she could come up with was that it was "like the difference between real wood and Formica printed with a wood design."

From my own experience, nineteenth-century printing, especially of broadsides in the period of the Republic of Texas, often exhibits a tiny but discernible "bite" in the paper that gives the printing a faint three-dimensional effect on the surface of the paper. Printers achieved this bite by slightly wetting sheets of paper. This softens the sheets so that the type will imprint on them.[45] The process of printing from photoengraved plates, even if it is done on old paper from the same time period, makes the printing look flat on the paper and gives it a uniform tone that is not present in letterpress printing.

A short time after examining the suspicious broadsides at Jenkins's office, Larson got in touch with Tom Taylor, who confirmed that two of the broadsides were indeed fakes. She was able to show him another that was new to him.[46] When Buck asked Jenkins about the fake broadsides, this was the first that Jenkins had heard about Taylor's investigation into the forgeries. Jenkins told Buck that dealers and historians had debated for years about the authenticity of the Texas broadsides that had appeared on the market, since it was impossible to make any judgments about whether or not they were genuine. Nevertheless, he told Buck, he had continued to sell them in spite of these reservations, and always with the unconditional guaranty of return for his customers.[47] What Buck did not know is that no one in Texas had been debating the authenticity of the broadsides.

———•———

Jenkins took another trip to Nevada in February 1988 and staked his hopes on Amarillo Slim's Super Bowl of Poker. Jenkins the poker champion was never too tied up to visit with a reporter, and on this occasion Peter Alson from the *Village Voice* interviewed him.[48] Jenkins wore his trademark Stetson and chomped a cigar while he explained his strategy behind the $10,000 buy-in for the poker game. The game was no-limit Texas hold'em, which meant that at any given time a player could bet all their chips, and it was a freeze-out competition, which meant that no additional buy-ins were allowed; once you lost your chips, you were out of the game.

Jenkins stressed to Alson that he had won consistently in poker tournaments since first competing in 1983, not just because he understood the math behind the game but also because he thought he could govern his emotions while playing. What Jenkins found most amazing was that even the "Doyle Brunsons and the Johnny Chans go on tilt." Of course, what he didn't say was that both Brunson and Chan, unlike Jenkins, had actually won major poker championships. Jenkins concluded, "They are not always as iron-willed in their self-control as I'd expect." Alson noted that early casualties on that first day of tournament play were former champions Doyle Brunson, Johnny Chan, and Austin Squatty. Jenkins was very successful at getting reporters to write stories about his poker playing, just as he had been with getting publicity about his rare book dealings; he just wasn't as successful at the gaming tables as he told them. But in those pre-Google days, reporters gave him the benefit of the doubt. Of course, losing out on the tournament didn't stop Jenkins from continuing to place large bets in the many side poker games going on at the same time.

———•———

Before news of the forgeries reached the public, Jenkins was quick to dismiss any talk of forgery. One dealer who had bought a Texas

Declaration from Jenkins and had heard through the grapevine that some were forged called and asked him about it. Jenkins told the dealer that Taylor was an idiot who knew nothing about Texana and was only out to make trouble.[49]

Jenkins's treatment changed when the news of the forgeries broke with the publication of Gregory Curtis's "Forgery Texas Style: The Dealers Who Buy and Sell Historic Texas Documents Move in a World of Big Money, Big Egos and Big Mistakes," in the March 1989 issue of the widely read regional magazine *Texas Monthly*.[50] There was no way for Jenkins to dismiss the story any longer. He probably realized that he had a weak hand because of the many fakes he had sold, and he decided that he could no longer ignore Taylor's detective work.

Jenkins tried the same strategy of bluffing, though. He wouldn't just acknowledge being taken in by the fakes; he would go all in with his praise of Taylor's detective work, with one crucial difference from his earlier statement to William Buck, the claims adjustor. Earlier Jenkins had told Buck that dealers and historians had been debating for years about the authenticity of these broadsides. Now Jenkins omitted all discussion of this debate. It was an important omission, since in reality there had never been any public questioning or debate of this topic, because no one else had had any idea that the broadsides were forgeries.

First, Jenkins called Taylor and said, "Tom, I've been a fool."[51] He was at some pains to thank Taylor for uncovering the forgeries. When a reporter from the *Austin American-Statesman* followed up on the *Texas Monthly* story and asked Jenkins for a comment on the forgeries, he told them, "We were all taken in by this. I will take my share of the blame." Jenkins acknowledged handling as many as twelve of the forgeries. "We've been fooled by them for 20 years," Jenkins acknowledged, adding that "there had never been any reason to doubt them." Jenkins played the final hand of his bluff: "Now Tom, with his expertise in printing, has made the breakthrough. On behalf of all the booksellers, we have the highest praise and congratulations for Tom for his discoveries, and we are all, in the long run, going to benefit from his discoveries."[52] How would Jenkins's all-in bluff about the forgeries actually play with his customers and fellow dealers?

Although Austin Squatty was known as a careful player who did not often bluff, he could sometimes go all-in with a weak hand when he was feeling pressed. Jenkins preferred to cast himself as the thoughtful, conservative poker player rather than adopting the "riskier, cockier" styles generally used by the professional players. He acknowledged that his lack of intuition in poker sometimes hindered him. "A lot of people make subconscious decisions based on things they've seen done hundreds of times," he explained. "I don't have that kind of experience or intuition and think about every move I make. Sometimes it works against me."[53]

In Binion's World Series of Poker in May 1983, Jenkins was among the last seven players when he drew an ace/king of spades on his opening deal, which is considered a slightly stronger start than opening with a low pair. Jenkins decided to scare out the rest of the table and build a good start of chips for the final push of the game. He went all-in on this weak opening hand with a bid of $150,000 in chips, which should have scared out all but the strongest hands of cards. Tom McElvoy, who had an equal amount of chips on the table, called with a pair of sixes. Jenkins said, "He probably knew that I had either an ace/king or a baby pair (a very low pair) or else I would have suckered him in with a lower bet." Jenkins did not get any of the cards he needed to win, and McElvoy got his pot. Boosted by that success, McElvoy went on to win the World Series of Poker that year. Jenkins remembered with a bit of awe: "I don't think he could tell you why he went all in with such a small pair, but it's an example of the kind of below the surface brilliance that you encounter here." The intuition that underlay that brilliance of when to fold and when to bluff eluded Jenkins in poker and in the arson investigation.

Despite Jenkins's claims of being taken in by the forgeries like every other rare book dealer, the Travis County district attorney's office decided to open an investigation into his connections with the forgeries. Some of the pressure to open the investigation came from Governor Bill Clements, who had purchased a forgery of the Texas Declaration from Reese, who had bought it from Jenkins.[54]

The ATF chemical analysis from the arson investigation also came back from the lab. It showed that a volatile accelerant was used in the Jenkins fire, either alcohol or acetone.[55] The fire investigators had already learned that Jenkins was several years delinquent on his federal tax returns.[56] Now they finally got their interview with Jenkins. First he vacillated between two stories, declaring that the rare book business was doing well, having shipped $237,000 worth of books so far in 1988, but adding that the company was doing poorly with its debts, which were approaching nearly $4 million.[57]

Jenkins insisted that there was no way he would profit by a fire, since the insurance proceeds would still leave him nearly a million dollars short of what the debt required, and he would still have to declare bankruptcy. The investigators pressed him about his poker playing in Las Vegas, but Jenkins insisted he was usually a winner. He claimed that he was in the black for 1987 and so far in 1988. The investigators wanted to confirm his story, so they asked him which casinos he played in most often. Jenkins refused to tell them. Then they asked him to take a polygraph examination. Jenkins adamantly refused: "I will never take one because I don't believe in them."[58]

That statement left the investigators wondering if Jenkins really was a high-stakes poker champion, or if he was someone hiding large debts to the casinos. It was around this time that the investigators began using this subheading in their reports on Jenkins: 18 U.S. Code Section 844 (i). This part of the U.S. Code is felony arson.

———•———

While the ATF investigators were waiting for Jenkins's financial records, they met with his longtime friend and occasional attorney, J. P. Bryan Jr. Bryan had a successful career investing in oil wells, beginning when he was still a law student at UT-Austin. His great-aunt gave him three small oil wells in South Texas to help him through law school. In the early 1960s oil was $1.50 a barrel, so when Bryan approached some brokers to purchase the wells they eyed the young college kid, guessed he probably wanted a new sports car, and offered him $1,500 cash. "Nope," J.P. said, "This is what we're going to do. You're going to give me $10,000 cash for the 3 wells and I'm going to retain a 10 percent share in each well." And that is what they did.[59]

J.P. was ready to listen with interest to whatever the arson investigators had to say, but he wasn't prepared when they said, "Jenkins is a liar." "Now, wait a minute," J.P. said, sure that they were speaking hastily. But the investigators were indignant and told J.P. that the book dealer was lying. Their visit ended abruptly, but J.P. remembered their final words: "We're going to indict Jenkins for arson." After their visit J.P. called Jenkins, who was desperate for any way out from under the federal investigation. J.P. advised him to withdraw his insurance claim. Bryan thought that, if there was no insurance fraud, there could be no arson charges.

The ATF investigators soon found out about Jenkins's new strategy. In late September one of them spoke with Lloyds of London and found out that Jenkins had not filed the paperwork to make a formal claim for his fire losses. An employee of the Jenkins Company confirmed that his boss had told them he "was not going to go through the hassles of filing a claim regarding his losses from fire." He had decided not to file a formal claim. Unfortunately for Jenkins, this did not end the investigation. The building offices were rented, the owner of the building was still filing insurance claims for his losses, and thus the arson investigation into Jenkins would continue.[60]

The financial repercussions of the news about the forgeries began to affect the Jenkins Company as customers started returning fake broadsides. For example, the Barker Texas History Center at the University of Texas identified two forged broadsides among those they had purchased. The forgeries were the Travis "Victory or Death" letter and an emigration broadside for settlers to Texas, which was supposed to have been printed in New Orleans in 1836 and for which the Barker Center had paid nearly $11,000.[61] Jenkins

honored the returns and let the Barker Center choose an equivalent value of other books to replace the forgeries.

The forgery revelations seriously damaged the business image
and reputation of the Jenkins Company. Jenkins typically exhib-
ited at the Boston Book Fair in November, but that year (1988)
he cancelled the book exhibits, though he still attended.[62] Even
though the Jenkins firm was in financial straits, he still picked up
dinner and drinks tabs during his visit to Boston. One evening
Jenkins invited a group of bookseller friends to dinner (Michael
and Elaine Ginsberg, Franklin and Mary Gilliam, and Howard
and Phyllis Mott), and over their protests he insisted on paying the
entire bill. After the dinner Mary Gilliam looked askance as Jenkins swung his feet out from under the table and proceeded to take
hundred-dollar bills out of his cowboy boots to pay for the meal.[63]

Franklin Gilliam was not convinced by Jenkins's bravado and
in a private moment after the dinner asked him how he was holding up in the face of accusations of arson and forgery. Franklin,
after all, had known Johnny Jenkins from the very beginning days
in Austin when he had sold the young dealer an incunable leaf
from the *Catholicon* that Jenkins had cut up into one-inch-square
"own a bit of history" pieces. Jenkins looked at him and said, "Our
backs are to the wall."[64]

During this Boston visit Jenkins had to face the ABAA's board
of governors to answer allegations about the forgeries for the
ethics committee. He was serving, after all, as the security officer
and liaison to the FBI for the ABAA. The ABAA had already
formed the Ad Hoc Questioned Imprints Committee to deal with
the forgeries, among whose members were Jennifer Larson and
Tom Taylor.

Jenkins played the same bluff on the board of governors that he
had used on newspaper reporters when the Texas forgeries were
uncovered earlier that year. He told them that everyone owed a
debt of gratitude to Tom Taylor for his work in uncovering the
forgeries.[65] Jenkins claimed that, when he was notified by Tom
earlier that year (1988), he immediately circulated a list of the
Texas forgeries to Texana dealers, collectors, and librarians so that
everyone would know. Jenkins tried to shift the blame to Simpson Galleries and Dorman David. He also reminded the board of

his role in ending David's archival theft rings in Texas. Perhaps Jenkins believed that his statement would save his reputation and membership, but after the board meeting he still resigned under pressure as security officer of the ABAA.[66]

———•———

David Hewett, a reporter for the *Maine Antique Digest*, heard about the Texas forgeries at the ABAA Boston Book Fair and decided to do a story. Despite its regional name, the monthly *Maine Antique Digest* is one of the most widely read periodicals in the antiquarian world, with tens of thousands of subscribers and plenty of pass-along readers, and it is known for taking on hard-hitting stories. Hewett talked to J. P. Bryan Jr., who was surprised at how many people the reporter had spoken to and the quantity of information he had gathered about the forgeries. Later Bryan called Jenkins and told him about the upcoming story. Jenkins was shocked and told Bryan that, if this article came out, Jenkins's reputation would be ruined. Jenkins said, "I might as well take a .45 and blow my brains out."[67]

  Hewett's article was the cover story in the January 1989 issue of the *Maine Antique Digest* and was widely read from coast to coast by booksellers and librarians. Hewett interviewed both Dorman David and Jenkins, and this time Jenkins did not try the bluff of thanking Tom Taylor for exposing the forgeries. Instead, he denied ever buying the printing plates for the forgeries from Dorman David.[68]

———•———

That December (1988) the ATF investigators were still trying to get the Jenkins Company financial records. They wanted to see if Jenkins had any financial motivations for setting the fire, though they already believed it was arson. In mid-December the investigators were told by employees that Jenkins was unavailable until the first of the year. A few days later the lead investigator for the ATF called the offices and stressed the urgency of seeing Jenkins. Employees relayed the message to Jenkins, who had his wife Maureen call the investigator. She told him that they were in Lake Tahoe (where Jenkins was playing poker), but they would have the records ready on their return in mid-January.[69]

By the end of January the ATF had both the firm's and Jenkins's financial records, and they arranged for an ATF auditor (Charles Beaty of the Dallas office) to begin going through the paper trail. The auditor took only a few days to confirm that there were major discrepancies between the general ledgers of the firm and their tax returns. Based on that, and the evidence of arson, the investigators next met with the U.S. attorney's office to discuss bringing charges against Jenkins.[70]

———————— · ————————

The *Maine Antique Digest* story had another unexpected repercussion. When Bob French got a copy and heard about the troubling financial problems Jenkins was facing, he decided he did not need to hold onto his forgeries for leverage over Jenkins.[71] There were four forgeries that Jenkins had sold French: Travis's February 24, 1836, proclamation "To the Citizens of Texas" ($5,500), which appeared to be a photocopy on old paper; "Texas!! Emigrants Who are Desirous of Assisting Texas" (New Orleans, 1836, for $2,750), which appeared to be letterpress printed; the first printed document from Stephen F. Austin in 1821 to the colonists ($6,500), which appeared to be letterpress printed; and the "Declaration of Causes of the People of Texas" (November 7, 1835, $7,500), which appeared to be photocopied on old paper. Together these fakes had been sold to French for $22,250.[72] French served Jenkins with notice on January 18, 1989, from his attorneys in Midland with a demand for immediate payment. Together with other misdescribed books that Jenkins had sold him, French wanted payment of over $38,000.[73]

Jenkins had deliberately sold French the forgeries, but as in every called bluff he was prepared to pay his lost bet, albeit this time with some difficulty. Jenkins's other attorney wrote to French, "As you know from the FDIC judgement, John is in severe financial straits and unlikely to survive without bankruptcy. He considers the French claim a matter of honor, and is extremely desirous of settling it." Jenkins's attorney proposed a settlement of $18,000, with checks enclosed for $9,000 now and $9,000 in sixty days. French seems to have accepted this offer of repayment as his best possible course given Jenkins's financial troubles.[74]

———•———

Despite his ATF investigation and other financial problems, Jenkins could not resist the call of another poker tournament. He went to Caesars Palace in Las Vegas for Amarillo Slim's Super Bowl of Poker in late January 1989. The buy-ins for the beginning games were lower (only $225) and rebuys were permitted, meaning that you could stay in the game as long as you could keep buying chips. There were 183 players who started the early games, and by 11:30 P.M. on January 31 two players were left in the Omaha game—John Jenkins and Lyle Berman of Minneapolis. Jenkins went all-in with a pair of jacks; Berman followed with his pair of tens. Each waited in the smoke-filled casino for the flop. The first card was a king, then a five, then an ace, then a three—so far no advantage to either player. Jenkins was almost certainly whispering "jack, jack" to himself when the final card was played—a jack. Jenkins took a pot of $99,050 (Berman took second place and $39,620). Jenkins must have certainly thought his luck had turned. He now had the $10,000 buy-in money for the Super Bowl tournament, plus lots of extra funds to play in the side games. But Jenkins did not win again. He lost his $10,000 buy-in for the Super Bowl of Poker final game; he almost certainly incurred more large losses at the betting tables and side games.[75]

———•———

Sometime in 1976, Jenkins had sold William Reese a forged Texas Declaration of Independence for $15,000 and even let him take it on approval to show to a customer. In other words, if the document didn't sell, Reese could return it to Jenkins and owe nothing. At the time, Reese thought Jenkins was doing him an enormous favor by letting him sell the document. He took the broadside to Dallas and sold it for $30,000 to a very pleased Governor William

Clements for his Texana collection. Reese later acknowledged his naiveté; he should have wondered at the time why Jenkins didn't just sell it directly to Clements himself. Years later in 1988, as news of the forgeries spread, Governor Clements returned the broadside for a refund to Reese, who returned it to Jenkins—and waited for a refund.

In one of Reese's last visits with Jenkins (around January 1989), he was still trying to get reimbursed by Jenkins, who told him that money was tight and asked if he would take some rare books in trade. After Reese said he would, Jenkins looked at him and asked, "Bill, do you think I was the forger?" Reese politely but noncommittedly replied, "Honestly, Johnny, I don't know." Then Jenkins said, "Don't you think I would have charged a lot more for them if they were actually real?"[76] That was as close to a confession to the Texas forgeries as anyone ever got from Jenkins.

The ATF auditor continued to uncover large inconsistencies between Jenkins's tax returns and business records, and the ATF provided this information about the Jenkins case to the assistant U.S. district attorney. Around the same time, the ATF agents were planning to subpoena the casinos in Las Vegas for John's poker debts, based on information they had gathered about his gambling habits.[77]

Because the ATF investigators were going over his finances, Jenkins hired the best tax attorney he could find. George A. Stephen (1920–2006) was a nationally recognized tax law expert who had retired as chief of intelligence of the IRS, but even he could not make the investigation go away.[78] The ATF investigators already thought Jenkins was a liar, and his attorney's denials only convinced them they were close to finally making Jenkins fold, especially when they heard the following from his attorney: "Mr. Jenkins was very distraught over the accusations that he may have started this fire and was concerned for his family and reputation."[79]

Everything was coming apart for John Jenkins. First the forgeries, then the arson investigation, and now there were also debts from his business. On April 10, 1989, the NBC Bank of Austin placed foreclosure notices in public view on his buildings and three-acre property at 7111 South Interstate 35. Jenkins had defaulted on a $600,000 loan, and the bank scheduled a public auction of his property at the Travis County courthouse steps on May 2.[80] His employees must have wondered what Jenkins had up his sleeve now to take care of these problems. Kevin MacDonnell remembered that Jenkins could be backed up against a wall with no clear way out, and then he could turn around and draw a picture of a door on the wall and walk through it. Whoever was watching him would be left wondering, How in the hell did he do that?[81]

———•———

The week before Jenkins died, his attorney, George Stephen, met with the ATF auditor and investigators again. Jenkins was ready to meet with the ATF, he told them, and he was probably ready to come clean on his gambling debts and the financial status of the Jenkins Company. He might even submit to a polygraph examination. Stephen stressed that Jenkins was extremely distraught, and he told them something that Jenkins had mentioned to him; if they tried to indict him, he would commit suicide.

The ATF investigators told the attorney that he should prepare Jenkins to be indicted. What they did not tell Stephen at this time was that they had already met with the assistant U.S. attorney about criminal charges. They were already preparing the indictments against Jenkins for arson, which typically would be served by a U.S. marshal.[82]

———•———

The Saturday before Jenkins died, he came into the office with a grin and an optimistic attitude, which must have been reminiscent of the teenage days when he sang "You Are My Sunshine" in his morning showers. His rare book manager, Michael Parrish, felt encouraged enough by his manner to ask him how Jenkins felt about the company's balance sheet. Jenkins smiled and told him he had a plan for fixing all of his finances, and everything was going to be all right.[83]

That last Saturday night Jenkins called cousin Ken Kesselus and asked him to go hunt for Edward Burleson's grave near Bastrop the next morning. Kesselus had no reason to suspect that Jenkins was anything but in a good frame of mind. They were jointly authoring a book on Edward Burleson, one of the heroes of the Texas Revolution, and were excited about finishing it. Each of them had written alternating chapters, and they were going to take two full weeks in May to finish the book and make sure that the chapters had a consistent approach and style.[84]

John told him that he intended to search Roger's Park, an old cemetery about one mile from the FM 969 bridge over the Colorado River. Ken reminded him that they had already searched that cemetery, and the only gravestone they found had Roger's name on it. Besides, he reminded John, he was the Episcopal priest for Bastrop, and he had church services to conduct on Sunday mornings. "Oh right," said Jenkins, as though he had forgotten. Kesselus figured that Jenkins wanted to tie up some loose ends by finding Burleson's grave before the book was finished.[85] Maureen remembered that John ended up leaving Austin for Bastrop just after 12:30 P.M. on Sunday.[86]

Apparently sometime that Saturday, Jenkins learned from his attorney that the ATF was about to have him indicted for the arson. He called his closest friend, J. P. Bryan, and told him that he was going to be ruined, reputation and all, and he mentioned suicide. Bryan argued with him and told him that was nonsense, that people got off on arson charges all the time. "Sure, they can show it was arson," Bryan told Jenkins. "But they can't as easily show that you were the arsonist. You can fight this thing, Johnny." But Bryan felt that something was different about Jenkins's reaction to his advice this time; usually John was the first one to fight for his reputation and honor, but for some reason he did not want to do so now.[87]

What Jenkins did not tell Bryan was the thing that he least wanted the world to know. It was not that he had done the forgeries, nor even that he had started the fire in his office. Instead, it was that he was not the poker champion who had been featured on the covers of so many gambling and other publications, and the ATF indictment and trial would reveal that to the world. Though Jenkins would have been the first to deny it, he transitioned in the early 1980s from someone who wagered on friendly home games to someone who compulsively bet at poker tables. A commonly accepted definition is that problem gamblers cannot limit their money and time in a pursuit that negatively affects themselves, their businesses, and their families. This summarizes the final ten years of Jenkins's life quite well.

Why did Jenkins become a problem gambler? Researchers at Harvard Medical School used gamblers' brain scans and found that winning money from wagering rewards their brain in ways very similar to those in addicts receiving an infusion of cocaine. In other words, gambling provides a mental reward similar to that for drug users. The researchers also confirmed that, the higher the risk, the greater the emotional payoff for the gambler. But the more a problem gambler plays, the harder it becomes to activate the brain's pleasure receptors. So, the player has to increase the risk and the odds to get a bigger emotional payoff.[88] Some hint of this is given in the many times Jenkins told journalists that he was unable to relax in traditional vacation settings: "I can't go lie in the sun because I would go completely crazy." But at a poker table he could be completely relaxed.[89] I think what Jenkins meant by "relaxed" was the enjoyment of an adrenaline rush from winning a risky bet.

Casino gambling debts are closely held secrets, and Jenkins had lines of credit at more than twenty casinos. After Jenkins's death, two close friends of his independently approached Benny Binion and asked him if Jenkins had left a lot of markers (debt) from his poker playing. Binion told each of them that no, Jenkins didn't have any gambling debts, which was technically true.[90] By the time Jenkins's friends asked Binion about his debts, there were none, because the casinos had been paid with money from a secret life insurance policy that Jenkins left to pay his poker wagers. An inside informant who was in a position to know firsthand (and who asked to remain anonymous) confirmed to me that Jenkins's poker gambling debts at the Las Vegas casinos totaled nearly a million dollars at the time of his death, and it was a point of honor with Jenkins to be sure that those debts were paid after his death. That was John's deepest secret. He took it with him to his death in the Colorado River late on a Sunday afternoon, April 16, 1989.

Epilogue

I went to the river on a January day in 2018 to pay my respects at the place where Jenkins died. The FM 969 highway that crosses the Colorado River just a few miles west of Bastrop is still a small two-lane farm road. Under the bridge is a pullout for fishermen.

The average river flow (when there are no floods or upstream dam releases) is around 300–400 cubic feet per second, so the drift speed for a fishing boat is usually 1–2 mph.[1] By comparison, a fast walk is 3–4 mph, and a slow amble would be around 2 mph. On this sunny day with a light breeze I threw two sticks out into the river to watch the flow. The current moved so slowly at this point that the breeze blew both sticks upstream. Jenkins's corpse would not have drifted very far in the river from where he was shot.

The river couldn't answer my real question, the one that had followed me through the years since Jenkins died. Had John shot himself here? Or had someone helped him? To find those answers, I started with the Bastrop County sheriff's office. The data clerk pulled up my request on the computer and told me that they no longer had any investigative files on the case. The death had been ruled a suicide, and a subsequent sheriff had decreed that the department would keep suicide files for only five years. They destroyed Jenkins's file in 1994. The only thing the computer record had were the names of Kaye Freeman, who found the body, and Robert Donnell, who found the wallet and turned it into the sheriff's department. Calvin Trillin had talked at length to Donnell, but he never mentioned Freeman in his *New Yorker* article.

Kaye Freeman lives in the rural countryside about thirty miles from Waco, Texas, and she has no landline telephone number. More interesting was that, before Freeman found Jenkins in the river, she had an arrest record that included assault and larceny. Now I knew that I needed to find Freeman and ask her about Jenkins.

I set out on a cool overcast February day. The address turned out to be a remote country road with mobile homes and trailers, none of which had any numbers. I have rarely felt as self-conscious as I did that afternoon, driving up and down that lane in my BMW. Some of the mobile homes had small crosses in the front yard; some of the trucks had small Confederate flag stickers. I could not have stuck out more if I had had a bumper sticker that said "OUTSIDER." I had raised steers in Wyoming and even had a cowboy hat and boots, both of which, unfortunately, were at home.

I decided on a strategy of asking at the nicest mobile home first, then working down from there. The first man at the door I tried looked over my shoulder at my car in the driveway before answering my question: "Nope. Never heard of her. Doesn't live on this street." At the next mobile home down the street I could hear the TV playing inside, but no one answered my knocks. At the next mobile home a woman in the yard said she had never heard of Kaye but would ask her husband, who also said he hadn't.

The mobile home across the street from theirs was Kaye Freeman's place. I could see someone watching me from the curtains as I walked up. Before I got to the wooden porch, she came outside and asked in a loud voice who I was looking for. I said I was looking for Kaye Freeman. She looked closely at me and said, "Is this about my going back to prison?"[2]

"No, ma'am," I said. "I'm looking for the woman who was unlucky enough to find a body in the Colorado River."

Kaye broke into a large grin. "Oh," she said. "That was me. Come on in."

In April 1989, Kaye Freeman was twenty-one years old, just barely old enough to tend bar in Bastrop at the 1832 Tavern on Saturday nights. On that particular Sunday afternoon the skies were bright blue with no wind, so she and her husband and his brother took their poles to their favorite fishing spot, just a few miles west of town where the bridge crosses the Colorado River.[3]

They usually parked under the bridge in the shade, but that afternoon a gold Mercedes 450SL was already parked there with both its front doors open. A briefcase lay open on the driver's seat, and papers had blown out of the car and into the river. They looked around but, not seeing anyone, took their fishing gear and some bottles of Budweiser to the river.

Freeman cast into the river and her hook got stuck on something. When she pulled up on the line, Jenkins's body bobbed to the surface. She screamed, "I hooked a dead body!" Her brother-in-law, who was fishing a short distance away, knew she played practical jokes and said, "Quit bullshitting, Kaye." She replied, "Come look at all the blood pouring out in the water, that's why the fish aren't biting." Jenkins's body lay parallel to the riverbank. It had been submerged long enough for snapping turtles to bite small pieces of skin from the back of his hand. The turtle bites reminded Freeman of her grandmother's folklore; if a snapper bites you, they won't let go until it thunders.

A drowned body or someone shot to death in the water sinks almost immediately to the bottom. Corpses rarely rise back to the surface until the gases have built up days later. If Freeman had not hooked Jenkins's body, he likely would have remained undiscovered in the murky river water for several days.[4]

I went to the former Bastrop County sheriff's ranch in Red Rock, Texas. Con Keirsey is in his late eighties now, but he clearly remembered the Jenkins case. He still runs steers on his hundred-acre ranch and is proud to wear his fifty-year-old brown felt cowboy hat made by the American Hat Company. "Not an LBJ or a politician's cowboy hat," he said, recalling Jenkins's white Stetson with the tall sides. He remembered when Calvin Trillin came to talk to him after Jenkins's death. "That feller from New York; it was scribble, scribble and after 30 minutes he left."[5]

Keirsey retired as a captain from the Austin police force; he had spent his last ten years there working in the homicide division, so violent deaths were nothing new to him. His family has deep roots in law enforcement. Keirsey is a member of the Chickasaw tribe from Oklahoma, and he remembers his grandmother speaking Comanche. Keirsey's great-uncle, Ben Collins, was a U.S. Indian marshal. The Oklahoma outlaw Jim Miller ambushed and killed his great-uncle with a shotgun in 1906. Keirsey moved to Bastrop County to enjoy his retirement, but the sheriff there kept pestering him to become a deputy. Only a short time later the sheriff died, and Keirsey became acting sheriff. He won the next election, then remembered why he had retired and did not run again.

When Keirsey arrived at the crime scene, Jenkins's body was still in the river. As they took the body out of the water, the justice of the peace (who was also the coroner) pulled up, and seeing the blood on Jenkins's head, before examining the body, he pronounced out loud at the scene that it was "death by blunt force instrument." Keirsey thought it was idiotic to rule on the death before examining the body.

Keirsey searched the dead man's Mercedes-Benz and belongings. He found no cash or credit cards in Jenkins's wallet, only a driver's license and a fire marshal's business card.[6] Jenkins's gold Rolex watch was missing too. Besides the open briefcase and scattered papers, there was a map with the Roger's Park cemetery circled in pencil. The sheriff also found a receipt from a convenience store purchase that Jenkins had made earlier that afternoon for a sandwich, a bottle of Coke, and a bag of ice. The half-eaten sandwich and pop bottle were in the car, but there was no sign of the bag of ice.

Sheriff Keirsey called in special divers from the Austin police department who used powerful magnets from Bergstrom Air Force Base to search for the missing gun.[7] Keirsey told reporters that the Lower Colorado River Authority had tentatively agreed to hold the water upstream at the dams at Austin. That would lower the river by a couple of feet, "which will help us a lot."[8] The divers did not find the gun that killed Jenkins, but they found plenty of other things in the river. They found the keys to his Mercedes about four feet from the bank.[9] Jenkins's cousin, Richard Kesselus, who thought someone murdered Jenkins, figured that since Jenkins never backed down from a fight he threw his car keys in the river to frustrate a robber.[10]

The divers also turned up a Rolex watch (but not Jenkins's gold Rolex), a golf club, and a hatchet. There were other mysteries found in the river, though none were related to Jenkins. The divers turned up several pieces of Reed and Barton silver flatware (stolen from a dinner party and then ditched into the river in a fit of conscience?) and a plastic evidence bag of bullets from the Bastrop County sheriff's office. Despite the sheriff's investigation, the justice of the peace (who had lost the sheriff's race to Keirsey the previous year) insisted on ruling the death a homicide since the pistol was not found.[11]

When the Travis County coroner examined Jenkins, he found one gunshot wound 5/16 inch in diameter. The coroner located the entry wound "3/4 inch above and 3/4 inch to the right of the external occipital protuberance"—in layman's terms, about three inches behind Jenkins's right ear and just below a plane even with his ear canal.[12] If Jenkins had twisted his head to the left and held the pistol with his right hand, this would have been an awkward, but not difficult, shot.

The coroner found other evidence consistent with a self-inflicted gunshot. He noted that Jenkins's entry wound "was surrounded by markedly blackened and charred margins." There was also "markedly heavy gunpowder burning around the entrance," a sign that the gun was pressed to the head. Jenkins had a .38 Special, the same one he had posed with in front of the Eberstadt vault. The range of entry wounds made by this caliber of gun in skeletal remains (0.32–0.72 inches) is close to the range of that found by the coroner in Jenkins's head—5/16 (0.3125) inch.[13]

Sheriff Keirsey knew that if someone had shot Jenkins he probably would have stood back a short distance from the victim, but in this case the gun was pressed next to Jenkins's head. If Jenkins had been shot by someone standing near the river, there would have been some splatter or blood somewhere on the riverbank, but there was not a speck anywhere. After the shooting there should have been "some ground disturbance, some sign of a struggle or dragging of a body" to the river.[14] They found none.

The nature of the shooting bothered Keirsey even more than the missing gun. He believed Jenkins was standing in the river when the shot was fired. "If somebody else did it he went into the water with Jenkins and waded back out," said Keirsey. "But there was no sign of anybody coming out of the water," no muddy footprints on the bank.[15] The sheriff had a good understanding of how a murder scene differed from a suicide. In his ten years working in the homicide division for the Austin police, the department had investigated three hundred to four hundred homicides and nearly a thousand suicides. Con Keirsey tends cattle on his hundred-acre ranch and no longer fights against crime. When the Chickasaw honor a warrior who has distinguished himself, they present him with an eagle feather. To honor Keirsey, they gave him the tribal name of *hatak ossi*: "Eagle Man."[16]

———•———

Had Jenkins ever discussed suicide and, particularly, ways to make it look like something else? At least one former employee stressed Jenkins's optimistic nature and denied they had ever heard him mention suicide at work. However, another employee who remembered Jenkins's optimistic attitude also remembered Jenkins coming out of his office after reading a thriller novel and discussing ways to make a suicide look like murder.[17]

Methods for faking a suicide once came up at one of Jenkins's poker games. J. P. Bryan played poker at Jenkins's home on Niles Road at least twice. On one of those occasions, the suicide exclusionary clause for life insurance policies was being discussed because it had just been ruled unconstitutional. Because Bryan was an attorney, the others at the table were asking for his thoughts on the change. One fellow brought up the story of the man who faked his suicide by making it look like murder. Jenkins spoke up: "I have the perfect suicide. You get a boat, tie the gun to a balloon, and the guy shoots himself in the back of the head." Then the balloon would float the gun downstream until it leaked enough air and sank. The suicide exclusion clause wouldn't matter since the death would look like a murder.[18]

When Bryan heard that Jenkins was found shot, he asked where he was shot. He was not surprised that it was in the back of the head. A couple of years after this poker table talk, when Jenkins was being investigated by the ATF for arson, he asked Bryan again about the suicide exclusion rule to be sure that he understood how it worked. The suicide exclusion clauses on Jenkins's life insurance policies had already expired before his death, so there was no monetary need to make his death look like a murder—only, perhaps, a theatrical one.[19]

Once Jenkins planned to take his life, he seems to have drafted a trial suicide or disappearance note in the form of a letter to his secret business partner, Robert A. Venable. Jenkins apparently intended the letter to be discovered among the papers on his desk. I only ran across it in his archive.

The surviving letter is a photocopy and begins on the second page, which is undated. No copy of the first page was found, and presumably it was never typed. The top margin of the page has the addressee, "Robert A. Venable, Page 2." In addition, the bottom of the page has "JHJ/st"—apparently meant to suggest that this letter was typed for Jenkins by his secretary, Sheri Tomasulo. And to be sure that everyone knew that Jenkins had written it, he stapled his handwritten draft in blue ink to the photocopied page. The letter is memorable. It begins at the top of page 2 in the middle of a sentence, "which is why I finally decided to chuck all responsibility. My address for personal correspondence will be c/o Fritz Bormann, Avenida Nueva Dritte Reich, Rio de Janeiro, but he will not accept any legal service and I will be using an assumed name until the heat is off."[20]

The astute observer will immediately note some inside jokes in this address. Fritz is a name as common in Germany as Joe would be in the United States. Bormann was a famous Nazi. "Avenida Nueva" is a Spanish term that translates as "New Avenue" and would not be used in a Portuguese-speaking country like Brazil; the correct term in Portuguese is "Avenida Nova." Also, "Dritte Reich" is a German term meaning "Third Reich." In other words, Jenkins was saying that he could be found staying with an escaped Nazi in Brazil at "New Third Reich Avenue."

Was there a reason why Jenkins chose Brazil, besides as an inside joke? Though Brazil has an extradition treaty with the United States that lists thirty-four crimes, arson is the only felonious offense in the United States not listed within the treaty's articles—in other words, it is extradition-proof.[21] Jenkins was probably counting on his former classmate Venable to get his inside joke about being one of the boys in Brazil.

The letter from Jenkins continues, "In the United States I will be represented by Don Yarbrough, provided his law license is reinstated after his release on parole." This detail is telling. Donald B. Yarbrough was a 1964 University of Texas law school graduate who was elected in 1976 as an associate justice of the Texas Supreme Court at the age of thirty-five after giving only one political speech and spending less than $400 on his statewide campaign; Texans assumed that because of his last name he must have been related to the well-known progressive senator Ralph Yarborough, and thus he won the election.

Shortly after being sworn in, Yarbrough was indicted for forgery and perjury, and after being convicted in 1978 he failed to appear for sentencing and fled with his family to Granada, where he was safe from extradition (and where he began attending medical school). One easily sees Yarbrough's allure for Jenkins. However, Yarbrough messed up. He went on a class fieldtrip in 1983 to visit the medical school in St. Vincent, which happens to be a U.S. territory; consular officials arrested him and extradited him to Texas, where in 1986 he was sentenced to six years in prison, which is where he was when Jenkins typed this letter.[22]

Jenkins concludes with this warm wish for his partner: "I hope that this total loss of all your investment will not in any way affect our friendship."[23] To find out more about this letter, I talked to Sheri Tomasulo, who Jenkins listed as the typist. She was certain that she had never seen or heard of that letter, but she said that Jenkins was an expert typist and could easily have done it himself.[24]

It would have been completely in keeping with Jenkins's gallows humor to draft this letter while considering his possible suicide. It is doubtful that he thought the letter would fool any officials. Just as likely, he probably intended to use it to thumb his nose at his investigators from beyond the grave. Though his references to Brazil and Yarbrough are playful, they clearly show that he had at one point considered fleeing prosecution, just as Yarbrough had, by researching which country would be safest for him.

Jenkins the magician would have loved to amaze the world with a disappearing act. Jenkins the realist knew that his affairs were too tangled and the humiliation too galling. Besides, the financial risk to his family of the life insurance companies deciding not to pay his policies if no body was found was too great. Perhaps it was also too hard for him to imagine living in a faraway place where he couldn't speak the language. Whatever else was right or wrong with Jenkins, he was still a faithful son of Texas.

———•———

Sheriff Keirsey said that a large-caliber gun was missing from Jenkins's office after his death.[25] J. P. Bryan remembered chatting with Jenkins's son Jay sometime after the funeral. Jay was holding a .38 caliber bullet in his fingers, and J.P. watched him for a moment, then asked, "Did your father have a pistol?" Jay said, "Yes, it was a .38." J.P. asked him, "Do you have it?" Jay shook his head. "No, all I have is this bullet."[26] Had Jenkins's pistol been tied to the missing bag of ice so that it would float away until the ice melted and then sink? That would not be too different from the hypothetical gun tied to a balloon mentioned by Jenkins years earlier. Fortunately for Jenkins, this is one mystery about his death that will remain to taunt biographers, historians, and detectives.

———•———

At college Jenkins kept a diary. On New Year's Day in 1959, he examined his three worst faults: "I enter the New Year with the same three sins that have always been with me—selfishness, hatefulness, and conceit." It is to Jenkins's credit that he could identify these in himself. He believed he had not tried nearly as hard as he should to improve himself and wondered if these traits would "always haunt" him, despite his best efforts.[27]

But, although Jenkins had self-defeating traits, he was also capable of great unselfishness to his friends. Throughout his life Jenkins was personally generous, whether in picking up the check for expensive dinners or in personal favors to employees. Michael Parrish remembered that Jenkins once gave him the company car, free of charge, when he and his family needed the help. Parrish never thought to ask for it; Jenkins just offered it to him. Kevin MacDonnell remembered that after his first year of employment at the Jenkins Company he had set aside a beautiful copy of the first edition of Henry David Thoreau's *Walden*, which he was saving to purchase from the company. When he mentioned the book to Jenkins, he insisted that he take it as Jenkins's gift to him, no payment required. By the time of his death, Jenkins's friends knew well his big-hearted nature.

Foolishly bold in the face of danger was another of Jenkins's attributes. He certainly showed no fear in experiences that terrified others, whether he was racing cars or standing in a lightning storm. Once Jenkins and his cousin Kenneth Kesselus canoed down the Colorado River on an overnight trip. They were looking for the old haunts of their Texas family heroes when a violent lightning and thunder storm started striking all around them. Kesselus sat there shaking in fear of death when Jenkins pointed our that here they were doing something they really enjoyed, reliving things their ancestors did decades ago. Jenkins said in the middle of the storm, "Being struck by lightning wouldn't be a bad way to go."[28] Jenkins was calm when faced with the danger of that death. His emotional rewards did not come from betting his life against fate. Instead, Jenkins took chances for the thrill of embellishing his image, to enjoy the praise and adulation of others.

What did Jenkins think about revealing the truth about historical figures? On the one hand, he loved embellishing stories. Kenneth Rendell was once at dinner with Jenkins and a group of friends when John started a story. Rendell called him out on it: "Johnny, you're so full of shit it's unbelievable." Jenkins said his story was the whole truth and nothing but the truth—as he remembered it.[29] On the other hand, his cousin and coauthor Ken Kesselus said that Jenkins felt that writers should not keep secrets about historical figures "because nobody owns the truth." Kesselus quoted Jenkins: "History belongs to everyone."[30] Even Jenkins's own hidden parts.

There is a famous character in literature who mirrors many of Jenkins's personal attributes—Jay Gatsby. In the summer between Jenkins's junior and senior years of college he listed nearly fifty influential books he had read in 1961. One of the books on his reading list was F. Scott Fitzgerald's *The Great Gatsby*.[31] In the novel, Gatsby was a generous host and friend, just as Jenkins was in real life. Gatsby lived large and wonderfully as long as no one knew the criminal background behind his sophisticated life, just like Jenkins.

Jenkins was Gatsby's huckster cousin. He adorned his status with luxury cars, hundred-dollar bills, and a half-joking sign in his Austin mansion that read, "Better Nouveau Riche Than No Riche." Jenkins used his self-deprecating manner to appear modest but he continually aspired to public recognition as a historian, rescuer of stolen Audubons, or champion poker player. Like Gatsby, Jenkins most feared the exposure of the crimes—arsons, forgeries, and gambling losses—behind his good-old-boy mask.

What were the long-term effects of Jenkins's archival thefts and forgeries on collecting and the historical legacy of Texas? The most serious damage to the cultural legacy of Texas history is the theft of original letters and documents. Jenkins and his partner in crime, Jaime Platon, raided the Texas state archives while they were both working as interns. No doubt, at some point Dorman David became aware of what they had done, and he soon had his own thieves raiding county courthouses and archives around Texas. In 1991, with the financial assistance of a local collector, the Texas state archives began a complete inventory of all the stolen documents.[32] Today the list still has nearly 850 original documents of Texas history missing. The stolen documents include more than thirty letters by Stephen F. Austin (the founder of Texas, who died in 1836) and nearly fifty letters by Sam Houston (the commander at the Battle of San Jacinto and first president of the Republic of Texas).[33] This is a staggering loss.

What about Jenkins's effect on the American antiquarian book trade in the later part of the twentieth century? After all, he was president of the Antiquarian Booksellers Association of America and brought the image of rare books and rare book sellers into popular media. Though the printed Texas forgeries sold by Jenkins were not a cultural loss in the same sense as the stolen manuscripts, they were a betrayal of the deep trust Jenkins's customers and friends placed in him. There were nearly sixty copies of at least fifteen different forgeries or outright fabrications of Texas historical broadsides sold to unsuspecting collectors and institutions, and most of those came from Jenkins. One might think that cheating every major collector of Texana would have caused them to stop collecting. For Bob French in Midland, it did.

But for most Texana buyers, there was no real long-term effect. Serious collectors are by nature avaricious and are always in pursuit of the rare, and so they are already prepped to believe in the next opportunity. If anything, the value of genuine Texas printed documents suddenly increased in price. Jenkins sold his fake Texas Declarations of Independence for $15,000–$30,000 each, but a year after the exposure of the fakes a genuine Texas Declaration sold in 1991 for $75,000 to a collector in Dallas—and the collector flipped it two years later for $150,000 to the Gilder Lehrman collection (now at the New York Historical Society).[34] If the collector had waited a few more years, he might have seen his copy realize the $750,000 that the last genuine copy brought at Sotheby's in 2004.[35] And the even rarer Travis "Victory or Death" broadside? Jenkins sold his fakes for around $5,000, but a genuine one sold for $299,000 in the same sale in 2004 at Sotheby's.[36]

Jenkins's willingness to defraud his friends is one of the more difficult aspects of his character to fathom. It certainly left associates like William Reese feeling that Jenkins had betrayed him by selling him the fake Declaration. "I really thought we were friends," Reese said, with a note of sadness in his voice. The forged Texas Declaration hung on his office wall as a bookseller's version of a *memento mori*—not "remember you must die" but *memento posse dicipi*—"remember you can be tricked." Reese thought it a macabre reminder of when he looked up to and trusted Jenkins.[37]

In the early Middle Ages the most coveted collectibles were not rare books or art but religious relics, and the temptation to sell fakes was enormous. One enterprising ninth-century Italian deacon, Deusdona, sold the court of Charlemagne the bodies of St. Peter, St. Marcellinus, and St. Hermes. A Frankish cleric from around the same time, Felix, is also recorded selling the same saints' bodies. Some of the sums paid were equivalent to small fortunes in modern currency.[38]

Texas history was Jenkins's religion. John, like the vicar, conjured the authority, and the customers who marveled at his rarities supplied the faith. Is this a facsimile printing of a Texas broadside? Or is it the authentic printed reliquary of a pivotal moment in Texas history? A passion for the Lone Star State drew Jenkins to rare books, but somewhere in the journey he became a counterfeit curate who lied about his relics.

Bluff, bluster, and self-deception dominated Jenkins's life. Whether he was making up a story about writing his first book in secret, or buying cheap antiquarian books as puffers for a collection, or selling forged Texas broadsides, or exaggerating his inventory for his bankers, or lying to the arson investigators, or telling everyone he was a champion poker player, no detail of his life was too sacred for Jenkins to embellish. Many of Jenkins's friends never knew his Bastrop cabin was a high school graduation gift from his parents; Jenkins told them he bought it with the royalties from his first book. The monetary payoffs for each of these scams were never as important to Jenkins as the emotional payoff from taking one more risk to enhance his own image.

Poker dates back to the 1730s in England, where it had the suitable name "brag." It is an apt name for a card game of storytellers. Jenkins could tell tall, entertaining stories, but he never learned how to tell poker tales. Poker players tell and read stories with raised eyebrows, a second glance at their cards, or by shuffling and restacking their chips. Each player hopes to tell a convincing enough story to fool the other players into surrendering their chips, or to read the other players' stories well enough to know when they should fold. When one longtime tournament player said that "Squatty's strength is his short stack game," he was paying Jenkins the ultimate player's compliment.[39] Even when the flop didn't give Jenkins any cards, and his bluffs weren't sticking, he still held out hope that the river—the last card dealt in the hand—would save him.

A card game for money that relied on tall tales would seem to be Jenkins's natural métier. But, although poker's storytelling made

Jenkins feel at home, it was a place he could never fully inhabit. The game's pots burned him more often than not. Poker was the last refuge of the original Texas bluffer, and the price it extracted from Jenkins's life of bluster became his ultimate unpayable wager. Squatty's final stack was short and the river was dry.

———•———

Jenkins picked a place to die imbued with a great and dreadful sense of his family history. In 1833 someone murdered Jenkins's great-great-grandfather near a Bastrop farm on the west bank of the Colorado River, and the assailant remained mysterious.[40] In 1890 a gunfighter in Bastrop ambushed and killed his great-grandfather.[41] Did the allure of a mysterious death and his feeling of being ambushed by the ATF appeal to Jenkins's sense of family and theater? The only thing found in Jenkins's wallet at the river besides his driver's license was the business card of the Texas state fire marshal investigator.[42] For Jenkins's final hand, the wallet showed the card that called his bluff. Perhaps he intended it as a very private message to the arson investigators: this is on you.

Elm, willow, and scrub oak trees still crowd the banks of the viridescent Colorado River where Jenkins died. Large snapping turtles yet sun their dappled green shells on limestone rocks in the quiet flow. What Fitzgerald said of Gatsby applies equally to Jenkins. At the end John beat his boat against the current, but it still bore him ceaselessly back into his past.

I imagine that in John's final moments he stepped into the river until the water was over his waist, shivering until he found his footing. He stood with the pistol pressed to the back of his head and looked across the river toward his home in Central Texas where his two ancestors died violently. Alice Roosevelt Longworth said about her father Theodore's need for attention that he always wanted to be the corpse at every funeral.[43] This time Jenkins got his wish. The gun's muzzle flashed, his arms splayed, and Johnny's life ended with a headline-worthy splash.

Notes

Prologue

1. These and the following details of the discovery of Jenkins's body are drawn from my interview with Kaye Freeman, February 20, 2018, near Waco, Tex., and from Calvin Trillin, "American Chronicles: Knowing Johnny Jenkins," *New Yorker*, October 30, 1989, 79–97. The *New Yorker* sent Calvin Trillin to Texas around this time, and he interviewed many eyewitnesses, some of whom have since died.

2. Terrance Stutz and Melinda Henneberger, "Rare Book Dealer Found Shot to Death," *Dallas Morning News*, April 18, 1989, 7A. "Body Found in Colorado River near Bastrop," *Austin American-Statesman*, April 17, 1989, is the source for the time of discovery of Jenkins's body. That article also quoted an unnamed official (probably the Bastrop justice of the peace) saying that the body "suffered several blows to the back of the head"—which was not true.

3. Bryan Woolley, "Enigmatic Ending: Book Dealer's Flamboyant Lifestyle Ignites Speculation about His Death," *Dallas Morning News*, April 28, 1989, 1A, 15A.

4. Ron Tyler quoted in Joe Vargo and Monty Jones, "Sheriff Calls Death 'Bona Fide Mystery': Austin Bookseller Found in River, Shot in Head," *Austin American-Statesman*, April 18, 1989, A1.

5. The "one scholar" was William W. Newcomb Jr. (1921–2010), professor emeritus of anthropology at the University of Texas and former director of the Texas Memorial Museum.

6. A brief biography of Bosse by his son Erik appeared in Aldredge Book Store Catalogue 113, noting his death on April 20, 2000, after a battle with cancer, but that the store would continue the "wise ass" slogan of Dick Bosse by offering "used books at antiquarian prices."

7. John Holmes Jenkins, *Audubon and Other Capers: Confessions of a Texas Bookmaker* (Austin, Texas: Pemberton Press, 1976), 78.

8. Ashley Cheshire, "A Dealer in Rare Books, He Lived with Flair and Died in Mystery," *Fort Worth Star-Telegram*, April 23, 1989, 21, 24.

9. J. Lynn McKinney, "Wheeler-Dealer's Death Ruled Homicide by Bastrop Co. Peace Justice Henderson: Official Says Noted Austin Book Dealer a Murder Victim," *Bastrop County Times* 97, no. 17 (April 27, 1989): A1, A16.

10. Cheshire, "Dealer in Rare Books," 21, 24.

11. Telephone interview with T. Michael Parrish, October 24, 2017; interview with Michael Ginsberg, June 17, 2017, North Easton, Mass.

12. Cheshire, "Dealer in Rare Books," 21, 24.

13. D. Wead, *All the Presidents' Children: Triumph and Tragedy in the Lives of America's First Families* (New York: Atria Books, 2003), 107.

14. McKinney, "Wheeler-Dealer's Death Ruled Homicide," A1, A16.

15. Brian Smith, "Super Bowl of Poker Exceeds Expectations," *Player's Panorama*, February 16, 1989, B7.

16. W. Thomas Taylor, *Texfake: An Account of the Theft and Forgery of Early Texas Documents* (Austin: W. Thomas Taylor, 1991), 110, has a list of the genuine and forged copies of the Travis "Victory or Death" letter.

17. Ibid., 104–6, has a list of the genuine and forged copies of the Texas Declaration of Independence.

18. "Dinner to John Holmes Jenkins, Esq. Yale Westerners" (New Haven, Conn.: Yale Corral of the Westerners, February 4, 1977). The keepsake was almost certainly written by the Beinecke curator of Western Americana, Archibald Hanna.

19. Conversation of the author with John H. Jenkins at the Texas State Historical Association Annual Meeting in Lubbock, Tex., March, 1989.

20. Oscar Wilde, "Pen, Pencil and Poison," in *Collected Works of Oscar Wilde: The Plays, the Poems, the Stories and the Essays including De Profundis* (London: Wordsworth Editions, 1997), 949.

Chapter 1

1. Interview with informant, February 2018. All interviews with this person were conducted in confidentiality, and the name of the interviewee is withheld by mutual agreement.

2. "Ex-councilman Dies in Austin," *Austin American-Statesman*, October 22, 1984, 16.

3. Undated newspaper clipping from the *Beaumont Advertiser* with Holmes Jenkins's letter of mid-October 1961, Box 2, Folder 18, John Holmes Jenkins Papers, DeGolyer Library, Southern Methodist University, Dallas, Tex. (hereafter Jenkins Papers).

4. See University of Texas press release for Jenkins's book, May 22, 1958, Box 1, Folder 7, Jenkins Papers. The federal minimum wage was $1.00 per hour.

5. One of Jenkins's reports can be found in *Numismatist* 68 (1955): 280.

6. The letter from Jenkins on coin cleaning can be found in *Numismatist* 68 (1955), 1101; the quote is from his typescript biography, Box 1, Folder 1, Jenkins Papers.

7. Scott Travers, *The Coin Collector's Survival Manual*, rev. 7th ed. (New York: Diversified, 2015).

8. John Holmes Jenkins (hereafter JHJ in archival contexts), "Books I Have Read," Box 1, Folder 3, Jenkins Papers.

9. Ibid.

10. JHJ, Box 1, Folder 18, Jenkins Papers.

11. JHJ, Box 1, Folder 19, Jenkins Papers.

12. *The Scribbler* (Dick Dowling Jr. High School student newspaper), May 25, 1955, in Box 1, Folder 4, Jenkins Papers.

13. Interview with Maureen Jenkins, February 22, 2018, Austin, Tex..

14. Telephone interview with Buford Barr, February 18, 2018.

15. Kenneth Kesselus, quoted in Woolley, "Enigmatic Ending," 15A.

16. Kent Conwell, "Business Woman Rita Ainsworth Was the Madam with the Heart of Gold," *Beaumont Enterprise*, September 20, 2006, http://beaumontenterprise.com/news/article/Business-woman-Rita-Ainsworth-was-the-madam-with-770714.php (accessed February 16, 2018).

17. Telephone interview with Mark C. Wilson, Houston, Tex., February 16, 2018.

18. JHJ, Beaumont High School, Composition IV, September 30, 1957, "Getting Ready for Our Vacation," Box 1, Folder 5, Jenkins Papers; JHJ to his uncle, Morris Rector, September 1, 1957, Box 1, Folder 26, Jenkins Papers.

19. JHJ, Box 1, Folder 24, Jenkins Papers.

20. JHJ to his parents, June 15, 1956, Box 1, Folder 24, Jenkins Papers; JHJ to his mother, n.d., but summer 1956, Box 1, Folder 24, Jenkins Papers.

21. JHJ, manuscript account of his life for *Junior Historian*, circa 1973, Box 3, Folder 22, Jenkins Papers.

22. JHJ to his mother, n.d., but summer 1956, Box 1, Folder 25, Jenkins Papers.
23. Ibid.
24. On Carlson, telephone interview with Mark C. Wilson, February 16, 2018.
25. JHJ, manuscript account of his life for *Junior Historian*, circa 1973, Box 3, Folder 22, Jenkins Papers.
26. J. Frank Dobie, "Foreword," in John Holmes Jenkins III, ed., *Recollections of Early Texas: The Memoirs of John Holland Jenkins* (Austin: University of Texas Press, 1958), xiii. Jenkins's book also got a blurb in the *New Yorker*; see "Recollections of Early Texas," *New Yorker*, September 27, 1958, 79.
27. JHJ, Box 1, Folder 36, Jenkins Papers.
28. JHJ, manuscript account of his life for *Junior Historian*, circa 1973, Box 3, Folder 22, Jenkins Papers. Jenkins kept the project a secret from his parents only for the first three months in 1955 when he started; at Christmas 1955 he gave his parents a typed preliminary draft of the book.
29. Lucile O'Donnell to JHJ, March 31, 1983, Box 10, Folder 36, Jenkins Papers. O'Donnell attended that author event in 1958 and wrote about it to Jenkins twenty-five years later.
30. JHJ to his parents, May 1, 1962, Box 2, Folder 14, Jenkins Papers.
31. JHJ to "Barclay," January 9, 1959, Box 2, Folder 1, Jenkins Papers.
32. JHJ, manuscript account of his life for *Junior Historian*, circa 1973, Box 3, Folder 22, Jenkins Papers. The Junior Historians of Texas was an educational program for students in grades 4 through 12 started by Walter Prescott Webb in 1939 and sponsored by the Texas State Historical Association. See "Junior Historians of Texas," *Texas State Historical Association*, https://tshaonline.org/education/students /junior-historians/home (accessed December 26, 2018).
33. JHJ to his parents, October 28, 1958, Box 1, Folder 30, Jenkins Papers.
34. Ibid.
35. JHJ to his parents, October 29, 1959, Box 2, Folder 4, Jenkins Papers.
36. Typed note from Dorman Winfrey on letterhead of the Eugene C. Barker Texas History Center, January 24, 1961, Box 2, Folder 13, Jenkins Papers. There is a similar permission note from Winfrey in Box 2, Folder 12, Jenkins Papers.
37. JHJ to his parents, September 19, 1960, Box 2, Folder 9, Jenkins Papers. Jenkins's book on Burleson was finished after his death

by his cousin and coauthor, Kenneth Kesselus, and published as *Edward Burleson: Texas Frontier Leader* in 1990 by the Jenkins Publishing Company.

38. JHJ to his parents, September 19, 1960, Box 2, Folder 9, Jenkins Papers.

39. Typed statement from Dorman Winfrey to University of Texas Certified Personnel Office, September 7, 1960, Box 2, Folder 11, Jenkins Papers.

40. JHJ to his parents, January 11, 1961, Box 2, Folder 14, Jenkins Papers.

41. JHJ to his parents, n.d., circa September 1961, Box 2, Folder 14, Jenkins Papers. Alan Gribben's biography, *Harry Huntt Ransom: Intellect in Motion* (Austin: University of Texas Press, 2010), does not mention Dorman Winfrey or John H. Jenkins Jr. (though it does have a passing reference to the Jenkins Company at 117).

42. JHJ to his parents, n.d., circa September 1961, Box 2, Folder 14, Jenkins Papers.

43. JHJ to his parents, November 21, 1960, Box 2, Folder 9, Jenkins Papers. The collection of documents Winfrey and Jenkins were negotiating for was not identified in the papers.

44. Little is known of Platon. He graduated from the University of Texas Law School in 1960, and in 1962 Jenkins's mother wrote that she had heard that Jaime was going to a Jesuit school in 1962 (Sue Jenkins to JHJ, July 13, 1962, Box 3, Folder 1, Jenkins Papers). The only other record found for Platon was a death notice in San Juan, Puerto Rico, in 2005.

45. JHJ personal diary, January 2, 1959, Box 28, Folder 7, Jenkins Papers.

46. Robert W. Akers, "It's Like This," *Beaumont Enterprise*, September 8, 1960, Box 2, Folder 12, Jenkins Papers; JHJ to his parents, August 30, 1960, Box 2, Folder 9, Jenkins Papers.

47. Akers, "It's Like This."

48. Interview with confidential informant, October 2017. The cigar story comes from Terry Belanger, who heard it from Jenkins; interview with Terry Belanger, February 9, 2018, Pasadena, Calif.

49. JHJ to his parents, n.d., circa 1959, Box 2, Folder 2; and July 9, 1961, Box 2, Folder 15, Jenkins Papers. The actual invoice for the typewriter shows that Jenkins paid $169.00, so Jenkins gave his parents an exaggerated version of the savings.

50. JHJ to his parents, October 30, 1958, Box 1, Folder 30, Jenkins Papers.

51. JHJ to "Barclay," January 9, 1959, Box 2, Folder 1, Jenkins Papers.

52. JHJ to his parents, April 13, 1961, Box 2, Folder 14, Jenkins Papers.

53. JHJ to his parents, January 11, 1960, Box 2, Folder 9, Jenkins Papers.

54. JHJ to his parents, October 29, 1959, Box 2, Folder 4, Jenkins Papers.

55. JHJ Selective Service form, November 16, 1961; and JHJ scholastic report, Box 1, Folder 6, Jenkins Papers. Additionally, in 1959 Jenkins received a D and a C in two American history classes—two classes that should have come easily to him.

56. JHJ to his parents, March 31, 1961, Box 2, Folder 14, Jenkins Papers.

57. JHJ notes, Box 3, Folder 4, Jenkins Papers; JHJ personal diary, September 3, 1985, Box 28, Folder 6, Jenkins Papers. The cabin was located at Bastrop Town Tract 11 on 0.29 acres.

58. Interview with Maureen Jenkins, June 17, 2018, Austin, Tex.

59. The notice is found in Box 2, Folder 11, Jenkins Papers.

60. Sue Jenkins to JHJ, n.d., Box 2, Folder 4, Jenkins Papers.

61. The Colorado River crested nearly 34.5 feet above flood stage. Undated copy of newspaper clipping from *Beaumont Journal* (circa November 1960), Box 2, Folder 13, Jenkins Papers.

62. Holmes Jenkins to JHJ, November 28, 1960, Box 2, Folder 13, Jenkins Papers.

63. Sue Jenkins to JHJ, n.d., circa early October 1961; and Holmes Jenkins to JHJ, n.d., circa mid-October 1961, Box 2, Folder 18, Jenkins Papers.

64. JHJ to his parents, November 8, 1961, Box 2, Folder 15, Jenkins Papers.

65. JHJ to Maureen Mooney, n.d., circa April/May 1962, Box 2, Folder 20, Jenkins Papers.

66. JHJ to Maureen Mooney, n.d., circa April 1962, Box 2, Folder 20, Jenkins Papers.

67. Copy of the ticket, January 3, 1962, with Holmes Jenkins's note, can be found in Box 2, Folder 20, Jenkins Papers. Maureen Mooney to JHJ, February 28, 1962, Box 2, Folder 20, Jenkins Papers.

68. JHJ to Maureen Mooney, n.d., circa May 1962, Box 2, Folder 20, Jenkins Papers.

69. JHJ to Maureen Mooney, n.d., circa early April 1962, Box 2, Folder 20, Jenkins Papers.

70. R. E. Wallace to JHJ, April 18, 1962, Box 2, Folder 20, Jenkins Papers.

71. JHJ to Dale Johnson, n.d., circa May 1962, Box 3, Folder 1, Jenkins Papers.

72. Interview with Maureen Jenkins, February 22, 2018. Various invoices for honeymoon purchases and shipping charges can be found in Box 3, Folder 3, Jenkins Papers.

73. JHJ to his parents, March 5, 1960, Box 2, Folder 9, Jenkins Papers.

74. Interview with Kenneth Kesselus, February 21, 2018, Bastrop, Tex.

75. JHJ to his parents, March 5, 1960, Box 2, Folder 9, Jenkins Papers. For more on the collecting bubble in 1950-D Jefferson nickels, see Arlyn Sieber, "On the Watch for 1950-D Jefferson Nickels," in *The Instant Coin Collector: Everything You Need to Know to Get Started Now* (Iola, Wis.: Krause, 2013), 154.

76. JHJ to his parents, November 8, 1961, Box 2, Folder 15, Jenkins Papers.

77. J. C. Adams to JHJ, October 10, 1961, Box 2, Folder 18, Jenkins Papers.

78. Invoice from JHJ to the University of Texas, December 18, 1961, Box 1, Folder 6, Jenkins Papers.

79. Sue Jenkins to JHJ, n.d., circa early November 1961, Box 2, Folder 18, Jenkins Papers.

80. Documentation, March 15, 1962, Box 1, Folder 6, Jenkins Papers.

81. Interview with Maureen Jenkins, February 22, 2018.

82. Prior to this name it had been Jenkins and Smith; Smith is not known.

83. Various complaint and refund letters (including the larger quote from John J. Cantees, July 15, 1961) can be found in Box 2, Folder 19 (and others in Box 3, Folder 3), Jenkins Papers.

84. JHJ to "Dan," August 11, 1961, Box 2, Folder 19, Jenkins Papers.

85. Better Business Bureau of Austin to JHJ, March 14, 1963, Box 3, Folder 3, Jenkins Papers.

86. JHJ to his parents, November 26, 1962, Box 3, Folder 2, Jenkins Papers.

87. Interview with J. P. Bryan Jr., February 21, 2018, Galveston, Tex. See "Leon Green," *Tarlton Law Library: Jamail Center for Legal Research*, http://tarlton.law.utexas.edu/first-year-societies/leon -green (accessed February 25, 2018).

88. Interview with J. P. Bryan Jr., February 21, 2018.

89. J. P. Bryan Jr., "Collections and Collecting," *Proceedings of the Philosophical Society of Texas* (2003), www.pstx.org/index.php?option =com_content&view=article&id=293:collections-and-collecting &catid=24&Itemid=189 (accessed October 18, 2017). See "The Bryan Museum: The Romance of the West," *Bryan Museum*, www .thebryanmuseum.org (accessed December 26, 2018).

90. Jaime S. Platon to JHJ, November 11, 1960, Box 2, Folder 13, Jenkins Papers.

91. *Numismatic News* (Iola, Wis.), Monday, December 5, 1960, 45, Box 2, Folder 13, Jenkins Papers. In 1991 the Texas state library and archives compiled a comprehensive seventy-five-page list on their website of stolen documents, including many related to financial affairs of the Republic of Texas: www.tsl.texas.gov/sites/default /files/public/tslac/arc/missinglist.pdf.

92. See items 1100, "Republic of Texas Paper Currency," offering nine notes, and 1101, "Same. Government of Texas," offering five notes. W. M. Morrison, Bookseller, *List 175* (Waco, Tex.: ca. 1962), 40.

93. Jaime S. Platon to JHJ, November 11, 1960, Box 2, Folder 13, Jenkins Papers.

94. In his letter Platon goes to some length to ridicule Winfrey (knowing or suspecting that Jenkins would be receptive?) and to accuse him of having plagiarized his research and paper for an article, "The Texan Archive War of 1842," in the *Southwestern Historical Quarterly* 64, no. 2 (October 1960): 171–84. Platon to JHJ: "That one was written by me and I shudder at DHW's audacity to put his name on it, especially since all of my contributions were straight from a thesis I found in the archives." See Hope Yager, "The Archives War in Texas" (Master's thesis, University of Texas, 1939). I read the article that Platon mentioned; though Winfrey did not mention Platon or give him a coauthor credit, he did cite Hope Yager's thesis throughout the work. Most likely Winfrey realized later that Platon had cribbed Yager's work and gave her the credit instead.

95. JHJ, manuscript account of his life for *Junior Historian*, circa 1973, Box 3, Folder 22, Jenkins Papers.

Chapter 2

1. Manuscript notes for a talk by JHJ, Box 3, Folder 11, Jenkins Papers.

2. Unsigned chattel mortgage between John H. Jenkins and James Mayo, Taft, Tex., June, 1963, Box 3, Folder 3, Jenkins Papers.

3. Interview with Maureen Jenkins, October 14, 2017.

4. Franklin moved the store to San Francisco in 1971; he once confided to me, "Why the hell I left Austin I'll never know."

5. Interview with John Critchton (proprietor of the Brick Row Bookshop), March 8, 2018, New York.

6. "Tall in Texas: Young Tycoon of Texana," *Austin Statesman*, August 18, 1963, 6.

7. Interview with Michael and Gail Ginsberg, June 21, 2017, North Easton, Mass.
8. John Holmes Jenkins, *Neither the Fanatics nor the Faint-Hearted: The Tour Leading to the President's Death and the Two Speeches He Could Not Give* (Austin: Pemberton Press, 1963), 1–2.
9. JHJ, "After Twenty Years—An Apology" (unpublished talk, circa 1983), 1, Box 3, Folder 15, Jenkins Papers.
10. Dawson Duncan, "Yarborough Snubs LBJ: Motorcade Rides," *Dallas Morning News*, November 22, 1963, 1. For more on Texas Democratic Party infighting during Kennedy's visit, see Robert A. Caro, "The Transition: Lyndon Johnson and the Events in Dallas," *New Yorker*, April 2, 2012: 32–49. Jenkins, *Neither the Fanatics nor the Faint-Hearted*, 2.
11. Jenkins, "After Twenty Years," 1.
12. Ibid., 2.
13. Bryan, "Collections and Collecting."
14. Jenkins, "After Twenty Years," 4.
15. The Jenkins Company, *Catalogue 3, John F. Kennedy: A Catalogue of Books, Articles, Autographs, Memorabilia* (Austin, Tex.: Jenkins, 1964).
16. Don Adams, "New Book Publishing Firm Here Centers on the Southwest," *Austin American-Statesman*, May 12, 1966, 29.
17. Undated Letter from NASA to JHJ, Box 3, Folder 16, Jenkins Papers.
18. 1966 U.S. Partnership Return on Income for Attal Antiques, Box 5, Folder 15, Jenkins Papers.
19. For the various agreements related to Witliff, see Box 6, Folder 1; and Box 5, Folder 22, Jenkins Papers.
20. Kenneth Kesselus, "Letter to the Editor," *Bastrop Advertiser*, August 10, 1967, 25.
21. Llerena Friend, "Book Reviews: *Cracker Barrel Chronicles*," *Southwestern Historical Quarterly* 69, no. 4 (April 1966): 546.
22. Undated inscription by JHJ, collection of Michael Heaston, Wichita, Kansas. I suspect that the county that did not exist was one that was later consolidated with another county in Texas; I have no clue about the omitted county.
23. This section is drawn from Jake Zeitlin, *Some Rambling Recollections of a Rambling Bookseller* (Los Angeles: Printed by Anderson, Ritchie and Simon for Occidental College, 1970), 8–9, along with other sources cited specifically. See also Donald C. Dickinson, "Zeitlin, Jacob 'Jake,'" in *Dictionary of American Antiquarian Book-dealers* (Westport, Conn.: Greenwood Press, 1998), 245–46.

24. Donald C. Dickinson, "Evans, Herbert," in *Dictionary of American Book Collectors* (Westport, Conn.: Greenwood Press, 1986), 108–9.

25. Donald C. Dickinson, "Howell, Warren R.," in *Dictionary of American Antiquarian Bookdealers* (Westport, Conn.: Greenwood Press, 1998), 100–102.

26. C. Dorman David personal diary, February 22, 1960, Box 9, Folder 26, Jenkins Papers. Of course, it is even more telling that Jenkins had David's diary among his own papers.

27. Larry McMurtry, *Books: A Memoir* (New York: Simon and Schuster, 2008), 74.

28. Gregory Curtis, "Forgery Texas Style: The Dealers Who Buy and Sell Historic Texas Documents Move in a World of Big Money, Big Egos and Big Mistakes," *Texas Monthly Magazine*, March 1989, 180.

29. McMurtry, *Books*, 74–75.

30. Ibid., 75.

31. JHJ letter for Jake Zeitlein birthday celebration, November 2, 1982, Box 7, Folder 25, Jenkins Papers.

32. Curtis, "Forgery Texas Style," 184; JHJ, "Dorman David Stories," undated and unnumbered typescript, Box 19, Folder 23, Jenkins Papers.

33. JHJ, "Dorman David Stories," undated and unnumbered typescript, Box 19, Folder 23, Jenkins Papers.

34. Ibid.

35. Undated promissory note from Dorman David to JHJ, Country Store Gallery, Box 9, Folder 25, Jenkins Papers.

36. Promissory note, October 17, 1964, from Dorman David to Country Store Gallery, Box 9, Folder 25, Jenkins Papers.

37. Note, August 31, 1964, by JHJ, Box 9, Folder 24, Jenkins Papers.

38. C. Dorman David and John J. Jenkins Joint Catalogue, *Texana: Manuscripts, Autographs, Documents, Offered for Sale by C. Dorman David and John H. Jenkins*, unnumbered and undated, in William Reese Collection, New Haven, Conn.

39. JHJ, "Dorman David Stories," Jenkins Papers.

40. For a later, more exaggerated version of this trade, see John Holmes Jenkins, *In Memory of My Friend, Price Daniel, Jr.* (Austin: Pemberton Press, 1981), also available in Box 3, Folder 20, Jenkins Papers.

41. Curtis, "Forgery Texas Style," 179.

42. Interview with Maureen Jenkins, February 22, 2018.

43. Ibid.; Jenkins Company, *American Celebration Catalogue* (Austin, 1976), preface; see also letter from JHJ to unknown, December 5,

1966: "As you know, I have been serving for the past eight months in counter-intelligence in the army," Box 9, Folder 24, Jenkins Papers.

44. Donald C. Dickinson, "Streeter, Thomas W.," in *Dictionary of American Book Collectors* (Westport, Conn.: Greenwood Press, 1986), 301–3.

45. See Michael Vinson, *Edward Eberstadt and Sons: Rare Booksellers of Western Americana* (Norman: University of Oklahoma Press, 2016); and Thomas W. Streeter to Henry R. Wagner, April 17, 1943, Streeter Papers, Box 15, American Antiquarian Society, Worcester, Mass.

46. For more on Thomas Streeter, see Edward Eberstadt, "The Thomas W. Streeter Collection," *Yale Library Gazette* 31 (April 1957): 147–53; and Frank Streeter, "Some Recollections of Thomas W. Streeter and His Collecting," *Gazette of the Grolier Club* 31 (1980): 40–50.

47. Sanka Knox, "Account of Magellan's Voyage Is Sold for $56,000," *New York Times*, October 26, 1966, 41.

48. Interview with Maureen Jenkins, February 22, 2018.

49. Maureen was able to buy one lot at the sale: Lot 394, a European periodical promoting immigration to Texas in the late 1850s, *Bulletin de la Societe de Colonisation Europeo-Americaine au Texas*, for $190.

50. Curtis, "Forgery Texas Style," 184.

51. Promissory note, n.d., by C. Dorman David to JHJ, Box 9, Folder 24, Jenkins Papers; JHJ, "Dorman David Stories," n.d., typescript, Box 19, Folder 23, Jenkins Papers.

52. Curtis, "Forgery Texas Style," 179.

53. Interview with Maureen Jenkins, February 22, 2018.

54. Typed agreement, February 25, 1965, signed by C. Dorman David and JHJ, Box 9, Folder 24, Jenkins Papers. The price was $2,000 cash, a promise of ten copies of every book printed by the Jenkins Company, an IBM electric typewriter, and two payments of $3,250 on David's behalf for a line of credit to Lake Jackson State Bank. The payments were made and settled by May 14, 1965.

55. Handwritten list of seven documents purchased by JHJ from C. Dorman David, September 28, 1967, including Ben C. Franklin document, December 21, 1836; James H. C. Miller–John W. Smith document, Bexar, July 31, 1835; Gail Border document, October 20, 1835; Sawyer Burnet document, August 17, 1836; Henry Smith document, December 28, 1836; and T. J. Rusk document, April 19, 1839, Box 9, Folder 25, Jenkins Papers.

56. JHJ to Dorman David, October 5, 1967, Box 9, Folder 24, Jenkins Papers.

57. Ibid.

58. Note from JHJ to C. Dorman David, January 16, 1968, Box 9, Folder 24, Jenkins Papers.

59. For 1968 sales figures, see tax returns in Box 5, Folder 21, Jenkins Papers. For contracts and lines of credit from Robert Venable in Dallas to Jenkins Publishing Company for $100,000, see January 16, 1969, Box 7, Folder 2, Jenkins Papers.

60. Details of this fire discussed below drawn from JHJ to Harris Masterson, August 26, 1975, Box 11, Folder 1, Jenkins Papers; and Roger Conger to JHJ, July 28, 1969, Box 9, Folder 21, Jenkins Papers. Roger N. Conger (1910–96) was president of Hammond Laundry Dry Cleaning Machinery Company until its sale in 1961. He was a Waco city commissioner from 1962 to 1965 and mayor in 1964/65. He also served on the board of directors of the Texas State Historical Association and was the author of several history books.

61. Donald C. Dickinson, "Lowdermilk, William H.," in *Dictionary of American Antiquarian Booksellers* (Connecticut: Greenwood Press, 1998), 131; Maria Luisa Cisneros, "Americana: Ex-libris," *Time*, February 23, 1970, 19.

62. "Flash on Jefferson's Libraries," *Quarto*, no. 9 (December 1944): 2.

63. Ralph Maud, *Charles Olson's Reading: A Biography* (Carbondale: Southern Illinois University Press, 1996), 87.

64. Dickinson, "Lowdermilk," 131.

65. The following account of Jenkins's Lowdermilk purchase is drawn from Herman Schaden, "Great Book Store Mystery," *Washington Star*, May 3, 1970, C-1, C-3, along with specific sources cited in this section.

66. Jenkins's purchases over three days of the auction: February 9, $1,990.00; February 10, $8,650.00; February 11, $1,700.00. Samuel T. Freeman of Philadelphia was the auctioneer and they had to send several dun letters until October 1970 for the final $2,000.00; see Box 10, Folder 21, Jenkins Papers.

67. Interview with Maureen Jenkins, October 14, 2017.

68. Ibid.

69. Herman Schaden to JHJ, March 6, 1970; and JHJ to Herman F. Schaden, March 11, 1970, Box 10, Folder 21, Jenkins Papers. Schaden seems to have been the first to suggest that Jenkins was transferring culture from the East to the West.

70. Interview with confidential informant, February 2018; interview with J. P. Bryan Jr., February 21, 2018, Galveston, Tex.

71. Richard Cornett, "Poker Unwinds Austin Squatty," *Las Vegas Review-Journal*, April 29, 1984, 3B.

72. Cedric Robinson to JHJ, January 29, 1971, Box 4, Folder 14, Jenkins Papers.

73. Robert Black to JHJ, February 12, 1971, Box 4, Folder 14, Jenkins Papers.

74. JHJ to Robert Black, February 3, 1971, Box 4, Folder 14, Jenkins Papers.

75. Ibid.

76. Robert Black to JHJ, February 12, 1971, Box 4, Folder 14, Jenkins Papers.

Chapter 3

1. Walter Goldwater, quoted in Phillip J. Wajda, "True Crime or Texas Tall Tale? Unraveling a 40-Year-Old Mystery," *Union College Magazine*, Summer 2011, 4–13. See also William R. Greer, "Walter Goldwater Obituary," *New York Times*, June 28, 1985, 16.

2. "Rizek Escapes Term in Prison," *Daily Home News* (New Brunswick, N.J.), December 20, 1957, 1.

3. "Indicted for Library Thefts," *College and Research Libraries News*, March 1964, 139; Wajda, "True Crime or Texas Tall Tale?," 11.

4. Wajda, "True Crime or Texas Tall Tale?," 10; Charles P. Everitt, *Adventures of a Treasure Hunter* (Boston: Little, Brown, 1951), 49–50. John E. Scopes and Company book shop was at 23 Steuben Street in Albany.

5. Wajda, "True Crime or Texas Tall Tale?," 10. Also, email communication from Wayne Sommers (June 28, 2018): "Ken Rosenberg, a young Albany dealer just starting out at that time told me that Jim Rizek had bought the Scopes inventory from the bank, which was the executor." Rizek divided the inventory into thirds; whichever third Jenkins purchased, he obviously felt that Rizek had culled the rarities from his portion.

6. Interview with Donald N. Mott, February 9, 2018, Pasadena, Calif.

7. Wajda, "True Crime or Texas Tall Tale?," 7.

8. Kenneth Paull was released from prison on May 27, 1971.

9. Wajda, "True Crime or Texas Tall Tale?," 11.

10. Ibid., 10–11; JHJ to Edwin K. Tolan (Union College Library), July 9, 1971, Box 19, Folder 22, Jenkins Papers.

11. Telephone interview with Sheri Tomasulo, October 2017. This detail was confirmed as well by Michael Heaston and Kevin Mac-Donnell, both former employees of the Jenkins Company.

12. Wajda, "True Crime or Texas Tall Tale?," 11.

13. JHJ to Edwin K. Tolan (Union College Library), July 9, 1971, Box 19, Folder 22, Jenkins Papers.

14. Ibid.

15. Ibid.

16. JHJ to Solomon R. Shapiro, July 19, 1971; and JHJ to Edwin K. Tolan (Union College Library), July 14, 1971, Box 19, Folder 22, Jenkins Papers.

17. Edwin K. Tolan, "Recovery of the Stolen Audubon Plates," *Friends of the Union College Library Newsletter*, September 9, 1971; and JHJ to Edwin K. Tolan (Union College Library), July 14, 1971, Box 19, Folder 22, Jenkins Papers.

18. JHJ to Solomon R. Shapiro, July 19, 1971, Box 19, Folder 22, Jenkins Papers.

19. George A. Spater, president of American Airlines, to Congressman J. J. Pickle, September 1, 1971, Box 19, Folder 22, Jenkins Papers; Tal Luther, T. N. Luther Books, to JHJ, August 2, 1971, Box 19, Folder 25, Jenkins Papers.

20. JHJ to Solomon R. Shapiro, September 16, 1971; and Solomon R. Shapiro to JHJ, September 23, 1971, Box 19, Folder 25, Jenkins Papers.

21. *Congressional Record: Proceedings of the 92nd Congress*, vol. 117, no. 125, part II, Wednesday, August 4, 1971.

22. Edwin K. Tolan, "Recovery of the Stolen Audubon Plates," *Friends of the Union College Library Newsletter*, September 9, 1971; and JHJ to H. Joseph Houlihan, Morris Book Shop, Lexington, Kentucky, September 17, 1971, Box 19, Folder 22, Jenkins Papers.

23. *Ground-Breaking Ceremonies for the Addition to Schaffer Library, Union College*, June 2, 1973; "Address: Skullduggery in the Book Trade: The Audubon Caper, by John H. Jenkins, Austin, Tex. Presentation of the Union College Founders Medal to John H. Jenkins," in Box 19, Folder 22, Jenkins Papers.

24. David Gilley and K. Oxford Abbey, "Diogenes Syndrome," spec script for *Kojak* TV series, CBS, Box 5, Folder 25, Jenkins Papers.

25. Inscribed *Kojak* spec script in the collection of the author. Jenkins signed it to Fred White Jr., no date.

26. Untitled typescript by JHJ, n.d., Box 4, Folder 12, Jenkins Papers.

27. Mike Cox, "Texfake Exposes Theft, Forgery of Rare Documents," *Austin American-Statesman*, October 13, 1991, H8. Even though

Cox did not name the document and map thief in his column, William Gerald Gray's name and information were published with his arrest in Austin on August 2, 1971; see Sara Howze, "Archivist Notes Theft Hazards: Current Probe On," *Austin Statesman*, August 8, 1971, A1, A4. It is a matter of public record that Gray was convicted on December 22, 1971. He was not imprisoned but instead received five years of probation.

28. "Drama in a Texas Library," *Centre Daily Times*, n.d. [ca. August 1971], 4.

29. Dorothy Sloan Rare Books, *Auction 23 Americana: High Spots of Texas, the West, Mexico and the Borderlands* (April 4, 2013), Lot 240.

30. Taylor, *Texfake*, 27–28.

31. *Sale of Rare Texas Historical Manuscripts and Autograph Materials Being Letters, Documents, and Broadsides from the Collection of C. Dorman David. To Be Sold to the Highest Bidder at the Warwick Hotel, Houston, Fontaine Ballroom, June 22, 1971* (Houston, 1971). Copy in the author's collection.

32. Eugene C. Barker, ed., *The Austin Papers October, 1834–January, 1837*, vol. 3 (Austin: University of Texas Press, 1926), 8; *Sale of Rare Texas Historical Manuscripts and Autograph Materials*, 9.

33. Roger Conger to JHJ, June 18 and June 23, 1971, Box 9, Folder 21, Jenkins Papers.

34. Marge Crumbaker, "Texana Sale Nets $23,000," *Houston Post*, June 24, 1971, 6, photocopy in Box 9, Folder 25, Jenkins Papers.

35. To his credit, Grizzard later voluntarily returned his documents to the State of Texas when news of David's thefts was uncovered. Taylor, *Texfake*, 43.

36. JHJ to Dorman David, July 2, 1971, Box 4, Folder 24, Jenkins Papers.

37. David Hewett, "Forgeries and Fraud in Texas," *Maine Antique Digest*, January 1989, 30A: "John Jenkins acknowledges that he aided authorities in an investigation that resulted in David's eventual incarceration."

38. Tim Fleck, "Rare Papers Target of Official Scrutiny," *Houston Chronicle*, June 15, 1972, 3:1.

39. Receipt from C. Dorman David to JHJ, July 5, 1972, Box 9, Folder 25, Jenkins Papers: "Sold to John Jenkins the following [list of seven books and letters, only Texas item is "Incomplete 1838 Abstract" of lands]. Signed, C. Dorman David, 7–5–72."

40. Patrick Beach, "Following the Paper Trail," *Austin American-Statesman*, April 7, 1998, E1, E8. Eventually in 1980 David turned

himself in to the authorities and did thirteen months in the prison at Huntsville, Tex.

41. Interview with William Reese, March 11, 2018, New York. Jackson owned forty sections (each section is 640 acres, or one square mile) and leased another hundred sections from the Bureau of Land Management.

42. Preface to *25th Anniversary Catalogue, Frontier America Catalogue 42* (Albuquerque: Fred White, Jr., 1992), 1.

43. See Michael Vinson, "A Passion for Western Americana: Remembering Fred White, Jr., Seven Years Later," in Michael Vinson, *Western Americana Catalogue 2003* (Afton, Wyo., 2003), 1–3. Fred White Jr. died February 5, 1996.

44. Interview with William Reese, November 13, 2017, New Haven, Conn.

45. The dates of the letters of recommendation for Jenkins are as follows: Jake Zeitlin (January 18, 1972); Kenneth Rendell (November 9, 1971); Michael Ginsberg (October 4, 1971), Box 4, Folder 14, Jenkins Papers.

46. JHJ to Kenneth Rendell, n.d., Box 4, Folder 14, Jenkins Papers.

47. Sotheby Parke-Bernet, "Albert Einstein, an Important and Large Collection of Autograph Manuscript Notes, Princeton, N.J., ca. 1950–1954" (November 28, 1972), Lot 155.

48. Interview with Kenneth Rendell, November 10, 2017, Boston, Mass.

49. Ibid. The catalogue record at the Harry Ransom Center for the Einstein scientific manuscript collection shows that they figured out that the manuscripts had been torn in half, since the record indicates 326 pages on 163 leaves, the result of tearing the larger quarto leaves in half so that they were octavo page size.

50. Dick Bosse to JHJ, January 3, 1973, Box 4, Folder 22, Jenkins Papers. The other Southwest chapter members were Ray S. Walton, vice-chairman; Fred White Jr., secretary-treasurer; W. M. Morrison; Wilson Bookshop (Robert A. Wilson); Gail Klemm Books; Dick Bosse (Aldredge Book Store); Dorothy McNamee (Overland Bookshop); Jack Potter, bookseller; and Conway Barker, autograph dealer.

51. JHJ to Steve Weissman, December 6, 1974, Box 4, Folder 15, Jenkins Papers.

52. Mike Cox, "Word Wildcatter Leaves Legend: Writer-Publisher Pumped Texas History, Lore to Produce Rich Bounty," *Austin American-Statesman*, April 23, 1989, D4. Sometimes Jenkins would

tell a slightly more believable version, that his poker game began with Prohibition in Austin in 1921.

53. Interview with Donald N. Mott, February 10, 2018, Pasadena, Calif.

54. Interview with Bill Cotter, April 10, 2018, New York.

55. Interview with Terry Belanger, February 10, 2018, Pasadena, Calif.

56. Dick Mohr to JHJ, June 29, 1973, Box 10, Folder 32, Jenkins Papers, about expenses related to the poker game at the Los Angeles Book Fair: "I paid $672.80 to the Ambassador Hotel which includes room rent, liquor, and bartender. You owe me one quarter of that."

57. Interview with Donald N. Mott, February 10, 2018; interview with William Reese, February 11, 2018, Pasadena, Calif.

58. Interview with confidential informant, February 2018.

59. Note sheet in JHJ's hand from the lesson with Thorp, collection of the author, Santa Fe, N.Mex.

60. See, for example, JHJ to Lou Weinstein, May 3, 1975, Box 9, Folder 53, Jenkins Papers: "Mike and I are planning to leave here about May 31 for Vegas, from whence I will fly to New York for the June 3rd Board meeting [ABAA]. Why don't you join us?"

61. Interview with Michael and Gail Ginsberg, June 21, 2017; interview with Maureen Jenkins, February 22, 2018.

62. Interview with Maureen Jenkins, February 22, 2018.

63. Interview with J. P. Bryan Jr., February 21, 2018, Galveston, Tex. Jenkins also taught Bryan the card counting system he had learned from Thorp.

64. Interview with confidential informant, February 2018.

65. Ricky Jay, *Cards as Weapons* (New York: Darien House, 1977), inscribed in ink on the title page, collection of the author, Santa Fe, N.Mex.

66. Interview with Kenneth Kesselus, February 21, 2018.

67. Kenneth Kesselus to JHJ, n.d, but apparently 1970s, Box 3, Folder 22, Jenkins Papers; interview with Kenneth Kesselus, February 21, 2018.

68. Everett L. DeGolyer Jr. to JHJ, January 17, 1974, Box 9, Folder 29, Jenkins Papers.

69. JHJ to Everett L. DeGolyer Jr., January 21, 1974, Box 9, Folder 29, Jenkins Papers.

70. Email from Kevin MacDonnell to the author, August 27, 2018. MacDonnell worked for Jenkins from 1980 to 1986 and often witnessed this practice.

71. JHJ to Archibald Hanna, June 19, 1975; and Archibald Hanna to JHJ, June 23, 1975, Box 9, Folder 49, Jenkins Papers.

72. JHJ to Richard Harwell (then curator of Georgiana at the University of Georgia Library in Athens), February 14, 1976, Box 9, Folder 51, Jenkins Papers.

73. JHJ to *Times Literary Supplement*, March 22, 1975, Box 11, Folder 19, Jenkins Papers.

74. JHJ to John Mayfield, June 4, 1975, Box 10, Folder 30, Jenkins Papers.

75. John Mayfield to JHJ, June 13, 1975, Box 10, Folder 30, Jenkins Papers.

76. JHJ to John Mayfield, July 3, 1975, Box 10, Folder 30, Jenkins Papers.

77. Charles Hamilton Autographs, *Auction. October 10th* (New York, 1974), Lot 361.

78. Anderson Galleries, *The Library of the Late H. Buxton Forman* (New York, October 4–7, 1920), Lot 1291.

79. See John Carter and Graham Pollard, *An Inquiry into the Nature of Certain Nineteenth Century Pamphlets* (London: Constable, 1934); also Nicholas Barker, John Collins, and John Carter, *A Sequel to an Enquiry into the Nature of Certain Nineteenth Century Pamphlets by John Carter and Graham Pollard: The Forgeries of H. Buxton Forman and T. J. Wise Re-examined* (London: Scolar Press, 1983).

80. See Vinson, *Edward Eberstadt and Sons*.

81. "Notes on Rare Books," *New York Times*, June 29, 1924, 19.

82. The following account, through the final Eberstadt transaction, based in part on Robert A. Venable, untitled four-page typewritten draft about the deal, apparently written circa September 1975, collection of the author, Santa Fe, N.Mex.

83. Robert Reinhold, "Murchison: A Fortune Lost," *New York Times*, March 5, 1985, D1, D6.

84. Interview with Michael and Gail Ginsberg, June 21, 2017.

85. Ibid.

86. JHJ to Rita Marsales, Fondren Library, Rice University, July 14, 1975, Box 11, Folder 1, Jenkins Papers.

87. Robert Sheehan, "Charles Allen, Jr.," in *Wall Street People: True Stories of Today's Masters and Moguls*, vol. 2, edited by Charles D. Ellis and James R. Vertin (New York: John R. Wiley and Sons, 2001), 26–30.

88. The following account from Lindley Eberstadt's perspective drawn from my interview with William Reese, March 11, 2018.

89. The marked Streeter auction catalogues showing the three-way cooperation are in the collection of William Reese, New Haven, Conn.

90. Interview with Michael and Gail Ginsberg, June 21, 2017.

91. Jenkins gave a campaign talk and fundraiser for former Texas attorney general John Luke Hill for his governor's campaign in 1977. See Jon Ford, "Hill Fund Gets $300,000," *Austin American-Statesman*, September 16, 1977, F18: "Austin publisher John Jenkins, who was treasurer for the 'Good Job, John Hill Reception,' predicted a $300,000 profit off the event."

92. Interview with Michael and Gail Ginsberg, June 21, 2017.

93. In their rush to pack up the rare inventory, Jenkins and his crew apparently packed up only eighteen of the nineteen Eberstadt offices that held inventory. After Jenkins left with the tractor-trailer, an Eberstadt employee gradually took the rare book stock in the nineteenth office to his home and stored the books in his attic, telling his children not to disturb them until after he died. He probably justified it by figuring that he was stealing from Jenkins, not the Eberstadts. Eventually in the early 2000s these rare materials came back into the market. William Reese was the one who figured out how it was that Eberstadt materials were reappearing and told me this story.

94. Interview with confidential informant, June 2018.

95. Interview with Michael and Gail Ginsberg, June 21, 2017.

96. Ibid.

97. William H. Goetzmann, Stiles Professor in American Studies, to F. Warren Roberts, August 25, 1975, Box 20, Folder 1, Jenkins Papers.

98. See Robert A. Caro, *The Years of Lyndon Johnson: Means of Ascent* (New York: Vintage Books, 1991), 424.

99. "University May Buy Rare Books," *Brownsville Herald*, October 23, 1975, 4.

100. JHJ to Allan Shivers, Chairman, Board of Regents, University of Texas, October 15, 1975, Box 11, Folder 36, Jenkins Papers. Jenkins Garrett, a prominent Fort Worth attorney who collected Mexican War materials, used his influence with the regents to divert the Mexican War part of the Eberstadt purchase to the University of Texas at Arlington.

101. Jerry Carroll, "Genteel World of the Rare Book Dealer," *San Francisco Chronicle*, January 25, 1983, 19. The "tall man of patrician mien" line is from Carroll.

102. Wayne Warga, "Record Prices: Theydunit at a Whodunit Book Auction," *Los Angeles Times*, December 15, 1981, part V, 1, 6. The underbidders on *A Study in Scarlet* were James Pepper and Peter Stern.
103. William Reese, one of the most knowledgeable booksellers I have ever known, told me this. I did reach out to the other much older unidentified bookseller, who is still living, to confirm this anecdote, and he vehemently denied ever trying to buy the Eberstadt collection with Warren Howell. Personally, I suspect the advancement of years and the desire to control one's past can dim memory.
104. Interview with Michael Ginsberg, June 17, 2017.
105. Interview with Kenneth Rendell, November 10, 2017, Boston, Mass.
106. Interview with Michael and Gail Ginsberg, June 21, 2017.
107. Color photograph from the collection of the author, Santa Fe, N.Mex.
108. JHJ to Dorman Winfrey, Director, Texas State Library, March 8, 1974, Box 11, Folder 19, Jenkins Papers.
109. Thomas N. Bonner, President, Union College, December 30, 1975 to JHJ, Box 11, Folder 29, Jenkins Papers.
110. Press release, n.d, ca. July 1976, Box 11, Folder 29, Jenkins Papers.
111. Thomas N. Bonner, President, Union College, June 13, 1976, [untitled declaration for John Holmes Jenkins III], collection of the author, Santa Fe, N.Mex.
112. JHJ to Thomas Bonner, Union College, January 6, 1976, Box 11, Folder 29, Jenkins Papers.
113. Telephone interview with Sheri Tomasulo, October 2017.
114. Interview with Kenneth Rendell, November 10, 2017.
115. Wolfgang Saxon, "Hans Peter Kraus, 81, Book Dealer and Collector," *New York Times*, November 2, 1988, D27.
116. Interview with Kenneth Rendell, November 10, 2017.
117. Ibid.
118. Interview with Donald N. Mott, February 10, 2018.
119. "Death Notice, Carolyn Manovill," *New York Times*, March 20, 2001, A23.
120. Jenkins kept the wrongly colored triple-decker *Whale* at his house until Kevin MacDonnell took over the literature department of the Jenkins Company in the early 1980s; then Jenkins instructed him to take the volumes to a San Francisco book fair, where they were sold to an unfortunate collector.
121. Jenkins, *Audubon and Other Capers*, 82.
122. Hewett, "Forgeries and Fraud in Texas," 29A–30A.

123. Taylor, *Texfake*, 107–11.
124. Joe B. Frantz, "Peace, John Robert," in *The New Handbook of Texas*, vol. 5 (Austin: Texas State Historical Association, 1996), 104.
125. Years later in the 1990s, Ray Walton was caught stealing from other antiquarian booksellers during setup at the Austin Antiquarian Book Fair. Walton's modus operandi was to carry a box of books around to other dealers' tables as though he were on his way from unloading his car. Then when they were distracted he would quickly place one of the dealer's more valuable Texas books in his box and shuffle off.
126. John Peace to JHJ, October 31, 1973, Box 10, Folder 43, Jenkins Papers.
127. The source of the consignor's name was an employee of Parke-Bernet Galleries who asked to remain anonymous.
128. Hewett, "Forgeries and Fraud in Texas," 29A–30A.
129. Receipts or photocopies of these forgeries are found in Box 10, Folders 41, 42, and 43, Jenkins Papers. See also Taylor, *Texfake*, 81, 102, 106, 110.
130. Taylor, *Texfake*, 102. For the illustration of the forgery, see the University of Texas prospectus, *A Collection on Texas and the American West* (Austin: University of Texas System, 1977), 10.
131. See the Beinecke Library acquisition card for the broadside, which is catalogued at *Broadsides 4to Zc 52 835czd*, Yale University, New Haven, Conn. Dawson purchased it (Lot 542, "Texas Broadside,") on June 29, 1975, at a Parke-Bernet sale in Los Angeles, Calif. (a copy of the Parke-Bernet invoice is also at the Beinecke).
132. See Taylor, *Texfake*, 76–77 (Columbia Jockey Club); 84–87 (Town of Houston); 145 ("Glorious News!"). There is one more fabrication, 115–16 ("A Public Meeting"), from 1838 about the first church in Galveston. All of the known copies of the church in Galveston fabrication came through Ray Simpson but, again, Jenkins was a constant consignor to Simpson's auction galleries through the 1970s.
133. Interview with Michael Heaston, September 12, 2017, Wichita, Kans. Heaston was manager of the Jenkins rare book department from 1976 to 1980.
134. Interview with Michael Ginsberg, June 17, 2017.
135. Stutz and Henneberger, "Rare Book Dealer Found Shot," 7A.
136. Check stubs showing payments from Jenkins Publishing Company to C. Dorman David, Box 7, Folder 2, Jenkins Papers. The stubs do not indicate anything about what was purchased by Jenkins (such

as "printing plates for forgeries"), but they are for the same time period as David said he sold the plates to Jenkins.

Chapter 4

1. Interview with Michael Thompson, February 9, 2018, Pasadena, Calif.
2. Interview with William Reese, February 11, 2018.
3. Interview with Stuart Bennett, February 8, 2018, Pasadena, Calif.
4. Email from T. Michael Parrish to the author, June 19, 2018.
5. Interview with William Reese, November 13, 2017.
6. Cover photograph and headline for *Southwest Airlines Magazine*, January 1985.
7. J. D. Reed, "The Clothbound Collectibles: Rare Volumes Outperform Gold, Diamonds, Stocks," *Time* 119, no. 17 (April 26, 1982): 83.
8. Interview with Kevin MacDonnell, February 23, 2018, Austin, Tex.
9. JHJ, "Making Movies," lecture given to University of Texas Law School, March 8, 1984, unpaginated, Box 3, Folder 26, Jenkins Papers.
10. Ronald Powell, "A Rare Bird in Old Books," *Austin American Statesman*, July 18, 1977, 9.
11. JHJ, "Description of Trinity University/Jenkins University Project," Box 8, Folder 11, Jenkins Papers. The university project description does not describe what Jenkins actually intended to do with it.
12. Dick Stanley, "Jenkins Make His Dreams Come True: Books, Films, Space Projects Keep Him Going," *Austin American-Statesman*, March 8, 1983, 3.
13. JHJ, "Dorman David Stories," unnumbered typescript, n.d., Box 19, Folder 23, Jenkins Papers.
14. The following discussion of Jenkins's movie adventures is drawn in part from JHJ, "Making Movies," Box 3, Folder 26, Jenkins Papers.
15. Jeff Guinn, *Go Down Together: The True, Untold Story of Bonnie and Clyde* (New York: Simon and Schuster, 2009), 364.
16. Margalit Fox, "Larry Buchanan Dies at 81: B-movie Schlockmeister," *New York Times*, December 19, 2004, 56.
17. "Larry Buchanan Biography," *Internet Movie Database*, www.imdb .com/name/nm0118041/bio?ref_=nm_ov_bio_sm; "*The Other Side of Bonnie and Clyde*, Full Cast and Crew," *Internet Movie Database*, www.imdb.com/title/tt0063399/fullcredits (both accessed April 21, 2018).
18. Interview with Maureen Jenkins, February 22, 2018. Years later one of the poker players' wives was convinced that her husband was

hiding his share of the film's profits during the divorce proceedings. Actually, Jenkins had won her husband's share of the movie profits in a poker game years earlier.

19. Interview with confidential informant, February 2018.

20. JHJ, check dated January 27, 1978, to Thomas Steinbeck for $15,000 for rights to *Cannery Row*, Box 5, Folder 19, Jenkins Papers.

21. Ronald Randall to JHJ, January 4, 1977, Box 7, Folder 25, Jenkins Papers.

22. Tobias Rodgers, Quevedo Rare Books and Manuscripts, to JHJ, October 7, 1977, Box 10, Folder 46, Jenkins Papers.

23. Interview with Ken Rendell, November 10, 2017.

24. Telegram from Ray and Carolyn Walton, April 18, 1980, to JHJ at the New York Hilton, Room 3655, Box 3, Folder 7, Jenkins Papers: "Congratulations on your inauguration as president of the ABAA. We send our warmest regards and wish we could be with you."

25. Larry Besaw, "Austin Rare Book Dealer Recovers Missing Goods," *Austin American-Statesman*, November 20, 1979, 19.

26. JHJ, *Rare Book and Manuscript Thefts: A Security System for Libraries, Booksellers, and Collectors, by John H. Jenkins, President, A.B.A.A.* (New York: Antiquarian Booksellers Association of America, 1981). Jenkins also conveniently profited from the pamphlet; he had his publishing company print five thousand copies and billed the association for $2,700; invoice dated March 24, 1982, for 5,000 6 × 9 booklets, $2,725.22 to the ABAA, in Box 4, Folder 23, Jenkins Papers.

27. JHJ, "Rare Books and the Law," typescript of undated talk, Box 3, Folder 29, Jenkins Papers.

28. I take the expression from Willa Cather's *Death Comes for the Archbishop*. Literally the phrase refers to the whipping of cats and can mean someone sent to do dirty work. It also has connotations of the more commonplace herding of cats and the difficulty of training cats to do anything.

29. Interview with Victoria Dailey, February 9, 2018, Pasadena, Calif.

30. Telephone interview with T. Michael Parrish, October 24, 2017.

31. Interview with Kevin MacDonnell, February 23, 2018.

32. Trillin, "Knowing Johnny Jenkins," 84.

33. Interview with William Reese, November 13, 2017.

34. Henry R. Wagner, *The Plains and the Rockies: A Bibliography of Original Narratives of Travel and Adventure, 1800–1865*, 3d ed., revised by Charles L. Camp (Columbus, Ohio: Long's College Book Company, 1953). The bibliography was updated in 1982. See Henry R. Wagner & Charles L. Camp, *The Plains and the Rockies:*

A Critical Bibliography of Exploration, Adventure and Travel in the American West, 1800–1865, 4th ed., edited by Robert L. Becker (San Francisco: John Howell–Books, 1982).

35. Klaus W. Werner invoices from John Howell–Books (1968–71) and the Jenkins Company (1975), collection of the author. Werner spent over $18,000 in that first visit purchasing rare books from the Eberstadt Collection.

36. Calvin Trillin astutely noted that Jenkins had "an abiding interest in quantity" rather than quality. Trillin, "Knowing Johnny Jenkins," 84.

37. Interview with William Reese, February 11, 2018.

38. JHJ, "The Adventure of Americana," unpublished typescript, n.d., circa late 1970s, Box 3, Folder 14, Jenkins Papers.

39. Ibid.

40. Jon Ford, "Hill Fund Gets $300,000," *Austin American-Statesman*, September 16, 1977, F18.

41. Jenkins Company invoice, May 27, 1979, Box 9, Folder 54, Jenkins Papers.

42. JHJ to Henry Miller, August 7, 1972; Henry Miller to JHJ, August 21, 1972; and JHJ to Henry Miller, September 14, 1982, Box 10, Folder 31, Jenkins Papers.

43. Henry Miller to JHJ, January 31, 1973, Box 10, Folder 31, Jenkins Papers.

44. Joyce Howard, ed., *Letters from Henry Miller to Hoki Tokuda Miller* (New York: Freundlich Press, 1986).

45. An uncorrected copy of this catalogue is in the collection of Kevin MacDonnell, Austin, Tex.

46. Emily Grover, "Roberts, Francis Warren," *Texas State Historical Association*, https://tshaonline.org/handbook/online/articles/frogr (accessed April 11, 2018).

47. Jenkins Company check no. 2363 to Warren Roberts for $7,500.00, January 9, 1978, Box 7, Folder 17, Jenkins Papers.

48. Email to author from Kenneth Rendell, October 4, 2017.

49. Donald C. Dickinson, "Feldman, Lew David (1906–1976)," in *Dictionary of American Antiquarian Bookdealers* (Westport, Conn.: Greenwood Press, 1998), 65–66.

50. Email to author from Kenneth Rendell, June 11, 2018.

51. This story was told by Clark to Kevin MacDonnell while they were driving to a library reception sometime after the incident. Email from Kevin MacDonnell to the author, July 1, 2018.

52. Gayle Reaves, "Chaos Charged: UT Audit Blasts HRC Operations," *Austin American Statesman*, December 16, 1978, A1, A8.

53. Email to author from Kenneth Rendell, October 4, 2017.

54. Dorman Winfrey to JHJ, October 8, 1970, Box 11, Folder 9, Jenkins Papers.

55. Ralph W. Yarborough to JHJ, undated note, Box 12, Folder 40, Jenkins Papers.

56. I know from experience on my first book, *Edward Eberstadt and Sons*, that Reese is a very close reader of manuscripts, and my book was far better for his extensive corrections and suggestions.

57. William S. Reese, "Review of John H Jenkins, *Basic Texas Books: An Annotated Bibliography of Selected Works for a Research Library*," *Papers of the Bibliographical Society of America* 79, no. 1 (1985): 141.

58. Interview with Kevin MacDonnell, February 23, 2018.

59. Collection of Robert H. Rubin, Brookline, Mass.

60. Interview with Ron Tyler, November 3, 2017, San Diego, Calif.

61. JHJ, "The Texas Revolution: The Need for Solid Research and a New Interpretation," unpublished typescript of a talk ca. 1979, Box 4, Folder 6, Jenkins Papers.

62. William C. Griggs to Archie McDonald, July 22, 1982, Box 9, Folder 37, Jenkins Papers.

63. JHJ to William Griggs, July 20, 1982, Box 9, Folder 37, Jenkins Papers.

64. JHJ to David Weber, Chair, Department of History, SMU, September 16, 1983, Box 12, Folder 6, Jenkins Papers.

65. Dan K. Utley, ed., *Archie P. McDonald: A Life in Texas History* (College Station: Texas A&M University Press, 2016).

66. Douglas Martin, "Amarillo Slim, Gambler with a Sly Wit, Dies at 83," *New York Times*, May 1, 2012, 16.

67. Ibid. The phrase "native Texan cornpone patois" is from Martin.

68. See Doug J. Swanson, *Blood Aces: The Wild Ride of Benny Binion, the Texas Gangster Who Created Vegas Poker* (New York: Penguin Books, 2014).

69. Michael Kaplan, "John Jenkins," unpublished typescript written October 1988, originally submitted to *GQ Magazine*, used by permission of the author, obtained via email April 17, 2018, collection of the author.

70. Richard Cornett, "Poker Unwinds Austin Squatty," *Las Vegas Review-Journal*, April 29, 1984, 2B–3B.

71. Email from Kevin MacDonnell to the author, August 27, 2018. MacDonnell worked for Jenkins from 1980 to 1986 and often witnessed this practice.

72. JHJ, "Rare Books and the Future," typescript of talk given to the Bridwell Library, Southern Methodist University, November 12,

1984, Box 4, Folder 1, Jenkins Papers. The same talk was given to the East Texas Historical Association in Kilgore, Tex., on February 23, 1985; to the University of Colorado, Boulder, on March 31, 1985; to the St. Louis Mercantile Library, on November 7, 1985; and to the Texas Library Association meeting in Fort Worth, April 9, 1986.

73. Interview with J. P. Bryan Jr., February 22, 2018.

74. JHJ to L. R. French Jr., n.d. [must be about July 5, 1987; French received the letter on July 7, 1987], Box 5, Folder 27, Jenkins Papers.

75. Interview with Kevin MacDonnell, January 11, 2018.

76. J. P. Bryan Jr. to JHJ, August 11, 1983, Box 9, Folder 15, Jenkins Papers.

77. JHJ to L. R. French Jr., August 14, 1984, Box 5, Folder 26, Jenkins Papers.

78. L. R. French Jr. to JHJ, September 5, 1984, Box 5, Folder 26, Jenkins Papers.

79. Jenkins's career poker tournament winnings can be found at the *Hendon Mob Poker Database*, https://pokerdb.thehendonmob.com (accessed April 2018).

80. "Squatty Strikes It Rich: Jenkins Aims for Win," *Poker Player*, 1984, 10.

81. Kaplan, "John Jenkins," October 1988 manuscript, collection of the author.

82. "Squatty Strikes It Rich," 10.

83. Kaplan, "John Jenkins," October 1988 manuscript, collection of the author.

84. Darrell Huff, *How to Take a Chance* (New York: W. W. Norton, 1959), 28–29.

85. JHJ to L. R. French Jr., January 4, 1985, Box 5, Folder 26, Jenkins Papers.

86. JHJ to Lindley Eberstadt, March 20, 1978; and Lindley Eberstadt to JHJ, undated handwritten reply on the March 20, 1978, letter, Box 9, Folder 29, Jenkins Papers.

87. Sotheby's, *Fine Printed and Manuscript Americana, including Books from the Library of Lindley Eberstadt* (New York, May 1, 1985). Lindley's library occupied Lots 140–231 in the sale.

88. Jenkins did buy Lot 142, a presentation copy of Stephen F. Austin's 1835 *Exposición al Público sobre Los Asuntos de Tejas*, for $12,000 for a customer (but not for inventory).

89. The information in this paragraph is drawn from conversations about that sale with Reese and other dealers over the years and from a marked copy of the auction catalogue (which shows prices paid and the purchasers) in the author's possession.

90. Interview with David Grossblatt, January 10, 2018, Dallas, Tex.

91. Email from Kevin MacDonnell, January 18, 2018. MacDonnell was one of the Jenkins employees who packed the books up that day in Dallas.

92. Kevin MacDonnell to David Farmer, August 29, 1991, collection of Kevin MacDonnell, Austin, Tex.

93. Interview with Michael Heaston, September 12, 2017.

94. Austin Fire Department, "Incident Report for Fire at 7111 South IH-35, December 24, 1985, 6 p.m.," collection of Kevin Mac-Donnell, Austin, Tex.

95. Kent Biffle, "Fire at Publishing House Is Untold Disaster for Texas," *Dallas Morning News*, January 5, 1986, 47A.

96. JHJ, Untitled talk on 4 x 6 notecards, ca. 1986, Box 3, Folder 11, Jenkins Papers. The quote also appears on page 1 of the Jenkins Company Catalogue 187, probably issued just a couple of months after the fire in early 1986. Ironically, or not, the catalogue shows the "fire truck" illustration from Ray Bradbury's *Fahrenheit 451*. In that novel, the fire truck carried kerosene and was called a salamander.

97. Joseph D. Porter, Investigator, "Texas State Fire Marshal Confidential Investigation Report, Case Number 71-SEP-053-S," December 29, 1987, collection of Kevin MacDonnell, Austin, Tex.

98. Biffle, "Fire at Publishing House," 47A. William MacKinnon was a collector living in Michigan who called the Jenkins Company on Christmas Day 1985, intending to leave an order on the telephone message machine. Maureen Jenkins answered the phone, told him about the fire and that she was standing in the shop's smoldering ashes. MacKinnon expressed his regrets for their misfortune and apologized. She said that it could have been worse, but that "all the good stuff" was in the fireproof vault. William MacKinnon, email to author, January 30, 2019.

99. This presentation copy apparently came from Dorman David; see C. Dorman David, *Catalogue 6*, item 59.

100. Interview with Kevin MacDonnell, Austin, January 11, 2018 (as told to Kevin by Ben Pingenot).

101. L. R. French Jr., to JHJ, June 26, 1986, Box 5, Folder 26, Jenkins Papers.

102. See "Statement of Thomas Michael Parrish, 6322 Bon Terra, Austin, Tex., 78731, made to Special Agent Charles E. Meyer, Bureau of Alcohol, Tobacco and Firearms, in the presence of State Fire Investigator Joey Porter, in Austin, Texas on November 5, 1987":

"During these trips to Nevada, he is absent from the business from about two to four weeks at a time [3–4 times per year]." Copy obtained through FOIA, collection of Kevin MacDonnell, Austin, Tex. See also *Texas State Fire Marshal Confidential Supplemental Report*, November 10, 1987, by Joseph D. Porter: "Jose Alvarez also explained that Mr. Jenkins was a professional gambler who would spend two to four weeks, three to four times a year, in Las Vegas." Copy obtained through FOIA, collection of Kevin MacDonnell, Austin, Tex.

103. Interview with Kevin MacDonnell, January 11, 2018.

104. Kent Biffle, "The King of Texas Books," *Dallas Morning News*, no date, but circa 1983, 6G.

105. Curtis, "Forgery, Texas Style," 184–85.

106. Interview with Kevin MacDonnell, January 11, 2018.

107. The following are sales totals from the Jenkins Company invoices to French for each year: 1984, $114,515; 1985, $236,450; 1986, $85,860; 1987, $119,390; Total $556,215. The invoices are in Box 5, Folder 26, Jenkins Papers.

108. The figures are found in a letter from John Pruitt, Attorney at Law, Route 2, Box 38, Manor, Tex., to Boldrick and Clifton, Attorneys at Law, Midland, Tex. [ca. February 4, 1989], Box 5, Folder 27, Jenkins Papers.

109. Kevin MacDonnell to David Farmer, August 29, 1991.

110. Ibid. The letter from Jenkins's attorney, John Pruitt, to French's attorneys, Boldrick and Clifton, in early February 1989 has the actual figures of $327,540.

111. Ibid.

112. L. R. French Jr. to Kevin MacDonnell, July 13, 1987, collection of Kevin MacDonnell, Austin, Tex.

113. JHJ to L.R. French Jr., about July 5, 1987, collection of Kevin MacDonnell, Austin, Tex.

114. Groucho Marx, quoted in Evan Esar, *20,000 Quips and Quotes: A Treasury of Witty Remarks, Comic Proverbs, Wisecracks, and Epigrams* (New York: Barnes and Noble, 1995), 230.

115. John Harris, "Publishing Company Hit by Fire," *Austin American-Statesman*, September 29, 1987, B-4.

116. Interview with Kevin MacDonnell, January 11, 2018; interview with former Manchaca fire captain Jeff Reeves, June 16, 2018, Austin, Tex.

117. JHJ to his parents, February 6, 1959, Box 2, Folder 2, Jenkins Papers.

Chapter 5

1. Joe Vargo, "Book Dealer Leaves Lenders Unpaid after Mysterious Demise," *Austin American-Statesman*, April 20, 1989, A1, A8; see also Ed Todd, "Judge Rules against FDIC: Millions in Loans at Stake," *Fort Worth Star-Telegram*, February 20, 1986, 1A–2A.
2. Don M. Lyda to Huffman Baines Jr., March 17, 1976, Box 5, Folder 7, Jenkins Papers: "Although I have never met John Jenkins, I have heard and read many fine things about him. Undoubtedly he will make an outstanding contribution to North Austin State Bank. Huff, I commend you on the very important part which you had in placing this outstanding individual on our board."
3. Certificate of authenticity, dated July 7, 1976, signed by William Simpson, Box 11, Folder 10, Jenkins Papers. Were these Persian rugs actually commissioned by the King Ranch but never collected from customs? Did it matter once Jenkins had the certificate of authenticity? Jenkins always preferred a good story to the truth.
4. Telephone interview with Sheri Tomasulo, October 2017.
5. Bureau of Alcohol, Tobacco, and Firearms (hereafter ATF), *Report of Investigation (Criminal Enforcement)*, October 28, 1987, suspect number 53110-88-1006 W. This and all ATF reports cited in this chapter were obtained through FOIA and are in the collection of Kevin MacDonnell, Austin, Tex. Today the name of the agency is the Bureau of Alcohol, Tobacco, Firearms and Explosives, but the abbreviation ATF is still used by the Bureau.
6. Email note from Tom Taylor to the author, August 25, 2018.
7. When I was a beginning antiquarian bookseller in 1992, I paid a courtesy visit to Ray Walton's home. He held court in his Barcalounger with a pizza box off to one side. His parting words of wisdom to me were that I could become a very good scout for him.
8. Lisa Belkin, "Lone Star Fakes: Forged Historical Documents Were Big Business in Texas until Arson and Murder Got in the Way," *New York Times Magazine*, December 10, 1989, 68.
9. W. Thomas Taylor, *Alone in the Vault: An Initiation into Bibliophilic Mysteries* (Dallas, Tex.: DeGolyer Library, 2009), [8].
10. Everitt, *Adventures of a Treasure Hunter*, 206.
11. Taylor, *Alone in the Vault*, [10].
12. Sotheby Parke-Bernet. *The Celebrated Collection of Americana Formed by the Late Thomas Winthrop Streeter* (New York, 1966), Lot 2; *Fine Books and Manuscripts Featuring Exploration and Travel* (New York: Bonham's, 2017), Lot 2.

13. The following Binion's account is drawn from Kaplan, "John Jenkins," October 1988 manuscript, 1–2, collection of the author.

14. ATF, *Report of Investigation (Criminal Enforcement)*, December 1, 1987, suspect number 53110-88-1006 W.

15. "Statement of Thomas Michael Parrish, 6322 Bon Terra, Austin, Texas, 78731, made to Special Agent Charles E. Meyer, Bureau of Alcohol, Tobacco and Firearms, in the presence of State Fire Investigator Joey Porter, in Austin, Texas on November 5, 1987," collection of Kevin MacDonnell, Austin, Tex.

16. *Texas State Fire Marshal Confidential Supplemental Report*, November 10, 1987, by Joseph D. Porter. Copy obtained through FOIA, collection of Kevin MacDonnell, Austin, Tex.

17. ATF, *Report of Investigation (Criminal Enforcement)*, February 11, 1988, suspect number 53110-88-1006 W. The lie detector examination was administered on February 2, 1988.

18. This section based on Taylor, *Texfake*, 4–6, and Belkin, "Lone Star Fakes," 70–72, along with sources cited below.

19. See Dorothy Sloan Rare Books, *Auction 15: The Daniel G. Volkmann, Jr., Collection of Fine Californiana*, February 16, 2005, Lot 111, "William B. Ide Manuscript Proclamation, June 15, 1846."

20. Russ Pate, "The City: The Inner Sanctum," *D Magazine*, March 1996.

21. *Texas Telegraph and Register* (San Felipe de Austin, Tex.), March 12, 1836, cited in Taylor, *Texfake*, 13.

22. Eric Korn reviewed the antiquarian book trade for the *Times Literary Supplement* and first used this delightful word to describe Jenkins's bluffs.

23. John Lukacs, "Poker and the American Character," *Horizon* 5, no. 8 (November 1963).

24. The Omaha hand with Pearson is described in Pete Peters, "Favorite Poker Stories," *Gambler's Times*, n.d, n.p. Copy in collection of the author, Santa Fe, N.Mex.

25. Elkan Allan, "Walter 'Puggy' Pearson," *Guardian*, April 17, 2006.

26. Joseph D. Porter, *Texas State Fire Marshal Confidential Supplemental Report*, December 29, 1987. Copy obtained through FOIA, collection of Kevin MacDonnell, Austin, Tex.

27. Belkin, "Lone Star Fakes," 66.

28. Anonymous, "Austin Column," *Austin Statesman*, June 22, 1967, A8.

29. Brad Buchholz, "A Name for Himself: Publisher Makes a Kind of Peace with His Orphan Past," *Austin American-Statesman*, January 13, 2008, J3.

30. Taylor, *Texfake*, 3.
31. On Taylor and Holman's investigation of this document, see Belkin, "Lone Star Fakes," 66.
32. For this account of the Binion game, see Kaplan, "John Jenkins," October 1988 manuscript, 5–14, collection of the author.
33. Belkin, "Lone Star Fakes," 72, describes Taylor's approach to examining the documents.
34. Taylor, *Texfake*,14–15. The original bill from the printers has been lost, but the Texas historian and bibliographer E. W. Winkler copied the bill in pencil on a photostatic copy of the Lamar copy of the Texas Declaration of Independence.
35. Taylor, *Texfake*, 43. Taylor later purchased this genuine copy and sold it to Dr. Paul Burns, a collector in Austin.
36. Hewett, "Forgeries and Fraud in Texas," 29A–30A.
37. Ibid.
38. Taylor, *Texfake*, 49.
39. Belkin, "Lone Star Fakes," 74.
40. Gregory Curtis was the first to speculate on Dorman David's motivations for revenge; see Curtis, "Forgery, Texas Style," 184–85.
41. Taylor, *Texfake*, 48–49.
42. The following account of Larson's participation is drawn from an email from Jennifer Larson to the author, April 2, 2018, and Jennifer Larson, notebook entry for January 21, 1988, collection of Jennifer Larson, Rochester, N.Y., along with other cited sources.
43. Taylor, *Texfake*, 60.
44. ATF, *Report of Investigation (Criminal Enforcement)*, February 11, 1988, suspect number 53110-88-1006 W.
45. See the *Telegraph and Texas Register*, December 17, 1836, where the printers complain about the effect of cold weather: "What will the public think of the devils of the press, when the very paper wetted down for publication, has been frozen?" Quoted in Taylor, *Texfake*, 26.
46. Taylor, *Texfake*, 46.
47. Ibid., 60–61, summarizes this March 7, 1988, letter to William Buck, a copy of which is found in the DeGolyer Library at Southern Methodist University, Dallas, Tex.
48. Peter Alson's report of this trip, cited in this section, is "The Score: The Real Deal: Sharks and Minnows at the Super Bowl of Poker," *Village Voice* 33, no. 15 (April 1988): 162–64.
49. Taylor, *Texfake*, 67.
50. Curtis, "Forgery Texas Style," 179.

51. Taylor, *Texfake*, 67.
52. Monty Jones, "Fake! Bogus Papers Sold as Real Texana," *Austin American-Statesman*, April 9, 1988, A1.
53. For Jenkins's self-characterizations in this section, see Kaplan, "John Jenkins," October 1988 manuscript, 8–9, collection of the author.
54. ATF, *Report of Investigation (Criminal Enforcement)*, August 2, 1988, suspect number 53110-88-1006 W. William "Bill" Krumpack was the Travis County special investigator who informed the ATF of this on July 8, 1988.
55. ATF, *Report of Investigation (Criminal Enforcement)*, April 14, 1988, suspect number 53110-88-1006 W: "Forensic Chemist Bill Dietz concluded that a light range distillate (alcohol or acetone) was found in a ball of cotton string which was discovered in the mail room."
56. ATF, *Report of Investigation (Criminal Enforcement)*, May 20, 1988, suspect number 53110-88-1006 W.
57. ATF, *Report of Investigation (Criminal Enforcement)*, June 15 and 17, 1988, suspect number 53110-88-1006 W.
58. Ibid.
59. Interview with J. P. Bryan Jr., February 22, 2018.
60. ATF, *Report of Investigation (Criminal Enforcement)*, September 23 and October 18, 1988, suspect number 53110-88-1006 W.
61. Don E. Carleton, Director, Barker Texas History Center, October 24, 1988 to JHJ, Box 4, Folder 24, Jenkins Papers.
62. Jenkins Company to ABAA, September, 1988, Box 9, Folder 2, Jenkins Papers.
63. Interview with Mary Gilliam, February 9, 2018, Pasadena, Calif.
64. Ibid.
65. JHJ to Antiquarian Booksellers' Association of America Board of Governors, November 2, 1988, Box 4, Folder 24, Jenkins Papers.
66. Hewett, "Forgeries and Fraud in Texas," 29A–30A.
67. Interview with J. P. Bryan Jr., February 22, 2018; also, Kevin Mac-Donnell had a phone conversation with Ben Pingenot on May 13, 1989, in which Jenkins had worried about the exposure of the *Maine Antique Digest* article about the forgeries and mentioned taking his life to Pingenot.
68. Stutz and Henneberger, "Rare Book Dealer Found Shot," 7A.
69. ATF, *Report of Investigation (Criminal Enforcement)*, January 6, 1989, suspect number 53110-88-1006 W.
70. ATF, *Report of Investigation (Criminal Enforcement)*, February 16, 1989, suspect number 53110-88-1006 W.

71. Kevin MacDonnell to David Farmer, August 29, 1991, collection of Kevin MacDonnell, Austin, Tex.

72. A list of the fake broadsides sold to French is found in Box 5, Folder 27, Jenkins Papers.

73. Law Offices of Boldrick and Clifton to JHJ, Midland, Tex., January 18, 1989, Box 5, Folder 27, Jenkins Papers.

74. John Pruitt, Attorney at Law, Route 2, Box 38, Manor, Tex., to Boldrick and Clifton, Attorneys at Law, Midland, Tex., circa February 4, 1989, Box 5, Folder 27, Jenkins Papers.

75. Smith, "Super Bowl of Poker Exceeds Expectations," B7.

76. Interview with William Reese, February 11, 2018.

77. ATF, *Report of Investigation (Criminal Enforcement)*, March 14, 1989, suspect number 53110-88-1006 W; Texas State Fire Marshal, [untitled Report on Jenkins fire investigation], n.d., but circa March 1989. Copy obtained through FOIA, collection of Kevin MacDonnell, Austin, Tex.

78. "George A. Stephen Obituary," *Austin American-Statesman*, May 7, 2006, 31.

79. Texas State Fire Marshal, [untitled Report on Jenkins fire investigation], n.d., but circa March 1989. Copy obtained through FOIA, collection of Kevin MacDonnell, Austin, Tex.

80. David Hewett, "John Jenkins Shot—Murder or Suicide?" *Maine Antique Digest*, June 1989, 10A.

81. Kevin MacDonnell, quoted in Cheshire, "Dealer in Rare Books," 24.

82. ATF, *Report of Investigation (Criminal Enforcement)*, May 2, 1989, suspect number 53110-88-1006 W: "There was sufficient evidence to indict Jenkins for the arsons, and it would not be necessary to call Jenkins before the Grand Jury." Even though this report was dated May 2, it was a summary of decisions reached in April about the Jenkins investigation.

83. Telephone interview with T. Michael Parrish, October 24, 2017.

84. Interview with Kenneth Kesselus, February 21, 2018.

85. Ibid.

86. Vargo and Jones, "Sheriff Calls Death 'Bona Fide Mystery,'" A1, A6.

87. Interview with J .P. Bryan Jr., February 22, 2018.

88. Hans Breiter, et al., "Functional Imaging of Neural Responses to Expectancy and Experience of Monetary Gains and Losses," *Neuron* 30, no. 2 (May 2001): 619–39; see also Johannes Hewig, et al., "Hypersensitivity to Rewards in Gamblers," Biological Psychiatry 67, no. 8 (April 2010): 781–83.

89. See, for example, Cornett, "Poker Unwinds Austin Squatty," 3B.

90. The two friends were Kenneth Rendell, who asked Benny Binion in 1989 if the mob had anything to do with Jenkins's death because of gambling debts (interview at Boston, November 10, 2017); and J. P. Bryan Jr., interview at Galveston, Tex., February 21, 2018. Benny Binion died December 25, 1989.

Epilogue

1. See "Flow Rates," *Bastrop River Company*, www.bastropriverco.com /flow-rates.html (accessed January, 2018).
2. Kaye Freeman's account drawn from my interview with her, February 20, 2018, near Waco, Tex.
3. Weather observations confirmed from *Wunderground.com* data for Austin, Tex., for April 16, 1989.
4. John L. Hunsucker and Scott J. Davison, "Time Required for a Drowning Victim to Reach Bottom," *Journal of Search and Rescue* 1, no. 1 (1993): 19–28. The usual sink time for an adult victim is five to ten seconds.
5. The following comments from Con Keirsey drawn from my interview with him, February 21, 2018, Red Rock, Tex.
6. Interview with Kevin MacDonnell, Austin, Tex., January 11, 2018; Kevin was told this by Joseph D. Porter, the Texas state fire investigator.
7. Carlos Vidal Greth and Joe Vargo, "Book Dealer's Life Read Like a Bestseller," *Austin American-Statesman*, April 30, 1989, A1, A8–A9.
8. Mary Lenz, "Authority to Lower River in Hunt for Missing Gun," *Houston Post*, April 20, 1989, 1.
9. McKinney, "Wheeler-Dealer's Death Ruled Homicide," A1, A16.
10. Interview with Kenneth Kesselus, February 21, 2018.
11. Woolley, "Enigmatic Ending," 1A, 15A; McKinney, "Wheeler-Dealer's Death Ruled Homicide," A1, A16.
12. Roberto J. Bayardo, M.D., "Medical Examiner's Report for John H. Jenkins," Office of the Medical Examiner of Travis County, April 24, 1989, collection of Kevin MacDonnell, Austin, Tex.
13. Hugh E. Berryman, O. C. Smith, and Steven A. Symes, "Diameter of Cranial Gunshot Wounds as a Function of Bullet Caliber," *Journal of Forensic Sciences* 40, no. 5 (September 1995): 751–54.
14. Woolley, "Enigmatic Ending," 1A, 15A.
15. Ibid.
16. Interview with Con Keirsey, February 21, 2018.
17. Hewett, "John Jenkins Shot—Murder or Suicide?," 10A. The employee was Dorothy Sloan: "John Jenkins was an optimist. No

matter how bad the circumstances, he always believed he'd weather the storm." Another employee (Kevin MacDonnell), however, recalled that at work one day Jenkins came out after lunch holding a Ludlum thriller novel, talking about how to make a suicide actually seem like a murder (interview with Kevin MacDonnell, January 11, 2018). I was unable to find the Ludlum plot mentioned by Kevin, but there is at least one known plot in literature of hiding a gun to make a suicide look like murder. In Arthur Conan Doyle's short story "The Problem of Thor Bridge," a wife, jealous of another woman's relationship with her husband, frames the woman for her death by shooting herself on a bridge and having the gun tied to a rock which afterward falls in the river, sinking the gun.

18. Interview with J. P. Bryan Jr., February 22, 2018.

19. Ibid. Ironically, Jenkins's life insurance company tried to deny payment to his widow. See Berta Delgado, "Collector's Widow Sues for Insurance," *Austin American-Statesman*, August 26, 1989, B1. See Cheshire, "Dealer in Rare Books," 24: "Jenkins' attorney, John Pruitt, said there was enough life insurance, all right, enough to pull Jenkins' diminished empire out of debt and provide for his wife Maureen and his teen-age son, but suicide didn't figure into it."

20. JHJ to Robert A. Venable, n.d., page 2 only, Box 12, Folder 1, Jenkins Papers.

21. The Brazil International Extradition Treaty with the United States was signed on January 13, 1961, and went into effect on December 17, 1964.

22. "Donald Burt Yarbrough (b. 1941), *Tarlton Law Library*, http://tarlton.law.utexas.edu/justices/spct/yarbrough.html (accessed May 30, 2019). Yarbrough died in Florida in 2017.

23. JHJ to Venable letter is a photocopy, but stapled to it in the archives is the original note card with Jenkins's cursive handwriting in blue ink. Robert A. Venable died in 1996 in Dallas, and I was unable to find his papers.

24. Telephone interview with Sheri Tomasulo, October 2017.

25. Interview with Con Keirsey, February 21, 2018.

26. Interview with J. P. Bryan Jr., February 22, 2018.

27. JHJ personal diary, Thursday, January 1, 1959, Box 28, Folder 7, Jenkins Papers.

28. Cheshire, "Dealer in Rare Books," 21, 24.

29. Interview with Kenneth Rendell, November 10, 2017.

30. Interview with Kenneth Kesselus, February 21, 2018.

31. JHJ, "Books Read in 1961," Box 2, Folder 18, Jenkins Papers.

32. James Grizzard was a Houston collector who provided the funding for an inventory of stolen documents at the Texas state archives in 1991: "Missing Materials from the Texas State Archives," *Texas State Library and Archives Commission*, www.tsl.texas.gov/arc /missingintro.html (accessed February 26, 2019).

33. The Texas state archives keeps an online list of stolen and missing documents at "Missing Materials from the Texas State Archives, December 12, 2008," *Texas State Library and Archives Commission*, www.tsl.texas.gov/sites/default/files/public/tslac/arc/missinglist .pdf (accessed February 26, 2019).

34. Dorothy Sloan Rare Books, *Catalogue 6* (Austin, 1989), item 56.

35. Sotheby's, *Fine Books and Manuscripts: Texas Independence Collection* (New York: June 18, 2004), Lot 24. The Declaration realized $764,000.

36. Sotheby's, *Texas Independence Collection*, Lot 39, realizing $299,200.

37. Interview with William Reese, September 29, 2017, New Haven, Conn.

38. Patrick J. Geary, *Furta Sacra: Thefts of Relics in the Central Middle Ages* (Princeton, N.J.: Princeton University Press, 2011), 45.

39. Kaplan, "John Jenkins," October 1988 manuscript, 13, collection of the author.

40. John Holmes Jenkins, ed., *Recollections of Early Texas: The Memoirs of John Holland Jenkins* (Austin: University of Texas Press, 2017), 20–21.

41. Thomas W. Cutrer, "Jenkins, John Holland," *Handbook of Texas Online* (accessed February 15, 2018); see also "The Bastrop Tragedy," *Austin Statesman* 20, no. 80 (November 12, 1890), 1.

42. Kevin MacDonnell visited the Bastrop Couny sheriff's office in 1992 and took notes on the Jenkins investigation file (before the file was destroyed by the county); collection of Kevin MacDonnell, Austin, Tex.

43. Wead, *All the Presidents' Children*, 107.

Bibliography

Archival Sources

Ginsberg, Michael. Private Collection, North Easton, Massachusetts
Heaston, Michael. Private Collection, Wichita, Kansas
Jenkins, John Holland. Papers. DeGolyer Library, Southern Methodist University, Dallas, Texas
Larson, Jennifer. Private Collection, Rochester, New York
MacDonnell, Kevin. Private Collection, Austin, Texas
Reese, William. Private Collection, New Haven, Connecticut
Rubin, Robert H. Private Collection, Brookline, Massachusetts
Streeter, Thomas W. Papers. American Antiquarian Society, Worcester, Massachusetts
Vinson, Michael. Private Collection, Santa Fe, New Mexico

Published Sources

Adams, Don. "New Book Publishing Firm Here Centers on the Southwest." *Austin American-Statesman*, May 12, 1966, 29.
Anderson Galleries. *The Library of the Late H. Buxton Forman*. New York, October 4–7, 1920.
Akers, Robert W. "It's Like This." *Beaumont Enterprise*, September 8, 1960, 8.
Allan, Elkan. "Walter 'Puggy' Pearson." *Guardian* (London), April 17, 2006.
Alson, Peter. "The Score: The Real Deal: Sharks and Minnows at the Super Bowl of Poker." *Village Voice* 33, no. 15 (April 1988): 156–64.
"Austin Column." *Austin Statesman*, June 22, 1967, A8.
Barker, Eugene C., ed. *The Austin Papers October, 1834–January, 1837.* Vol. 3. Austin: University of Texas Press, 1926.

Barker, Nicholas, John Collins, and John Carter. *A Sequel to an Enquiry into the Nature of Certain Nineteenth Century Pamphlets by John Carter and Graham Pollard: The Forgeries of H. Buxton Forman and T. J. Wise Re-examined*. London: Scolar Press, 1983.

"The Bastrop Tragedy." *Austin Statesman*, November 12, 1890, 1.

Beach, Patrick. "Following the Paper Trail." *Austin American-Statesman*, April 7, 1998, E1, E8.

Belkin, Lisa. "Lone Star Fakes: Forged Historical Documents Were Big Business in Texas until Arson and Murder Got in the Way." *New York Times Magazine*, December 10, 1989, 66–76.

Berryman, Hugh E., O. C. Smith, and Steven A. Symes. "Diameter of Cranial Gunshot Wounds as a Function of Bullet Caliber." *Journal of Forensic Sciences* 40, no. 5 (September 1995): 751–54.

Besaw, Larry. "Austin Rare Book Dealer Recovers Missing Goods." *Austin American-Statesman*, November 20, 1979, 19.

Biffle, Kent. "Fire at Publishing House Is Untold Disaster for Texas." *Dallas Morning News*, January 5, 1986, 47A.

———. "The King of Texas Books." *Dallas Morning News*, n.d. [circa 1983], 6G.

"Body Found in Colorado River near Bastrop." *Austin American-Statesman*, April 17, 1989, 3.

Bonham's. *Fine Books and Manuscripts Featuring Exploration and Travel*. New York, 2017.

Breiter, Hans, Itzhak Aharon, Daniel Kahneman, Anders Dale, and Peter Shizgal. "Functional Imaging of Neural Responses to Expectancy and Experience of Monetary Gains and Losses." *Neuron* 30, no. 2 (May 2001): 619–39.

Bryan, J. P., Jr., "Collections and Collecting." *Proceedings of the Philosophical Society of Texas* (2003). www.pstx.org/index.php?option=com _content&view=article&id=293:collections-and-collecting&catid=24 &Itemid=189.

Buchholz, Brad. "A Name for Himself: Publisher Makes a Kind of Peace with His Orphan Past." *Austin American-Statesman*, January 13, 2008, J3.

Caro, Robert A. "The Transition: Lyndon Johnson and the Events in Dallas." *New Yorker*, April 2, 2012, 32–49.

———. *The Years of Lyndon Johnson: Means of Ascent*. New York: Vintage Books, 1991.

Carter, John, and Graham Pollard. *An Inquiry into the Nature of Certain Nineteenth Century Pamphlets*. London: Constable, 1934.

Charles Hamilton Autographs. *Auction. October 10th*. New York, 1974.

Cheshire, Ashley. "A Dealer in Rare Books, He Lived with Flair and Died in Mystery." *Fort Worth Star-Telegram*, April 23, 1989, 21, 24.

Cisneros, Maria Luisa. "Americana: Ex-libris." *Time*, February 23, 1970, 19.

Conwell, Kent. "Business Woman Rita Ainsworth Was the Madam with the Heart of Gold." *Beaumont Enterprise*, September 20, 2006. https:// beaumontenterprise.com/news/article/Business-woman-Rita -Ainsworth-was-the-madam-with-770714.php.

Cornett, Richard. "Poker Unwinds Austin Squatty." *Las Vegas Review-Journal*, April 29, 1984, 2B–3B.

Cox, Mike. "Texfake Exposes Theft, Forgery of Rare Documents." *Austin American-Statesman*, October 13, 1991, H8.

———. "Word Wildcatter Leaves Legend: Writer-Publisher Pumped Texas History, Lore to Produce Rich Bounty." *Austin American-Statesman*, April 23, 1989, D4.

Crumbaker, Marge. "Texana Sale Nets $23,000." *Houston Post*, June 24, 1971, 6.

Curtis, Gregory. "Forgery Texas Style: The Dealers Who Buy and Sell Historic Texas Documents Move in a World of Big Money, Big Egos and Big Mistakes." *Texas Monthly Magazine*, March 1989, 180.

Cutrer, Thomas W. "Jenkins, John Holland." *Handbook of Texas Online*. https://tshaonline.org/handbook/online/articles/fje05

David, C. Dorman. *Catalogue 6*. Houston, n.d. [ca. 1960s].

———. *Sale of Rare Texas Historical Manuscripts and Autograph Materials Being Letters, Documents, and Broadsides from the Collection of C. Dorman David. To Be Sold to the Highest Bidder at the Warwick Hotel, Houston, Fontaine Ballroom, June 22, 1971*. Houston, 1971.

David, C. Dorman, and John J. Jenkins. *Joint Catalogue, Texana: Manuscripts, Autographs, Documents, Offered for Sale by C. Dorman David and John H. Jenkins*. Austin, ca. 1963.

"Death Notice, Carolyn Manovill." *New York Times*, March 20, 2001, A23.

Delgado, Berta. "Collector's Widow Sues for Insurance." *Austin American-Statesman*, August 26, 1989, B1.

Dickinson, Donald C. *Dictionary of American Antiquarian Bookdealers*. Westport, Conn.: Greenwood Press, 1998.

———. *Dictionary of American Book Collectors*. Westport, Conn.: Greenwood Press, 1986.

Dobie, J. Frank. "Foreword." In *Recollections of Early Texas: The Memoirs of John Holland Jenkins*, edited by John Holmes Jenkins III, ix–xiv. Austin: University of Texas Press, 1958.

Dorothy Sloan Rare Books. *Auction 15: The Daniel G. Volkmann, Jr., Collection of Fine Californiana.* Austin, 2005.

———. *Auction 23 Americana: High Spots of Texas, the West, Mexico and the Borderlands.* Austin, 2013.

———. *Catalogue 6.* Austin, 1989.

"Drama in a Texas Library." *Centre Daily Times*, n.d. [circa August 1971], 4.

Duncan, Dawson. "Yarborough Snubs LBJ: Motorcade Rides." *Dallas Morning News*, November 22, 1963, 1.

Eberstadt, Edward. "The Thomas W. Streeter Collection." *Yale Library Gazette* 31 (April 1957): 147–53.

Esar, Evan. *20,000 Quips and Quotes: A Treasury of Witty Remarks, Comic Proverbs, Wisecracks, and Epigrams.* New York: Barnes and Noble, 1995.

Everitt, Charles P. *Adventures of a Treasure Hunter.* Boston: Little, Brown, 1951.

"Ex-councilman Dies in Austin." *Austin American-Statesman*, October 22, 1984, 16.

"Flash on Jefferson's Libraries." *Quarto: Prepared in the Interests of Book Collecting at the University of Michigan*, no. 9 (December 1944): 2.

Fleck, Tim. "Rare Papers Target of Official Scrutiny." *Houston Chronicle*, June 15, 1972, 3:1.

Ford, Jon. "Hill Fund Gets $300,000." *Austin American-Statesman*, September 16, 1977, F18.

Fox, Margalit. "Larry Buchanan Dies at 81: B-movie Schlockmeister." *New York Times*, December 19, 2004, 56.

Frantz, Joe B. "Peace, John Robert." In *The New Handbook of Texas*, vol. 5, 104. Austin: Texas State Historical Association, 1996.

Frontier Americana. *25th Anniversary Catalogue 42.* Albuquerque, 1992.

Friend, Llerena. "Book Reviews: *Cracker Barrel Chronicles*." *Southwestern Historical Quarterly* 69, no, 4 (April 1966): 546.

Geary, Patrick J. *Furta Sacra: Thefts of Relics in the Central Middle Ages.* Princeton, N.J.: Princeton University Press, 2011.

"George A. Stephen Obituary." *Austin American-Statesman*, May 7, 2006, 31.

Greer, William R. "Walter Goldwater Obituary." *New York Times*, June 28, 1985, 16.

Greth, Carlos Vidal, and Joe Vargo. "Book Dealer's Life Read Like a Bestseller." *Austin American-Statesman*, April 30, 1989, A1, A8–A9.

Gribben, Alan. *Harry Huntt Ransom: Intellect in Motion.* Austin: University of Texas Press, 2010.

Guinn, Jeff. *Go Down Together: The True, Untold Story of Bonnie and Clyde*. New York: Simon and Schuster, 2009.

Hanna, Archibald. *Dinner to John Holmes Jenkins, Esq. Yale Westerners*. New Haven, Conn.: Yale Corral of the Westerners, February 4, 1977.

Harris, John. "Publishing Company Hit by Fire." *Austin American-Statesman*, September 29, 1987, B-4.

Hewett, David. "Forgeries and Fraud in Texas." *Maine Antique Digest*, January 1989, 29A–30A.

———. "John Jenkins Shot—Murder or Suicide?" *Maine Antique Digest*, June 1989, 10A.

Hewig, Johannes, Nora Kretschmer, Ralf Trippe, Holger Hecht, Michael Coles, Clay Holroyd, and Wolfgang Miltner. "Hypersensitivity to Rewards in Gamblers." Biological Psychiatry 67, no. 8 (April 2010): 781–83.

Howard, Joyce, ed., *Letters from Henry Miller to Hoki Tokuda Miller*. New York: Freundlich Press, 1986.

Howze, Sara. "Archivist Notes Theft Hazards: Current Probe On." *Austin Statesman*, August 8, 1971, A1, A4.

Hunsucker, John L., and Scott J. Davison. "Time Required for a Drowning Victim to Reach Bottom." *Journal of Search and Rescue* 1, no. 1 (1993): 19–28.

Huff, Darrell. *How to Take a Chance*. New York: W. W. Norton, 1959.

"Indicted for Library Thefts." *College and Research Libraries News*, March 1964, 139.

Jay, Ricky. *Cards as Weapons*. New York: Darien House, 1977.

Jenkins, John Holmes. *Audubon and Other Capers: Confessions of a Texas Bookmaker*. Austin, Texas: Pemberton Press, 1976.

———. *Basic Texas Books: An Annotated Bibliography of Selected Works for a Research Library*. Austin: University of Texas Press, 1983.

———. *Cracker Barrel Chronicles: A Bibliography of Texas Town and County Histories*. Austin: Pemberton Press, 1965.

———. *In Memory of My Friend, Price Daniel, Jr.* Austin: Pemberton Press, 1981.

———. *Neither the Fanatics nor the Faint-Hearted: The Tour Leading to the President's Death and the Two Speeches He Could Not Give*. Austin: Pemberton Press, 1963.

———. *Rare Book and Manuscript Thefts: A Security System for Libraries, Booksellers, and Collectors, by John H. Jenkins, President, A.B.A.A.* Introduction by Terry Belanger. New York: Antiquarian Booksellers Association of America, 1981.

————, ed. *Recollections of Early Texas: The Memoirs of John Holland Jenkins*. Austin: University of Texas Press, 2017.

————. [Untitled letter on coin cleaning.] *Numismatist* 68 (1955): 1101.

Jenkins Company. *American Celebration Catalogue*. Austin, 1976.

————. *Catalogue 3. John F. Kennedy: A Catalogue of Books, Articles, Autographs, Memorabilia*. Austin, 1964.

Jones, Monty. "Fake! Bogus Papers Sold as Real Texana." *Austin American-Statesman*, April 9, 1988, A1.

Kesselus, Kenneth. "Letter to the Editor." *Bastrop Advertiser*, August 10, 1967, 25.

Knox, Sanka. "Account of Magellan's Voyage Is Sold for $56,000." *New York Times*, October 26, 1966, 41.

Lenz, Mary. "Authority to Lower River in Hunt for Missing Gun." *Houston Post*, April 20, 1989, 1.

Lukacs, John. "Poker and the American Character." *Horizon* 5, no, 8 (November 1963): 8.

Martin, Douglas. "Amarillo Slim, Gambler with a Sly Wit, Dies at 83." *New York Times*, May 1, 2012, 16.

Maud, Ralph. *Charles Olson's Reading: A Biography*. Carbondale: Southern Illinois University Press, 1996.

McKinney, J. Lynn. "Wheeler-Dealer's Death Ruled Homicide by Bastrop Co. Peace Justice Henderson: Official Says Noted Austin Book Dealer a Murder Victim." *Bastrop County Times*, April 27, 1989, A1, A16.

McMurtry, Larry. *Books: A Memoir*. New York: Simon and Schuster, 2008.

Pate, Russ. "The City: The Inner Sanctum." *D Magazine* (Dallas, Texas), March 1996.

Powell, Ronald. "A Rare Bird in Old Books." *Austin American Statesman*, July 18, 1977, 9.

Reaves, Gayle. "Chaos Charged: UT Audit Blasts HRC Operations." *Austin American Statesman*, December 16, 1978, A1, A8.

"Recollections of Early Texas." *New Yorker*, September 27, 1958, 79.

Reed, J. D. "The Clothbound Collectibles: Rare Volumes Outperform Gold, Diamonds, Stocks." *Time*, April 26, 1982, 83.

Reese, William S. "Review of John H Jenkins, *Basic Texas Books: An Annotated Bibliography of Selected Works for a Research Library*." *Papers of the Bibliographical Society of America* 79, no. 1 (1985): 141.

Reinhold, Robert. "Murchison: A Fortune Lost." *New York Times*, March 5, 1985, D1, D6.

"Rizek Escapes Term in Prison." *Daily Home News* (New Brunswick, N.J.), December 20, 1957, 1.

Saxon, Wolfgang. "Hans Peter Kraus, 81, Book Dealer and Collector." *New York Times*, November 2, 1988, D27.

Schaden, Herman. "Great Book Store Mystery." *Washington Star*, May 3, 1970, C-1, C-3.

Sheehan, Robert. "Charles Allen, Jr." In *Wall Street People: True Stories of Today's Masters and Moguls*, Vol. 2, edited by Charles D. Ellis and Jame R. Vertin, 26–30. New York: John R. Wiley and Sons, 2001.

Sieber, Arlyn. *The Instant Coin Collector: Everything You Need to Know to Get Started Now*. Iola, Wisc.: Krause, 2013.

Smith, Brian. "Super Bowl of Poker Exceeds Expectations." *Player's Panorama*, February 16, 1989, B7.

Sotheby Parke-Bernet. *Albert Einstein, An Important and Large Collection of Autograph Manuscript Notes, Princeton, N.J., ca. 1950–1954*. New York, November 28, 1972.

———. *The Celebrated Collection of Americana Formed by the Late Thomas Winthrop Streeter*. New York: Parke-Bernet Galleries, 1966.

Sotheby's. *Fine Books and Manuscripts: Texas Independence Collection*. New York, June 18, 2004.

———. *Fine Printed and Manuscript Americana, Including Books from the Library of Lindley Eberstadt*. New York, May 1, 1985.

"Squatty Strikes It Rich: Jenkins Aims for Win." *Poker Player*, 1984, 10.

Stanley, Dick. "Jenkins Makes His Dreams Come True: Books, Films, Space Projects Keep Him Going." *Austin American-Statesman*, March 8, 1983, 3.

Streeter, Frank. "Some Recollections of Thomas W. Streeter and His Collecting." *Gazette of the Grolier Club* 31 (1980): 40–50.

Stutz, Terrance, and Melinda Henneberger. "Rare Book Dealer Found Shot to Death." *Dallas Morning News*, April 18, 1989, 7A.

Swanson, Doug J. *Blood Aces: The Wild Ride of Benny Binion, the Texas Gangster Who Created Vegas Poker*. New York: Penguin, 2014.

"Tall in Texas: Young Tycoon of Texana." *Austin Statesman*, August 18, 1963, 6.

Taylor, W. Thomas. *Alone in the Vault: An Initiation into Bibliophilic Mysteries*. Dallas: DeGolyer Library, 2009.

———. *Texfake: An Account of the Theft and Forgery of Early Texas Documents*. Austin: W. Thomas Taylor, 1991.

Todd, Ed. "Judge Rules against FDIC: Millions in Loans at Stake." *Fort Worth Star-Telegram*, February 20, 1986, 1A–2A.

Tolan, Edwin K. "Recovery of the Stolen Audubon Plates." *Friends of the Union College Library Newsletter*, September 9, 1971, 1.

Travers, Scott. *The Coin Collector's Survival Manual*, rev. 7th ed. New York: Diversified, 2015.

Trillin, Calvin. "American Chronicles: Knowing Johnny Jenkins." *New Yorker*, October 30, 1989, 79–97.

"University May Buy Rare Books." *Brownsville Herald*, October 23, 1975, 4.

University of Texas. *A Collection on Texas and the American West: Prospectus*. Austin: University of Texas System, 1977.

Utley, Dan K., ed. *Archie P. McDonald: A Life in Texas History*. College Station: Texas A&M University Press, 2016.

Vargo, Joe. "Book Dealer Leaves Lenders Unpaid after Mysterious Demise." *Austin American-Statesman*, April 20, 1989, A1, A8.

Vargo, Joe, and Monty Jones, "Sheriff Calls Death 'Bona Fide Mystery': Austin Bookseller Found in River, Shot in Head." *Austin American-Statesman*, April 18, 1989, A1.

Vinson, Michael. *Edward Eberstadt and Sons: Rare Booksellers of Western Americana*. Norman: University of Oklahoma Press, 2016.

———. "A Passion for Western Americana: Remembering Fred White, Jr., Seven Years Later." *Western Americana Catalogue 2003*, 1–3. Afton, Wyo., 2003.

W. M. Morrison, Bookseller. *List 175*. Waco, Texas [ca. 1962].

Wajda, Phillip J. "True Crime or Texas Tall Tale? Unraveling a 40-Year-Old Mystery." *Union College Magazine*, Summer 2011, 4–13.

Wead, D. *All the Presidents' Children: Triumph and Tragedy in the Lives of America's First Families*. New York: Atria, 2003.

Wilde, Oscar. *Collected Works of Oscar Wilde: The Plays, the Poems, the Stories and the Essays including De Profundis*. London: Wordsworth Editions, 1997.

Winfrey, Dorman. "The Texan Archive War of 1842." *Southwestern Historical Quarterly* 64, no. 2 (October 1960): 171–84.

Woolley, Bryan. "Enigmatic Ending: Book Dealer's Flamboyant Lifestyle Ignites Speculation about His Death." *Dallas Morning News*, April 28, 1989, 1A, 15A.

Zeitlin, Jake. *Some Rambling Recollections of a Rambling Bookseller*. Los Angeles: Printed by Anderson, Ritchie and Simon for Occidental College, 1970.

Index

CPSIA information can be obtained
at www.ICGtesting.com
Printed in the USA
LVHW091628070820
662639LV00005B/31/J